WILLIN'

WILLIN'

The Story of

LITTLE FEAT

BEN FONG-TORRES

DA CAPO PRESS

A Member of the Perseus Books Group

Designed by Jeff Williams
Set in 11 point Sabon by The Perseus Books Group

Library of Congress Cataloging-in-Publication Data

Fong-Torres, Ben.
    Willin' : the story of Little Feat / Ben Fong-Torres.
       pages cm
    Includes bibliographical references and index.
    ISBN 978-0-306-82131-8 (hardback) -- ISBN 978-0-306-82132-5 (e-book) 1. Little Feat
(Musical group) 2. Rock musicians--United States--Biography. I. Title.

ML421.L59F66 2013
782.42166092'2—dc23
[B]
                                                                                2013022269
Published by Da Capo Press
A Member of the Perseus Books Group
www.dacapopress.com

Da Capo Press books are available at special discounts for bulk purchases in the U.S. by corporations, institutions, and other organizations. For more information, please contact the Special Markets Department at the Perseus Books Group, 2300 Chestnut Street, Suite 200, Philadelphia, PA 19103, or call (800) 810-4145, ext. 5000, or e-mail special.markets@ perseusbooks.com.

10 9 8 7 6 5 4 3 2 1

CONTENTS

ACKNOWLEDGMENTS

This has been, by far, the most difficult project I've tackled. But the reason for this has little to do with Little Feat. Its members, past and present, and its associates—fellow musicians, managers, producers, record company executives and staffers—have been most helpful. So have family, friends, and fans.

My problems were personal, and they'll be briefly addressed soon enough. But I am grateful that, from start to finish, I found so many people willing to help—with personal stories, anecdotes, research materials, and suggestions for others who might shed additional light on this much-loved band.

I am including a list of all the people I interviewed. I'm not one to play favorites, but I need to note that, among the band, Bill Payne and Paul Barrere were especially helpful. Among Lowell George's family, Hampton, his brother, and two of his kids, Luke and Inara, were generous with their memories. So were his first wife, Patte, and the love of his life, Elizabeth, who gave as much as she could while steadfastly trying to guard her and their privacy.

There are a few musicians who did not respond to requests for interviews, but they were outnumbered by those who spoke with enthusiasm about a favorite band. Special thanks to Bonnie Raitt, Jimmy Buffett, Linda Ronstadt, John Sebastian, Tom Johnston of the Doobie Brothers, Page McConnell of Phish, and Van Dyke Parks.

I am also grateful that Lenny Waronker and Joe Smith, presidents of Warner Bros. Records; Peter Asher, the manager; and Russ Titelman and Ted Templeman, Little Feat's first two producers, granted time to me. Others who were especially close to the band as well as to Lowell George and who were of great help included Gene Vano, George's faithful roadie and driver; Martin Kibbee; his childhood friend and cowriter; journalists Bud Scoppa and Daisann McLane; and managers Cameron Sears and John Scher.

It was appropriate that one of my first interviews was with Lynn Hearne, who as a teenager in Southern California became a fan of rock bands and met Lowell George while he was in the Factory. She compiled binders full of Feat press clippings and memorabilia over the years, exemplified the lifelong Little Feat fan, and introduced me to the band's Grassroots movement.

There, I found Chris Cafiero, online keeper of all things Feat, along with two radio broadcasters, Ed O'Connell of WHCN in Connecticut and "Cerphe" Colwell of WHFS in Maryland, who shared their encounters with George as well as two others, Gary Bennett of KSHE in St. Louis, and David Moss, who each produced and hosted long-running Little Feat radio shows. Moss's son, Matt, is an example of Little Feat's reach into the current generation. He is the drummer in the band Steel Toed Slippers, who've opened for Little Feat and whose 2012 CD was coproduced by Feat bassist Kenny Gradney and Johnny Lee Schell, the guitarist who engineered Little Feat's latest, *Rooster Rag*.

For editorial assistance I thank my longtime friend Bobbi Cowan in Hollywood and Elizabeth Valente, a former student of mine when I taught a magazine-writing class at San Francisco State University; Elizabeth was invaluable in helping me cross the finish line. At the Perseus Books Group, Carolyn Sobczak and Josephine Mariea were wonderful in their capacities as project editor and copy editor, respectively.

In every book there are two women I thank. One is Sarah Lazin, my colleague for years from *Rolling Stone* who became one of the best literary agents in the business. I've been fortunate that she's kept me on her roster and led me to a Little Feat fan who happened also to be an editor at Da Capo Press. I am grateful that this editor, Ben Schafer, saw fit to entrust me with the assignment of telling the improbable story of the band that was always . . . willin'.

Second, and most of all, I thank Dianne, who had grown accustomed to my meeting and beating deadlines for my previous books and was shocked—shocked!—that I had to push my delivery date several times. But, of course, she understood. Soon after I agreed to the Little Feat project my family and I suffered a series of tragedies that were almost beyond comprehension. I won't get into it here; that's what personal websites and blogs are for. Suffice it to say that we miss my younger sister, Shirley, and my younger brother, Burton, and that we are taking turns visiting my mother at her nursing care facility in Oakland.

The personal losses took their toll on my work schedule and must have taxed everyone involved. But they also gave me additional empathy for the losses Little Feat's family endured, from band members like Lowell George, Richie Hayward, album cover artist Neon Park, road manager Rick Harper to family members like Fran Tate Payne, studio engineer, vocalist, and wife of Bill Payne.

Finally I thank the family members who, for the last two years, saw a particularly more rushed version of me than usual, including my sister Sarah and Dave Watkins; my niece Tina Pavao and her family, Matt and the girls; Maggie and Stella; my niece Lea; and my nephew Jason Watkins and his wife, Wendy Todd. My in-laws in Los Angeles saw me not at all except when I swung by to see Little Feat working on *Rooster Rag*. I look forward to longer visits with Robin and Chuck Ward as well as with Eileen and Richard Powers.

PROLOGUE

MY FIRST BOOK, MANY YEARS AGO, WAS ABOUT GRAM PARSONS, THE flawed country-rock pioneer whose legend continues, despite the fact that in a career that spanned eight years and several bands, including the Byrds and the Flying Burrito Brothers as well as a most harmonious pairing with Emmylou Harris, he never had a hit record.

My most recent book, just a couple of years ago, was about the Eagles, who followed in Parsons's footsteps but found all the success that was denied to Parsons.

And now, ladies and gentleman, we come full circle with Little Feat. Many music fans who still can recall the artists and sounds of the seventies may ask, "Little Who?" Like Parsons, Little Feat never scored a hit record. Like Parsons, Lowell George, the band's cofounder and leader, died too young and for no good reason. Like Parsons, Little Feat were favorites of music critics and disc jockeys and got radio exposure, especially on FM rock stations unencumbered by such restrictions as formats and formulas.

Songs like "Oh Atlanta," "Easy to Slip," "Rock and Roll Doctor," and "Dixie Chicken," with their finely tuned nods to all manner of American music, especially the sounds of the South, earned plenty of airplay. And when fellow artists began covering the songs composed by Lowell George and partners, including childhood friend Martin

Kibbee and keyboardist Bill Payne, Little Feat got just a little bit bigger.

The main song was "Willin'." Covered in 1975 by Linda Ronstadt on her breakthrough solo album, *Heart Like a Wheel*, it brought George (and his band) some acclaim—and precious time.

They seemed always to be running out of that commodity at their record label, Warner Bros., which issued their first album in 1970 and was famous for its patience with and coddling of favored artists, many of them musicians not interested in or capable of swimming in any mainstream. Captain Beefheart, the Mothers of Invention, Ry Cooder, Randy Newman, Van Dyke Parks, and Bonnie Raitt, who— hard to believe—produced excellent albums over a sixteen-year span but didn't make it until she moved over to Capitol Records, were loss leaders, whereas Jimi Hendrix, James Taylor, Black Sabbath, Van Morrison, and Joni Mitchell helped the label to rake in the dough.

Little Feat just raked. But with precious few rewards.

They got respect from rock critics, disc jockeys, and fellow artists. As Don Snowden noted in a 1977 appreciation: "Groups as stylistically diverse as Marshall Tucker and Led Zeppelin have publicly proclaimed the Feats as their favorite band. When Little Feat journeyed to Europe two years ago as part of a Warner Bros. package tour—a jaunt that saw them steal the show night after night from the headlining Doobie Brothers—the Stones made their first public appearance as a group in some five years to catch one of their shows. And yet Little Feat remains something of prophets without honor in their own land, still slogging around the country playing 3000-seat arenas."

To Marshall Tucker Band and Led Zep one could add Bob Dylan, Elton John, Eric Clapton, and the Rolling Stones; the Stones actually wanted to jam with Little Feat when they showed up at a concert one January evening in Amsterdam in 1975. George wouldn't go for that, but two years later Mick Taylor did join them onstage at the Rainbow Theater in London. Dylan caught them in 1974—on both coasts: at the Bottom Line in New York and at the Santa Monica Civic Auditorium. In 2000 Bill Payne, playing behind Phil Lesh on his tour with Dylan, ran into him: "'Hey, Billy,' Dylan shouted, 'do you remember the Bottom Line?' I said, 'Yes. You were sitting right off the center, on my side, and scared the hell out of me!'"

Paul Barrere remembers Robert Plant visiting Little Feat backstage in Birmingham, England, in 1976, then inviting the band to a party for the release of Led Zep's soundtrack album for *The Song Remains the Same*.

As for Clapton, the guitar god paid Little Feat a supreme compliment—and this was for the reformed, post-George Feats. He had joined them on stage in Rochester Hills, a Detroit suburb, in the fall of '92, playing on "Mellow Down Easy" and George's composition "A Apolitical Blues." As Barrere remembers it: "We ran into Eric at the hotel we were staying at. He found out we were playing the next night, so he stayed an extra day just to come and see our show and sit in with us."

But that wasn't the compliment. At the concert Payne remarked, "Gosh, we just saw you in New York." Said Clapton: "Well, I want my band to hear a *proper* band."

Considering that they never had a hit record and, thus, don't pop up on oldies or classic rock stations the way the Eagles, the Doors, the Stones, and, yes, the Doobies do, that there have been two tribute albums is a testament to Little Feat's standing among peers. In 1997 *Rock and Roll Doctor* included Feats compositions performed by Bonnie Raitt, Taj Mahal, J. D. Souther, Randy Newman, Allen Toussaint, Chris Hillman, Jennifer Warnes, Eddie Money, Jackson Browne (who's godfather to Lowell and Elizabeth's daughter, Inara), and Inara herself, backed by Ry Cooder and Van Dyke Parks.

In 2008 Jimmy Buffett helped produce *Join the Band*, a Feats tribute whose lineup included Emmylou Harris, Chris Robinson, Dave Matthews, Bob Seger, Brooks & Dunn, Vince Gill, Béla Fleck, and Inara George. Buffett, who did two songs, never met Lowell George, but Little Feat, he said, were "a band's band."

In 2010 Phish devoted its Halloween concert in Atlantic City to Little Feat. Phish has a tradition, of sorts, in which it performs another band's album in its entirety as its Halloween show. The band doesn't announce which work they'll be recreating; it's a nice Trick 'n' Treat surprise. And in 2010 it was a shock: Little Feat's *Waiting for Columbus*, a two-album live set issued in 1978. Phish, who'd never replicated a live album before, even included a horn section to represent Feat's sidekicks, the Tower of Power horns. A tricky treat, indeed.

Little Feat had devoted fans throughout Lowell George's run with them. And when a reformed version of Little Feat appeared a decade after George's passing, their fans reappeared too, giving them what they never achieved with George—a major hit album—and sticking with them through thick and thin . . . mostly thin. But a worldwide base of fans, many of them involved in Feat's "Grassroots" movement, continues to spread the word—and the music—online.

This book exists largely because of the Grassrooters and all the Featfans who buy their recordings and go to great lengths to catch their concerts. Little Feat fans have plenty of music, all the merchandise they might want to collect, and an abundance of news and other info by way of the band's website. But there's never been a book devoted to Little Feat—by that, I mean the entire band and its entire history, not just the story of Lowell George, who in both life and death has dominated the spotlight.

The story of Little Feat is the story of Lowell George—that's not in debate. But it is also the story of the other guys who made up the original quartet and who, from the beginning, helped create the music and set the tone of Little Feat. George logged almost ten years with the band. After he died there was a period of silence lasting eight or nine years. Little Feat, with different lead vocalists, has been together again since 1987—more than twenty-five years. Billy Payne, the original keyboard player, has been there throughout. Sharp of both physical features and musical mind, he's a story. So is Paul Barrere, whose motto could be the Little Feat album title *Ain't Had Enough Fun* and who takes pride in being the Little Feat who had his motorcycle accident before joining the band, unlike George and Richie Hayward, the original drummer and the undisputed rock star of the band. So is Kenny Gradney, the dapper bass man who came into the band with conga player Sam Clayton, an Aaron Neville minus the earring and angelic voice. (But Clayton, despite his protestations, can sing just fine.) And finally, so is the first bassist, Roy Estrada, who is serving a life sentence and spoke with me from inside a Texas penitentiary.

Little Feat's audiences today are made up mostly of music lovers who never saw them with Lowell George up front and who may have only a vague recollection of him as the guy who started the band, who wrote some great songs, and who was an exceptional guitarist, vocalist, songwriter, and record producer. They may think of him with hazy shades of respect, the way one might think of, say, Nick Drake, Syd Barrett, Alex Chilton, Brian Jones, Tim Hardin, Dino Valente, Laura Nyro, or, yes, Gram Parsons.

Great stories, all of them.

Speaking of stories, this book is full circle with *Hickory Wind*, my Gram Parsons biography, in another way. In my prologue I noted that, although Gram was quite the storyteller, he proved to be one of the least reliable sources on the subject of Gram Parsons.

From the research I've conducted for this book, I would resist calling Lowell George a fabricator of stories. But he contradicted himself on numerous occasions, sometimes giving two or three accounts of a single event. This may be because of memory loss, it may be because of drugs or alcohol, or he may have been having fun with a reporter. Or he may have been feeling hostile when he decided to steer that reporter wrong.

There is, for an extreme example, the story of Lowell's two grand-uncles, names unknown, who lived on a ranch in Nevada in the latter part of the nineteenth century and had their eyes on the same prize, a girl named Ella Mae. To determine who would win her, they did the brotherly thing: they fought a pistol duel. At exactly fifty paces they turned, aimed, and fired. Both hit their marks.

There was one George brother left, and when he was a teenager, his parents packed up and moved to Los Angeles. And there the George family line continued, resulting in another set of George brothers, Hampton and Lowell.

One of them, Lowell, told that story to a magazine writer, Daisann McLane, and she naturally used it in her *Crawdaddy!* magazine profile of him. It was, after all, a killer lead. She'd heard the story from a writer friend of Lowell's and brought it to George for confirmation and, no doubt, some embellishments. The profile was published in spring 1979. Within months George died, and *Rolling Stone* assigned McLane to write his obituary. She couldn't help retelling the essence of that story. And so it became legend.

Lowell's other brother, Hampton, is less of a yarn spinner than Lowell was. He, however, visited the anthropology department of the University of Nevada, Las Vegas, to which he had contributed family photos and archival materials. Researchers there showed him documents indicating that Edward and William Kiel, brothers of Hampton and Lowell's great-grandfather, died in 1900 at a family ranch in Vegas Valley. The original theory was a murder-suicide, but an exhumation and examination in 1975 determined that both had been murdered with shotgun blasts. Hampton spoke about some animosity between his family's and another family's ranch, possibly having to do with an unpaid debt.

Because the university, with the permission of the Kiel family, had investigated the matter—which a genealogy site refers to as the Vegas Valley's "oldest unsolved murder case"—in 1975, it's possible that Lowell got word of it and put his own twist on the story. But, Hampton said firmly, "A duel is not the truth." He then confessed, "It sounds good, though! Better a duel than a murder."

And although the investigation turned up no girl named Ella Mae, Hampton George did see, among the photos in the George family exhibit at UNLV, a shot of a young woman named Sadie—holding a shotgun.

Lowell, of course, wasn't the only one who toyed with facts. As I wrote in *Hickory Wind*: "I learned that double- and triple-checking, tracking down friends and friends of friends, relatives of relatives, only added to the confusion." In the case of George and Little Feat, clashing recollections came from everyone, from family members and childhood friends to bandmates, fellow artists, and music executives. Some stories that turned out to be untrue were innocent mistakes and misstatements, but there also were numerous ones, mostly self-aggrandizing, that appeared to be motivated by ego, by the desire to be a part of music history, or at least appear in a moment of it. As the character of Tommy DeVito, one of the Four Seasons, says in *Jersey Boys*: "We all remember it the way we need to."

I was commiserating with Bill Payne about this, and he said that if he were to write his own book, he'd promise up front that in the course of the story that the reader would encounter, "there are some truths to it." Or there might be some "magic realism" involved. Payne offered an example: "When I was going to Sunday school as a little kid, there was a little girl, and she and I were walking down the street and there was this cat that looked like he's about four to four and a half feet tall. Not possible, right, but that's what I remember seeing. This little girl Marilyn would skip down this one road . . . I would say, 'How do you run so fast?' and she would say, 'I was taken by this green ball of energy.'"

It's a ball of confusion, as the Temptations would say. What a mess. Fortunately, Little Feat's story is compelling enough and worthy of telling, so that the work of sorting everything out was a task I was honored—and more than willin'—to accept.

Chapter 1

THE CONTENDERS

IT BEGAN WITH A MOST UNSTEADY CELEBRITY STATION ID. IT MUST'VE been the first and only take:

"This is Lowell George, and livin-liv-*livin'* and listenin' to WHCN. And dig this."

Thus began George's visit to a rock station in Hartford, Connecticut, on the early evening of June 22, 1979. He was dutifully promoting a local club gig, which in turn would promote his solo album, his first since forming Little Feat some ten years before.

Sitting with the disk jockey, Ed O'Connell, George answered questions he'd been fielding for weeks, ever since Warner Bros. Records scheduled the album for release and the promotional machinery began to rev up.

The questions had to do with his band. It'd been reported that Little Feat had busted up for the third or fourth time and that this might have been the last time. After all, here was their leader out on the road, fronting a new band and performing songs from an album bearing only his name. And what about that album? Little Feat followers—many of them rock critics and DJs—had been hearing about it for at least two years. What took so long?

George could have flicked away the questions with a joke, a non sequitur, or even a plain old "No comment." But that wasn't his style.

O'Connell introduced his guest: "We've got Lowell George hanging out in the studio before he goes on stage tonight at the Hard Rock Stage West. Lowell George is willing to take your phone calls too. He's 'Willin'!'"

So he spoke with O'Connell about the pressures of meeting his record company's demand for Little Feat product, which he felt required not only his services as the producer but also the need to tour, to make the money that the records failed to do with their middling sales.

"I could have done it in two weeks if I'd been able to prepare myself for it, but I was never able to until last December. Then after all the back and forth, the group breaks up in February or March. The world's a weird, wild and wonderful place, and it seems to all happen to me. But it's all okay."

It was not. George was trying to maintain a balance between paranoia and optimism. He told O'Connell that he expected to complete Little Feat's latest album when he completed his tour—but his band had fallen apart. Bill Payne, the keyboard player and one of the four original members, and Paul Barrere, the guitarist, had already formed a new ensemble. They'd even recruited a guy who sounded kind of like Lowell George.

Still, he wasn't saying the band was over: "They're on the shelf, you might say. We've kind of backed off a little bit. Everybody hates everybody." Bands, he explained, "are always like that. Tell me a group that doesn't hate each other and I'll show you a group that's really bad."

Bands with no talent, he went on, "have this thing about how bad they are. But groups that argue about their music, about all sorts of unimportant things—there's usually talent there. So when the group got together and we started arguing, we knew everything's fine."

What, O'Connell asked, did his band argue about?

"'You parked too far, or too close to me, and I can't get out.' You name it. 'I don't like rehearsing down here; I have to drive forty-five miles.' 'Why are we recording out here, man? This is all the way out in the boondocks.' I said, 'Because we don't want the evil influences of the big city to get to us.' 'Well, whose idea was that?' 'Well, that was *your* idea.' 'Oh.'"

That kind of discourse, George reckoned, might be in the past. Payne and Barrere, he said, "got excited about playing with a band where nobody argues. What they don't remember is that you don't argue for maybe the first six months, and then you begin to argue, and it's all the same. The grass is not greener anywhere else."

But he was, essentially, on a green-grass tour, here on the East Coast. "There's gonna be a little gathering at the Hard Rock Stage West," said O'Connell, wrapping up the visit. "I get to play tonight," George said with some enthusiasm. "I get to play with my new band."

But George would only get to play a few more nights. A week after that interview on WHCN he died in his hotel room in Arlington, Virginia, across the Potomac River from Washington, DC.

Lowell George was thirty-four. The initial cause of death was heart failure. But few believed it was that simple. After all, the guy was thirty-four.

Well, they say time loves a hero.
But only time will tell.
If he's real, he's a legend from heaven.
If he ain't, he's a mouthpiece from hell.

Bill Payne and Paul Barrere wrote those words a few years before George's death. "Time Loves a Hero" became the title track of their sixth album, issued in 1977. That was the album that marked the passage of the band's leadership from George to others, notably Payne and Barrere.

But the arguing had begun long before then. Fighting could be traced back to the first album, when it was just the four of them: Lowell George, Bill Payne, Roy Estrada, who'd played bass alongside George in the Mothers of Invention, and Richie Hayward, who'd been part of an earlier band with George, the Factory.

There may even have been disputes at the first rehearsals in 1969. If there were, that would have been just the way George liked it.

Chapter 2

THE BIRTH OF LITTLE FEAT: MOTHERS AND IN-LAWS

LITTLE FEAT BEGAN WITH LOWELL GEORGE AND BILL PAYNE, THE latter being the only surviving, playing member of the original band. Or maybe it started with another of Lowell's childhood pals, Martin Kibbee, who didn't play in the band but did contribute several of their signature songs. Kibbee also played alongside George in the Factory, so maybe Little Feat began with that band, which also included Richie Hayward on drums.

Or was the genesis the Mothers and that iconoclastic mother of all musical invention, Frank Zappa? After all, he had produced a few demos and a single for the Factory and then hired Lowell George into his band, which included future Feat Roy Estrada on bass. And it was while playing guitar in the Mothers that George wrote Little Feat's most enduring song, "Willin'."

Two other bands figure in the early going: the Standells (of "Dirty Water" fame) and the Fraternity of Man ("Don't Bogart That Joint"). Lowell had a short, unhappy stint in the former and helped out on a Fraternity album. Kibbee and Hayward were actual members of Fraternity, and Billy Payne, like George, did a cameo.

But in the end—and in the beginning—it's Lowell George.

LAUREL CANYON, as Van Dyke Parks said in his *Song Cycle*, was "the seat of the beat." Nestled in the hills overlooking West Hollywood and the Sunset Strip, Laurel Canyon was where seemingly an entire generation of hipsters—artists, musicians, and others—lived, worked, and played, where music was created and made. But Laurel Canyon and its neighbor, twenty miles to the west, Topanga Canyon, were not the only places that pulsed in the mid-1960s; all of Hollywood and Los Angeles was a draw for young creative types looking for something different.

Stephen Stills was in New York in 1965, trying to put a band together and kept his ear to the radio. "I heard the Byrds," he said. "The sound of their electric guitars and voices made me think that L.A. was the place to be if I wanted to rock and roll." He wound up in Laurel Canyon and, after a nice run with Buffalo Springfield, wound up working with a Byrd, David Crosby. The Byrds, he said, were among thousands of musicians touched by the Beatles.

As Crosby told Anthony Fawcett in *California Rock, California Sound: The Music of Los Angeles and Southern California* (1979): "We heard that music; we said, 'Oh, really? . . . there are no rules. You can do anything.' And we instantly did. But it's that 'Hey, anything's possible' kind of feeling that was characteristic about California . . . and it drew us all. We all just sort of glommed together in one place . . . L.A. in the Sixties . . . From about 1964 to about 1968 it was mind-boggling. Every singer-songwriter of worth that I knew of was right here . . . it was the most creative scene that I can remember seeing."

As for his and Stills's future partner, Graham Nash, a native of Manchester, England, he saw Los Angeles while on tour with the Hollies in 1966. Nash soon left the band and returned to Los Angeles, landing in the canyon and living with Joni Mitchell. "There was no question about me being mystified by the place," he said. "I mean, the telephone rang just like in the movies."

Musicians came from here, there, everywhere. But Lowell George had been there all along. Now, having put together one of the dozens of garage bands that were writing and practicing away throughout the canyon (at one time there had to have been more bands than there were garages), he would visit friends there—whether they were Byrds or Monkees, Van Dyke Parks or Frank Zappa—who took up residence in a rambling house once occupied by Tom Mix, the hero in silent Western movies of the twenties and thirties.

That was the world, the era into which Lowell George was born. He was truly a child of Hollywood—the Hollywood of the forties, of RKO and MGM, of Pantages and the Brown Derby, and of Schwab's Pharmacy and the Grauman's Chinese Theater. It was the land of making people believe, and Lowell's family was in the middle of it. His father, Willard Hampton George, was widely known in the movie industry as the "furrier to the stars." Born in Nebraska in 1889, he moved to Los Angeles as a boy and was working in a fur shop in 1910. By 1918 he had his own store and had begun working with the first of the movie studios in Hollywood. His son Hampton, born in 1940, boasts, "Every movie from 1915 to '57, he provided the furs." And you can look it up. Online, he has at least three costume and wardrobe credits, for *Diamond Jim* in 1935, *It Happened on Fifth Avenue* in 1947, and *The Babe Ruth Story* in 1948. He also costumed Victor Mature in his first leading role as a fur-clad cave man in the 1940 film *One Million B.C.* What's more, Willard was known to be hunting pals with W. C. Fields, among others.

The Georges lived just above Grauman's Chinese Theater in the Santa Monica Mountains on Mulholland Drive between Laurel Canyon and Woodrow Wilson Drive. Although these are all familiar reference points to Angelenos now, back then they were nowhere, so the Georges were pioneers. "It was a ranch-style house," says Hampton. "Dad built it, and it was one of the first to build on Mulholland. Laurel Canyon Boulevard was a dirt road." Their neighbors included some of the movie stars who George would come to drape in chinchillas and foxes, and chief among them was Dan Duryea, who served as cub scoutmaster to both George boys between film and television roles. On the flip side of Duryea, who was married to the same woman for thirty-five years, there was Errol Flynn, who in 1940 built what he called Mulholland Farm just across the road from the Georges. Flynn's mountain home included a tennis court, swimming pool, barn, and a casino along with a house that reportedly contained secret passageways and two-way mirrors to satisfy the swashbuckling actor's voyeuristic instincts. Lowell didn't remember him that way, though. "He was a real character and a very nice man, too," he said. But the Georges didn't see much of Flynn, who fled the country in 1953 because he owed taxes to the IRS and alimony to two ex-wives—as well as money to Willard George for a chinchilla bedspread, said Hampton: "And he never paid him." There was other criminal activity from the Flynn estate: the actor, Lowell remembered, had a pet monkey. "He used to spot me eating an apple, swing across the telephone wires, drop down, steal the apple and run."

In a neighborhood without much traffic, Hampton and his little brother often pulled pranks. Once, when he was about twelve, Hampton put up a dummy on the street. "People would be curious and sneak up to it, and we'd throw water balloons at them." Another time Hampton filled a weather balloon "about twenty feet around" with water and placed it in the middle of the street "so the only way a car could go by would be to puncture the balloon, and it was almost like an ocean wave—in all directions." One Halloween night they set up a sheet that they'd maneuver so that what appeared to be a ghost would confront a driver heading up Mulholland. It was all make-believe.

Aside from scaring innocent strangers, Hampton says, Lowell had ordinary hobbies like studying World War II aircraft and building model and remote-controlled airplanes. "He was pretty much an all-American kid with some worldly interests."

George Sr., who had three ranches, including a chinchilla farm just behind the family home, took Hampton hunting. Lowell, however, Hampton recalls, couldn't go outdoors much because of asthma, so he stayed at home with their mother. Hampton remembers that she played a little piano around the house, but she was best known as a competitive swimmer and diver. "She was booked to go to the Olympics the year it was canceled due to World War II," he says. A year later, 1945, she gave birth to Lowell Thomas George, named after the famed broadcaster and writer who, in the early twenties, brought British Army captain T. E. Lawrence to worldwide fame as "Lawrence of Arabia." So their mother, Florence Louise George (Willard's second wife), preferred that her boys pursue more creative pastimes. "There was a domestic struggle going on," Hampton says. "My dad always wanted to take the kids hunting—ducks, deer, dove— and Mother wanted Lowell and I to take music lessons." And so, of course, they did.

They began with harmonica lessons, with Lowell getting a chromatic while Hampton tried the larger chord and bass harmonicas. At age ten Hampton realized that his five-year-old brother was gifted musically, whereas he was not. "I had no sense of rhythm," he said. "I could read and play music, but I'd sit in front of that metronome for hours and still couldn't do it."

No matter. Within a couple of years they were performing on stage—first at their Carpenter Avenue grammar school in Studio City along with the satiric writer and recording artist Stan Freberg. Then, Hampton says, "we played Ted Mack's Amateur Hour." (*The Original Amateur Hour*, as it was officially titled, was the *America's Got Talent* of the fifties.) It's been written that one of their rivals on the show was . . . Frank Zappa, and that both acts lost to a tap dancing girl. However, Liz George says Lowell told her about being on Ted Mack's show—and winning. Hampton doesn't remember whether or not they won, but he does say that they performed the usual harmonica repertory, including "Peg o' My Heart" and "The Hungarian Rhapsody," that they once shared a stage with the Harmonicats, and that Lowell was a natural: "Not only could he read and write music; he could play it by ear. He'd hear something once and play it right back. He was quite talented."

It wasn't quite that easy. Lowell, talking to a local paper in 1979, remembered his first music lessons, at age five: "A teacher taught me how to read music, and all the time I was faking it . . . playing by ear. He'd say, 'Hold that note.' And I'd go, *Hmm*. And he'd go, 'No, that's not it.' And then I would say, 'You play it first.' Which, in terms of reading, turned out to be a real drag. I never really did get to read a whole lot until I started playing flute."

Regardless, George was extraordinarily bright—and it wasn't just his brother saying so. Patte Stahlbaum, George's first wife, remained friends with Lowell's mother after their separation. One day, she recalls, the two were driving in Los Angeles when Florence George pointed to a building and said that Lowell had gone there. "That's a school for the gifted," she told Patte.

Over the years she learned some of Lowell's family history. His father, she said, favored Hampton "just tremendously"—taking him hunting, having him helping out on his farms—"so his mom over-compensated by doing a lot of stuff with Lowell. Lowell was always the chubby, not real popular guy through school, and in addition to that, his mom, in an effort to help him, had taken him to doctors who were prescribing Dexedrine and other medications for him to lose weight. So even in childhood his metabolism was all screwed up, and he needed a lot of affirmation that he was attractive and cool."

In 1956 Willard George died, at age sixty-seven, of a cerebral hemorrhage. He left his family in fine financial shape, having sold one of his ranches near Las Vegas, just before he died. (It was later owned by Howard Hughes and is now a state park.) A few years later Florence George married Andy Anderson, and the family moved, not far away, to a house on Outpost Drive.

Hampton went from Hollywood High straight into the military, leaving behind a classical guitar he'd never played; Lowell mastered it by the time he entered North Hollywood Junior High. There his friends included Martin Kibbee, a fellow music fan who aspired to play guitar, took note of his pal's musical talents, and kept in touch, to their mutual benefit, a few years down the road.

At Hollywood High Lowell took up the flute, playing it in the school orchestra and marching band. "I was a jazzer at that time," he said. "I played flute. Legitimate flute. I hated rock and roll then. At that point I was not . . . you know . . . it was the Frankie Avalon story . . . who wanted it? Who needed it?"

Not Lowell. As Kibbee remembers, his friend was into "gut-string guitar, coffeehouse, black turtleneck sweater groups. . . . He started out with the Beatnik, jazz, Herbie Mann type of thing."

Going to clubs, said Lowell, "I saw a lot of life and didn't know what I was seeing. I'd sneak into clubs, and Lenny Bruce would be opening for Sonny Rollins, and all I can remember is thinking, 'Boy, is this guy dirty.'"

Lowell may have been affecting cool, digging Rollins, Mann, and Rahsaan Roland Kirk, but at heart he was still the prankster who pulled tricks with Hampton on Mulholland. In his high school years, he once recalled, "What we used to do is go to the Beverly Hills Hotel and hang around the pool and order drinks, to the wrong room, and sign the check, and then beat it." Wild.

Lowell was also a clown in class. At least that's the impression he gave a fellow student named Elizabeth Osborne, who was a semester behind him but shared an English class with him when she was a junior.

"Oh, he was a cutup," she said. "For some reason there was a table next to the teachers' desk, facing out toward the class, and he was sitting at that table. . . . Maybe he was in trouble, and that's why he was sitting there." Elizabeth didn't become friends with the cutup and had no idea that she would wind up marrying him.

Paul Barrere, who also would figure heavily in Lowell George's future, entered Hollywood High the year after George had graduated. Through his older brothers, he heard about George's antics. Once, playing his flute in the school orchestra, Lowell turned his chart upside down and played it, amazing and amusing his fellow students—but not the teacher. "He got thrown out," said Barrere.

Besides music, George developed an interest in martial arts. "He was really into Japanese culture," says Hampton. "Karate, samurai—he had a collection of armor and swords and weapons." Lowell had also begun adding instruments to his repertoire, including saxophone, the sitar, and a Japanese flute, the shakuhachi. "He had a lot of instruments from around the world," says Hampton. When Hampton came home on a leave he and Lowell would go downtown, "to the Japanese part of town in L.A., and watch Samurai movies, or Toshiro Mifune films together." Hampton dismisses an oft-told story about having beaten up on his younger brother, only to return from military service to learn that Lowell had become an accomplished martial artist—and get a whipping from him. "That's nonsense," he says. "He did learn karate, but so did I when I was a paratrooper."

"That's not Lowell at all," says Elizabeth, the classmate who would later become Lowell's wife. He was not a violent person, she says. "Lowell always said, 'You never make contact unless you intend to do harm.' He was a very spiritual, extraordinary person. What Lowell *did* say to Hampton was, 'Oh, would you like to come and watch me in my class?' And he did. His brother was very respectful of Lowell's extraordinary abilities."

"He was a disciplinarian," Hampton added. "And 'Mr. Karate Man' meant it. The guy practiced."

One of Hampton's most vivid memories of their youth was when, in 1963, he and Lowell went to Asia with their mother and stepfather. Hampton was twenty-three; Lowell, eighteen.

They traveled by ocean liner—first class, of course—on the *SS Lurline* to Hawaii. "We went from Hawaii to Japan; we took another ship to Hong Kong, and we toured around Asia." Stopping in Nara, a city steeped in history—it was Japan's first capital, from 710 to 784, and graced with many temples and gardens—one day the brothers escaped the tourist trappings. "We took off from the parents and went to a nightclub, even though it was daytime," Hampton remembers. As they sat at the bar a performer joined them to ask for a glass of water. Lowell noticed his flute and asked whether he could play it. The musician had no problem. "Lowell whipped off a song, and the guy asked, 'What else do you do?'" Lowell looked toward the stage, where a guitar sat against a stand. "Lowell went up, and he picked up the guitar and played, 'Ojos Negros'—and sang it in Spanish!"

The George brothers were soon invited to join a table with several sumo wrestlers and their geishas, and they wound up drinking a little sake before rejoining their parents. It was an early lesson in the strange and seductive powers of music.

By now, Lowell had picked up the electric guitar—first, a Fender Mustang and, later, a Stratocaster. "I didn't start playing guitar till after high school," he asserted. "I was going to Valley Junior College [in Sherman Oaks, northwest of Hollywood] as an art major, mostly 'cause I really enjoyed working with my hands. Welding was great. . . . Anyway, one night, I modified my molecules and went to see the Byrds. And this particular night, [drummer Michael] Clarke got into a punch-out with (guitarist David) Crosby. He jumped right over the drums, climbed over the cymbals and tore him apart! And I thought, 'Gosh! These guys are having fun!'

"The next day, my molecules still modified, I went to school, looked at my art history book for the first time and took a test. I got the highest mark in the class and quit. It was just too easy."

Lowell also worked part time as an attendant at a gas station (in the early sixties there still was such an occupation). He didn't need a job, but according to Liz, his mother wanted her son to develop a work ethic.

The filling station experience would inspire a country-flavored song later on, and the sitar was part of his curiosity about the world—the entire world—of music. But he was well aware that, here in 1965, the pop pap that he had abhorred was giving way not only to the Byrds but also to the Beatles, the Stones, the Who, the Kinks, and many more from overseas. Everywhere, molecules were being modified and, along with London, New York, and San Francisco, Los Angeles was a center for what one glib headline writer would call a "youthquake."

While George, armed with his electric guitars, explored rock and its roots in country and blues music, his guitar-picking friend from his junior high school days, Martin Kibbee, was up north in Berkeley. He made friends with a handsome fellow guitar player, Warren Klein, and, after graduation, decided to leave his English lit studies behind and take a shot at music. He thought of Lowell and convinced Klein to go with him to Los Angeles.

Klein didn't need much coercion. Born in New York, he seesawed between interests in music and science. He studied electronic engineering in the US Navy, working for the Naval Applied Science Lab. During the evenings he was on his acoustic guitar, which he took up when he was a teenager; his teachers included Dave Van Ronk. One night he went to see his mentor at a hootenanny at the Gaslight in Greenwich Village. "And Dylan would come in, surrounded by a crowd of women. He'd be high as a kite, and he'd sing 'Masters of War,' and everybody would just go nuts. It was unbelievable"—and inspirational.

Music won out, and when a friend encouraged him to check out the music scene in California and offered space in a house in Berkeley, off he went. One of the roommates there was Kibbee, and after a year in town, Kibbee suggested heading south to Hollywood. (Contrary to stories Kibbee has told, the two never performed as a duo around Berkeley. In fact, Klein says, he never played in public at all, only around the house.) When Klein and Kibbee showed up in Los Angeles and declared their interest in working with George, he wasn't shocked or wary.

As they reunited, Kibbee envisioned a songwriting team with George. For their earliest efforts Kibbee called himself "Fred Martin," partly because "I wasn't sure this was good music at the time" and partly so that the printed credit would be "George-Martin," a nod to the Beatles producer.

The Beatles were a clear influence, Kibbee says, and so were the blues. "Basically, the Beatles and the Rolling Stones, we hit Howlin' Wolf. I know we studied those Howlin' Wolf records . . . and it finally started coming out. 'Forty-four Blues' was a song that transcended pop groups."

In George and "Martin's" hands, Chester (Howlin' Wolf) Burnett's Mississippi and the Fab Four's London blended with their own native town. As Kibbee put it: "We pretty much stuck with that influence, but it was grafted onto an odd Hollywood sensibility . . . with a kind of fractured look at lyrics. We would do songs out of Marx Brothers movies. There was a song, "Alone," in a Marx Brothers movie [*A Night at the Opera*] that we did a rock arrangement of."

As they wrote their first songs they put together a quartet, adding a drummer, Cary Slavin, to join Klein on guitar and Kibbee, who had added bass guitar to his repertoire; George played flute and piccolo as well as guitar. They gave themselves a dead-dull name, the Factory, and, with a $10,000 infusion from George and Kibbee (money from parents and grandparents, according to Kibbee), they bought a van and enough equipment to begin writing songs, rehearsing, and recording, all out of a rented house on Crescent Heights Boulevard in the Hollywood Hills.

Around this time Ira Ingber, teenaged brother of Elliot Ingber, who was friends with Kibbee and would figure in the Feat saga as part of the Fraternity of Man, dropped by. He was impressed, stating, "They were always recording . . . all of the instruments were miked permanently. They were all living there. I guess they just rolled out of bed and started recording. I thought it was so impressive that they had . . . probably a Revox, some kind of decent enough tape recorder, but the whole idea was so new to me. In those days you went into a recording studio."

The Factory would get into the studios soon enough, but they began by getting into the circuit of rock clubs that were opening around Hollywood and sending out their adventurous mix of Beatles and the blues, folk rock and acid rock, nods to Captain Beefheart and the Marx Brothers. Soon enough they drew the attention of Herb Cohen, an artists' manager who was working with Frank Zappa and the Stone Poneys, a country-rock band fronted by a knockout of a singer, Linda Ronstadt.

They trooped into a studio and cut three songs as an audition for Cohen and Zappa. George and Klein wrote two of the songs: "Candy Cane Madness" had Byrdsy guitar lines and more vocal harmonies than Little Feat would ever do, and "Changes" had George in Stones mode. The third song, "Hey Girl!," was solely a George composition and seemed aimed at Zappa with its ferocious lead vocals and Slavin's hard-charging drums.

No record deal was made, but Cohen agreed to manage them. Further, Zappa was interested enough in the band that he produced two of their other songs, both by George and Kibbee. It would be the fledgling team's first compositions to be recorded.

Zappa acted as producer on only a couple of sides, but his impact was immediate and clear. On "Lightning-Rod Man," a George-Kibbee song, Lowell sounded like a madman, in an asylum. As he said himself, "It's a cross between 'They're Coming to Take Me Away, Ha-Ha' and Ian and Sylvia . . . somewhere in the middle there." He was being facetious, but he did get some odd instructions from Zappa. Talking about the song, which he said was based on a Herman Melville short story, Kibbee recounted, "Zappa said, 'Forget Melville; sing it like Elvis.' 'OK, now, sing it like Little Richard.'"

Actually, he sang the opening lines kind of like Napoleon XIV, who laughed and screeched his way through his 1966 novelty hit, "They're Coming to Take Me Away." But there's no Ian & Sylvia—a Canadian folk duo of that period—within earshot.

The other Zappa production was another song by Lowell and Martin, "The Loved One," which was short on musical interest but featured a bit of eccentricity with George, at song's end, suddenly shouting. Zappa also performed on the song, playing prepared piano, its strings damped by a screwdriver wedged between them. He'd also pitched in vocals on "Lightning-Rod Man."

Soon after the sessions the Factory got a new drummer, Dallas Taylor, out of Denver and on his way, in two years' time, to backup glory with Crosby, Stills, Nash & Young. With the Factory, however, he had anything but glory.

Taylor was on board when the Factory began to be included on bills with Zappa's Mothers of Invention, including several concert events patterned after the Trips Festivals and Acid Tests that had taken place up north in San Francisco. The Los Angeles versions of these early gatherings of the hippie tribes included GUAMBO, or Great Underground Arts Masked Ball and Orgy, staged in July and followed a few weeks later by a "Son of GUAMBO."

In September came "Freak Out" at the Shrine Auditorium in downtown Los Angeles. The concert lineup itself was freaky. The producer chose to headline Little Gary Ferguson, billed as a "Sensational 7 Year Old" and never heard from again. Under *ALSO* on the concert poster was the Mothers, the West Coast Pop Experimental Band, Count Five (the only act that was on the charts at the time with "Psychotic Reaction"), and the Factory, credited with a song they never recorded: "Your Ma Said You Cried in Your Sleep Last Night," which was a 1961 hit single for Kenny Dino. The Turtles covered it in 1965.

Although Zappa looked the part for a "Freak Out," he was a serious musician with a disdain for the long-haired crowd. He had no interest in the sex-and-drugs lifestyle that was not simply emerging but actually exploding in major cities in the United States and around the world. Pamela DesBarres, who was part of the GTOs (Girls Together Outrageously), a performance group comprised mostly of groupies, had a theory: "When everybody got weirder, Frank got less weird. I think one of the main reasons he moved to Laurel Canyon was to make fun of it."

But a gig was a gig, so there were the Mothers—and the Factory.

And there was Lynn Hearne, a fourteen-year-old from Covina in the San Gabriel Valley, twenty-something miles from downtown Los Angeles. She was with a few girls, who mostly wanted to try to get autographs from the Count Five. But Lynn was more into the Mothers. The girls were all too young to attend the show, so they hung out in the parking lot. After her friends gathered autographs from the departing members of Count Five, they stayed near the backstage door until a security guard took pity on them—downtown was pretty sketchy in the midsixties—and let them in, just in time to see the Mothers.

That was fine by Lynn, who had no idea that she was about to become Lowell George's and, a bit later, Little Feat's first major fan. (She would also become known, in Feat circles, as Shag and, later, as Shaglyn.)

Sitting in a café in San Francisco, near carefully assembled binders of Little Feat memorabilia, she talks, more than forty-five years later, as though it was just the other night. "I went to this concert with a bunch of girls I had just met. So somebody's mother piled a bunch of us young girls into a station wagon and dropped us off. We stood outside getting autographs." After the guard let them in, saying, "Look, you're safer inside," Lynn was stunned. "Boy, was that a mind-blowing experience . . . because it was a full freak-out with all the body paint and all the freaky people, and I loved it.

"We all walked out and stood in the parking lot waiting for somebody's mom to show up . . . and it just got later and later, and there was this beautiful old vintage Morgan in the parking lot, so I gravitated to that, and we were looking at this car, and Lowell came out and saw all of us hanging around the car and wanted to know what we were doing. We said, 'Waiting for someone's mom,' and so he stayed with us until her mom came. He had his sweater on inside out, and my grandfather used to tell me that putting your clothes on inside out was bad luck, so I tried to pull that on Lowell, but he wasn't having it.

"So we're chatting it up. 'Oh, you were onstage? Let me have an autograph.' He said, 'I've never given an autograph before . . . I don't know what to write.' And I said, 'Write that.' I handed him a sheet of lined paper and a pencil, and he wrote, 'This is my first autograph. Lowell George.'

"He also wrote out the names of the guys in the Factory and his phone number and his address in the Hollywood Hills." This is what is known as light security.

The drummer at "Freak Out" was Dallas Taylor, but he was not long for the band. There are wildly varied stories about how Richie Hayward came to replace him. George said he met Hayward at the "Freak Out": "We had Dallas Taylor playing drums in the band at that time and he . . . had had an appendix operation. He was ripping his stitches while he was playing the drums. He was dropping the beats and slowing down, and I thought, 'Wow, this guy's terrible. I've got to get another drummer.' He was actually very good, but he was just ill. And I didn't find out until years later that he was bleeding through his shirt. I mean, he needed the money real bad, and he was so honorable that he wouldn't cop to the fact that he was sick.

"And Richie came up and said, 'That guy's no good. You need a good drummer. I'm your drummer.' . . . He was with a girl, Animal Huxley was her name—a relative of Aldous Huxley [she was the granddaughter of the author of *Brave New World* and *The Doors of Perception*]. Animal brought him to the concert." Soon Hayward was in the band.

But this is not how Hayward remembered it, nor Hearne. She says he attended the concert after spotting an ad in the *Los Angeles Free Press*, an underground paper, reading, "WANTED: Drummer. Must be freaky." Hayward himself told Robyn Flans at *Modern Drummer* magazine that he had spotted that ad when he was still a new kid in town but didn't make his first contact with the Factory at any concert. He went on to describe his journey from the Midwest to Hollywood.

Richie was born in 1946 in Clear Lake, Iowa, where a parade changed his life. He was three, he recalls: "The bass drum came by, and I felt it in my chest—in my guts. Then there was no stopping me; it was all I wanted to do."

How good for Richie that, even before kindergarten, he had his career mapped out. How bad for his parents, who'd taken him to that parade. "They weren't terribly discouraging," he recalled, but as he grew older "they did find it annoying to have me pounding on things in the basement all the time, while I neglected my studies and was turning into a young hooligan before their very eyes."

They did not relent, as so many parents did, and buy him his first instruments. So at the age of eleven, he said, "I mowed lawns and shoved rocks until I saved enough money to buy this Montgomery Ward drum set for $150. I remembered waiting for *months* for that thing to come in."

He learned more from pounding away on the set along with records than he would from teachers, although he did join his high school band. But, he said, "I never liked the discipline part of it."

"The first drummer who turned my head was Sonny Payne, who was with Count Basie," Richie said. "It was on some hokey black and white TV show, but I was mesmerized. The way he moved was hypnotic, energetic. Playing the drums became a passion for me right then."

Richie came to favor big-band drummers like Jack Sperling, whose résumé ranged from Bunny Berigan and Tex Beneke to Les Brown and Pete Fountain, and who doubled bass and tom-toms on his set, playing aggressively. Richie got good enough that, about a year after taking delivery of his first drums, he had a job playing a Shriners' New Year's Eve party: "We played old standards. I was younger than most of their children."

Rock and roll came in 1960, when, just as he was about to enter high school, he and a few friends started a band and played the kind of gigs a band could find in a small town in Iowa—frat parties and roller-skating rinks.

Within a few years he realized that as a young musician with aspirations to play the best drums he could and with the best musicians he could find, he was in the wrong place. "I wanted to be a drummer, and in 1964, 1965, there was no place for a drummer except the Ramada Inn lounge. So I had to go to a coast. It was either New York or L.A. I flipped a coin and it came up New York, so I flipped it again. I didn't want to say 'Youse,' and I didn't want cold weather in dirty big cities. So I came here to a dirty bigger city."

He was nineteen or twenty when he landed in Los Angeles. He knew one person—"vaguely, very vaguely"—in town and stayed with him until he got his first drumming gig with a bar band called the Rebels, playing covers of rock tunes at the Lucky Lady in Pasadena.

One day he spotted the ad in the *Free Press* seeking a drummer who "must be freaky." He had no clue what that meant, but he'd had enough of the Rebels, so off he went to the address in the ad.

"It turned out to be Lowell and this band, the Factory," he recalled. "I went in to audition and there was this long stairway going from the driveway up into the band house; it was in the hills just above Crescent Heights. There were like four drummers there with their kits, and all the Mothers were there except Frank: Don Preston, Ray Collins, Roy Estrada, and Jimmy Carl Black. They were all sitting in there getting big laughs out of all of this auditioning of drummers. It was a bit intimidating, but I got the gig."

The Factory, as Hayward saw it, was "a Sixties L.A. band: bell bottoms, big buckles, sandals." That, of course, was the costume of the day, and that was the band's look when they appeared on two television series early in 1967. In an episode of *Gomer Pyle, U.S.M.C.*, they played themselves, unbilled, as a rock band in a nightclub packed with young people doing the shimmy and the Frug. And in *F Troop*, the post–Civil War comedy series, they portrayed "the Bedbugs," a band brought into Fort Courage to play a military ball. George and Klein sling guitars—Klein frantically, as if he's been bitten by some bugs—while Kibbee is on what appears to be a two-string bass and Hayward thrashes away on a hatbox drum and a single cymbal. They make a lot of noise, destroying "Camptown Races" and less recognizable tunes, fend off an attack of vegetables and other missiles at one saloon, and run around a little as if they were in a Monkees episode. George gets several lines of dialogue until they are eclipsed by an upstart folk band, the Termites, who, a century before Dylan, sing "Mr. Tambourine Man." Fun stuff.

Herb Cohen made another Hollywood connection for the band with Marshall Leib, an A&R man—that is, talent scout—who'd been a member of the Teddy Bears, the vocal trio that had the hit "To Know Him Is to Love Him" in 1958, written by fellow Teddy Bear Phil Spector. According to Kibbee, Leib got the Factory signed to Uni Records, the future home of, among others, Neil Diamond and Elton John.

Leib took them into a studio and supervised the recording of a half-dozen tracks. But Martin Kibbee was not impressed. "He was a partner of Phil Spector," he said. "What he tried to foist on us was the 'Wall of Sound' meets the Byrds. It was sort of a mess."

From the few Factory recordings that exist, it's clear that the band could've been a contender. Even though the guys were still finding their way as songwriters and musicians, they could have been mistaken for such post-Byrds folk-rock bands as the Turtles or the Leaves. They could speed themselves up to punky, garage-band mode, echoing the Seeds, or sink into a bubblegum quagmire with clunky lyrics—"loneliness is only just a lie"—and tempos. Contrary to what Kibbee said, there was little of the bass-and-echo heavy "Wall of Sound" that was Spector's signature. The Byrds were a clear influence, but they were only a takeoff point.

From the start George—and his writing partners—had a sense of humor and an openness to novel sounds. In "When I Was an Apple" George portrayed the fruit, delighting in getting polished by a girl, taunting listeners who might wish they were the apple of the girl's eye, and ending with the sounds of an apple being eaten. Uni released it as the Factory's first single, putting on the flip side "Smile, Let Your Life Begin," a jaunty song with military-band drum riffs and George on piccolo. Nothing happened with the single, and Uni tried another release, "No Place I'd Rather Be," an understated love song by George and Warren Klein. For its B-side, it went again with "Smile." "No Place" also went nowhere, and within months the band, which never recorded enough songs for an album, would call it quits. As Kibbee recalled, "We were very dissatisfied with our deal and our producer, Marshall Leib."

But at least they had a couple of singles to show off. On St. Patrick's Day, 1967, six months after the "Freak Out" show, Lynn Hearne, the girl who'd acquired George's first autograph, appeared at his door. She was celebrating her fifteenth birthday and got her sister to drive her over. She did phone first, "and he said, 'Yeah, our band is over here. Come on over.' So we did, and they gave me a 45, and I got signatures of three of the four guys in the Factory, and I met Richie Hayward on my fifteenth birthday."

By the latter part of 1967, according to most accounts, the Factory was no more. Kibbee, Klein, and Hayward heard that a band called the Fraternity of Man was looking for a new rhythm section and, en masse, got the gig. They joined lead guitarist and vocalist Elliot Ingber and Lawrence "Stash" Wagner, who also played guitar and sang. Ingber, who was born in Minneapolis and had been in Los Angeles since 1958, had multiple connections with the young men who would become Little Feat. He'd been a member of the Mothers of Invention, playing on their debut, *Freak Out!*, in 1966, and he was friends with Martin Kibbee. Before the Factory rhythm section joined Fraternity of Man, Ingber and Wagner had composed "Don't Bogart Me," better known, especially after it appeared on the soundtrack of *Easy Rider*, as "Don't Bogart That Joint."

For Hayward, however, there was all too much Bogarting in the new band. "Of all things to be called, that band was definitely not a fraternity," he said. "There was a lot of dissension, to be quite nice about it. We didn't get along at all, and we didn't play terribly well either." Still, the Fraternity went on to make two albums, play the club circuit, and tour. All the while George pursued other interests.

While in the Factory he, along with Warren Klein, had begun taking sitar classes at Ravi Shankar's Kinnara School of Music, which had just opened a Los Angeles branch in the spring of 1967. Soon he was showing off his skills at gatherings at composer Jimmy Webb's house. Webb had scored big with "Up, Up and Away" and "By the Time I Get to Phoenix," so he was living large in a twenty-three-room mansion in the Hollywood Hills. It was the former Philippine embassy, a perfect rental for a nouveau riche musician.

Fred Tackett, a guitarist from Arkansas who was friends with Webb, was a regular visitor. "There was a party going on twenty-four hours a day," he recalled, "and you'd go downstairs and there'd be Jimi Hendrix asleep on a couch or Mitch Mitchell playing drums in the basement. Larry Coryell was part of that too. And Lowell would come by a lot." The first time Tackett saw George he was dressed all in white—not unlike Webb—and was sitting on the floor, playing a sitar.

When George wasn't playing or showing off the instrument, he was taking music courses at Los Angeles Community College. He wasn't thinking much about rock bands at the time, though a former classmate was thinking about him.

John Fleckenstein was playing bass in the Standells, a garage band that had done pretty well for themselves. They'd had a hit, "Dirty Water," late in 1966 and had appeared in a couple of movies, including *Riot on Sunset Strip*, a teen exploiter for which Fleckenstein, known as "Fleck," composed the title tune.

When drummer and lead vocalist Dick Dodd left in 1968, Fleck, who was still new to the Standells at the time, suggested George take over the singing. "We'd known each other all through middle school and high school," he said, "and I'd been doing things with Lowell since we left high school, so when that spot opened up, I actually pulled Lowell out—he was going to LA City College and studying music theory. I told him, 'You gotta quit and come be a rock and roll guy.'"

George later would recall the job offer, which would pay $500 a week. "My music teacher advised against it, pointing out that I had a B average," he said. "I asked him how much he was making, and he thought for a minute and said, 'Take the job.'"

"So he got in our group," said Fleckenstein, "But the Standells was kind of punk-pop, and Larry Tamblyn and Lowell had a different vision, and they kinda bumped heads."

The Standells: punk-pop. Lowell George: blues, rock, jazz, shaku-hachi, sitar . . . bump city.

Tamblyn, who played organ and did some lead vocals, recalled, "Having Lowell George in the group was quite a departure from our sound. It got a little more psychedelic."

Replacing Dodd, a former Mouseketeer who young girls found attractive, with the slightly portly George also had ramifications. As George recalled, "I only did about six or seven dates with them, and on one gig these Chicano girls, fourteen or fifteen, showed up and stood around the door and asked about Dickie Dodd. . . . they found out I'd replaced him, and I was in fear of my life for the next four gigs because these girls kept showing up. Shades of Charles Manson! I envisioned being attacked in my sleep."

Besides fearing potentially homicidal teenagers, George had other issues with the band—or vice versa. According to Tamblyn, it didn't help that on joining the Standells, he tried to become their leader. Tamblyn was one of only two original members of the group, which started in 1962. (This helps explain the name—those were the days of artists like Troy Shondell and groups like the Dovells, the Shirelles, and the Marcels.) They had evolved from their years of matching outfits and pompadours and had entered the sixties scene. Now, after one hit, they were coming apart as they dealt with Dodd's departure and problems with management.

"It was real enlightening," said George, "because it was a band in real decline. The other guys were bringing their hairdryers and mag-nifying mirrors along to gigs. They used to fluff up before the gig! I was stunned."

But George came up with his own ideas about hair. "We were re-hearsing about a week," Tamblyn recalled, "when Lowell announced his new vision for the Standells. He wanted us to revert to a greaser look, a parody of ourselves." George, he thought, "looked down upon the stuff we did. He wanted us to do a Sha Na Na thing."

Fleck didn't recall George wanting the guys to emulate the band that specialized in fifties oldies, complete with donning fifties drag. Nonetheless, said Tamblyn, "He and I argued about our differences. Essentially, he said 'my way or the highway,' and I stomped out."

But not right away. Although George's stint with the Standells lasted only a few months, Tamblyn did recall a few concerts, most notably one at Pierce College in Canoga Park in the San Fernando Valley. "It was an afternoon concert, outdoors," he said. "As part of the show, Lowell sat on the floor and played the sitar and sang." And, Fleck added, "he was playing the tablas. We put a little carpet down on the stage, and Lowell sat down and played. One of the songs that I wrote had a little part that we could put the sitar in."

George didn't make any recordings with the Standells, but during his time there he did go into a studio with Fleckenstein—to produce jingles for a Japanese candy. "A friend of mine worked at a commercials company, and they had a client who had 'Melody' candy bars in Japan. They wanted jingles, rock and roll stuff. Lowell and I just sat in his living room and wrote the songs, and then we'd go over and record them."

Many years later, while being interviewed for WHCN in Hartford, Connecticut, George remembered that assignment, adding a few additional details. "Yeah, and it was some guitar and rock 'n' roll, and I got three great background singers. What happened was, it turns out that the commercial got canned because in Japan they don't say 'Melody,' they say 'Merody.' And it got blanked three times. . . . And there went my commercial career."

And here, again, came Frank Zappa.

Chapter 3

"YOU GOT UGLY LITTLE FEET"

FRANK ZAPPA'S BAND WAS CALLED THE MOTHERS OF INVENTION, but that was a reinvented name that its label, MGM, forced because it protested to the original, more succinct, and slightly ruder "The Mothers." They had released their first album, *Freak Out!*, in 1966 and, under Zappa's forceful and exacting direction, issued four more recordings in the following two years: *Absolutely Free, Lumpy Gravy, We're Only in It for the Money*, and the fifties doo-wop send-up and tribute *Cruising with Ruben and the Jets*.

Mothers came and went, and the departure of a lead vocalist created an opening for Lowell George. Ray Collins left in late 1968, and Zappa thought of the guy who'd fronted the Factory, who played some mean guitar and had a way with words, whether he was speaking or singing.

Likewise, Zappa had made an impression on George when he served as producer for those Factory tracks. But soon after George joined the Mothers, around October or November of 1968, he mentally adjusted his job description. "No one could replace Ray," he told one writer in 1975. "He was a singer par excellence and had a sense of humor I couldn't hope to get near. So I really ended up playing more guitar than singing." Later, he told another reporter, "I was really performing no function in the band."

Still, he said, "It was very interesting to go out on the road and play with Frank Zappa. . . . One time we played . . . a girls college in Massachusetts . . . and one guy stood up and said, 'Fuck you, Frank Zappa' [for the sake of radio, George muffed the "f," saying "ruck" and, to these ears, 'hruck'], and some other guy jumped up from across the hall and went, 'You can't say "fuck you, Frank Zappa!" . . . You can't do that.' And somebody else jumped up and said, 'You wanna bet? He can say "fuck you" to anybody he wants to!' There were . . . maybe three thousand people in this hall, and pretty soon the whole place was rocking with people saying 'You can't say "fuck you" . . . ' And Frank turned around to me and said, 'What do we do now? The show's over. We did it already. This is what I was aiming at! This is what I wanted to happen!'"

Offstage George said his contributions were minimal. "Frank wanted some new faces in the group, but outside of a weird piece about a German border guard, I didn't get in the spotlight much," he said. "It didn't help that I was the second guitarist in a group with a famous lead guitarist. You can hear me play on the Mothers' album, *Weasels Ripped My Flesh*, but that's about it."

The "weird piece about a German border guard" was George's big moment as a Mother, as he played rhythm guitar and pretended to interview travelers crossing the border. The track was called "Didja Get Any Onya?," which, George pointed out in a radio interview, also featured bassist Roy Estrada and appeared on *Weasels*.

George did appear on two other albums, both issued after his departure. But credits, he said, were haphazard, at least when it came to his contributions. "Everything was in a state of flux," he told Andy Childs *of Zigzag*. "Those moments were never chronicled." George recalls playing on *Hot Rats* as well as singing on the oldie "WPLJ" in the album *Burnt Weeny Sandwich* but not being credited for either. And a photo of him was included in *Uncle Meat*, although he did nothing on that album.

But ultimately George and Zappa weren't meant to be. Although both appreciated a wide range of music and both would prove to be exacting workaholics, there was one crucial difference, as George's pal, Martin Kibbee, noted. Whereas Lowell was fun loving and free wheeling, drinking alcohol and enjoying drugs, "Frank was more a sober leader of a crew. Frank didn't take drugs."

Early in the history of the Mothers Zappa had been arrested on suspicion of inciting a riot. Said George: "He was paranoid that the band would get busted, so he never got high, and he always made a point of saying, 'You guys cannot get high,' although something other than that was expressed in the intent of his music. *Freak Out* was really high music."

But it wasn't paranoia that drove Zappa's stance against drugs; instead, he never was into them. Nor was he into the hippie scene or most of the pop and rock bands that sprouted in Los Angeles and in Laurel and Topanga Canyons or played the Whisky and the rest of the club circuit.

George, born and raised in and around Laurel Canyon, was pretty comfortable with the evolving culture of sex, drugs, and rock 'n' roll. He began to chafe under Zappa's autocratic, demanding ways, and his distant demeanor. By May 1969, just about half a year after he'd signed on, he was on his way out.

Pamela DesBarres, who gained fame when she wrote a book about her exploits as a groupie, told writer Barney Hoskyns that Zappa fired George for smoking marijuana "all the time," adding, "I don't even know what Lowell was really doing in the Mothers, because it wasn't his sort of music. I guess he saw it as a stepping-stone, which was what it turned out to be."

But Lowell himself said, simply, "I just never really got along with Frank, and one day we mutually decided it was enough. Frank suggested I start my own group . . . "

Before that day, however, George had composed "Willin'," his ode to truck drivers, whose protagonist suggested that he'd be open to a gift of "weed, whites, and wine." Many people consider that song the reason for George's departure. "I think Frank was both impressed and put off by the song because of the drug reference," said Bill Payne. "He was somewhat conservative on certain levels."

But George said he never showed the song to Zappa. "I was always smart enough not to submit it," he said. "But he did hear it once, and a few days later I was offered to start my own band, which was a nice way of firing me, I think."

Whatever the reason was, the split was amicable, enough so that, according to George, the two artists stayed in touch over the years. And before George decamped, Zappa asked him to do some production work for the GTOs, the band of groupies he'd signed onto Bizarre, one of two labels he'd formed in partnership with Warner Bros. (the other was Straight). And George did, working with some members of the Jeff Beck Group to give the girls some musical support on *Permanent Damage*. Two tracks bore George's stamp—and slide guitar: the countrified "Do Me in Once and I'll Be Sad, Do Me in Twice and I'll Know Better" and "I Have a Paintbrush in My Hand to Color a Triangle," a song about a ménage à trois involving a GTO and a Rolling Stone (Brian Jones).

But George didn't recall *Permanent Damage* as his finest moment. "There were no real singers in the GTOs, they were performers rather than singers," he said. "But that was the original Little Feat on those GTOs songs: Russ Titelman on guitar, Ry Cooder and me, and I go back to those two cuts we did and I gasp and cringe. They are hell on earth."

DesBarres has fonder memories. George, she said, did a lot on the GTOs' album. "Frank worked on the theater of the thing, but Lowell did the music," she recalled in an interview in the early nineties. George, she added, "was just a sweet-natured, angelic man. God, I just loved him, and I still have letters from him."

A lot of women loved George, and vice versa. Through the years numerous highly recognizable names would be linked with George's, including Linda Ronstadt, Bonnie Raitt, and Rickie Lee Jones. His admiration society, many of whom would sing and play with him in both recording studios and informal jams, also included Emmylou Harris, Nicolette Larson, and June Millington of the all-woman rock band Fanny.

But the first women were girls—girls in junior high school, fellow students at Hollywood High. Two of them would wind up marrying him. There was, of course, Elizabeth, Liz Osborne, who met him in high school. Before her there was Patte Price. She went to North Hollywood Junior High with Lowell, then to North Hollywood High, but she saw him at parties and other occasions.

Patte was the oldest of three Price sisters. She was born in 1945—the same year as George—and Pam was born in 1946, with Priscilla ("Prissy") in 1948. All three come into play in the Little Feat saga, and not only with George.

Pam Price was married to Richie Hayward, George's Factory mate, and the couple shared their apartment on Fountain Avenue with Pam's two sisters. In the late sixties they all were in their early twenties, and as Patte recalled, "Lots of musicians and friends would come by, and Lowell was one of them."

But before George began connecting with the Price sisters, there was another girl, Susan "Jonna" Taylor, whose brief relationship with him produced his first son, Forrest, in March of 1969.

Soon after Forrest was born his mother took off with him, and George would not meet him until 1978. In the meantime George gained entry into the Price club—but not with Patte. She was seeing others (including, at one point, Warren Klein). Instead, Lowell dated Prissy. But then Patte and her boyfriend broke up, Lowell and Prissy followed suit, and, one evening, Lowell invited Patte to join him at a recording studio. "I went, and we decided it was pretty serious." This was in 1968, and they married in 1970, the same year their son, Luke, was born.

Patte, who'd kept an eye on Lowell through the years, may have been the girl who knew him best. From her perch in the "popular group" in junior high, she saw that Lowell admired her. Although they attended different high schools, they saw each other at various events and would do a little flirting. That went on into young adulthood, at Fraternity of Man's house in Laurel Canyon and, finally, on Fountain Avenue. But theirs seemed to be more a budding friendship than a hot romance. It was compatibility, born out of familiarity. As she recalls, "I was interested in a couple of other guys [including Warren Klein] and Lowell spent time with Priscilla. He was always quite nice to me, and when my patella got shoved the wrong way by a dancer at an Alice Cooper event, resulting in a full-leg cast, Lowell was even nicer. He focused a *lot* of attention on me. He would try to teach me some keyboarding and generally just lasered in. Lowell was intelligent, goal oriented in terms of his music, and willing to express and share his vulnerability with me. He even cried when I told him at one point early in our lives at Ben Lomond that I didn't think it would work out."

Once they married, Lowell and Richie began hanging out more often, what with their Price connection and all. "So we started Little Feat," said Hayward.

Not so fast, though. Although Lowell and Patte were married and living in a two-bedroom house on Ben Lomond Drive near Griffith Park, Liz Osborne also was in the picture. She was now Liz Levy, having married Tom Levy, one of George's close friends from grammar school. Liz recalls crossing paths with George around the time of the Factory. Levy lived in a guest house above the Factory's communal home on Crescent Heights, and Liz went to Europe for a year and a half, attending college. She returned, married Levy, and had a son, Jed, before parting ways with Levy.

Years later Pam Price would put it perfectly in a comment for a profile of George in *People* magazine: "This is the most incestuous band I've ever heard of. It's a riot when the kids get together with all the different combinations."

During my phone conversation with Liz George about affairs of the heart—hers and Lowell's in particular—she made my head spin with a two-sentence summary: "This is how it is: my first husband, Tom, is married to my second husband's first wife's sister. And those two sisters are sisters of Pam, who was married to Richie." Another of those sisters—Prissy, the youngest—married Rick Harper, who served as road manager for both Fraternity of Man and Little Feat.

Liz George was reluctant to divulge much about her and Lowell's personal life, stating, "I loved his cartoon vision. I loved his writing, his music. I think he's an extraordinary writer, and we used to read poetry together. He's very charismatic."

It was at "the beginning of the seventies," she allowed, "that we realized that we were more than friends. Let's just say it was a segue."

Patte Price (now Patte Stahlbaum) would share something else. "Lowell was a guy who had a lot of baggage," she began. "His dad favored Hampton just tremendously, so his mom overcompensated by doing a lot of stuff with Lowell. Lowell was always the chubby, not real popular guy through school, and in addition to that, his mom, in an effort to help him, had taken him to doctors who were prescribing Dexedrine and other medications for him to lose weight. So his metabolism is all screwed up, and he needed a lot of affirmation that he was attractive and cool, and for that reason he just couldn't be monogamous . . . and although I'm positive he really cared for me, and I know he loved Luke, our child, he understood that I was hoping for a more monogamous relationship, and so he moved out. He told me he couldn't be what he thought I needed someone to be. And it was soon after that that Liz became more and more involved with him."

She adds, if it wasn't Liz, "it would have been someone else."

Tom Levy, for one, wished it had been someone else. When Liz moved in with Lowell, Levy severed his longtime friendship with his childhood buddy. According to Patte, he has not yet come to terms with either Liz or Lowell.

Patte knows this because Levy, rather ironically, wound up marrying a Price sister: Prissy.

When Lowell and Richie Hayward were married to Patte and Pam Price, respectively, they were brothers-in-law and formed the original core of what would become Little Feat. Candidates for the roles beyond guitar and drums surrounded them, and one was another Mother: Roy Estrada, who could play bass, if he wanted. And for keyboards there was a Mothers wannabe who, having failed to crack that band, had joined George in helping bail out the Fraternity of Man when recording its second album. George knew of his talent and put him on standby. But it would not be long before he too would join Little Feat.

When Bill Payne and George first met in 1969, Payne was twenty years old and had already been playing piano for fifteen of those years. Born in Ventura, west of Los Angeles and south of Santa Barbara, he remembers getting into music at about age five. His inspirations were his mother and a competitive streak—even at that early age.

His mother would put him on her lap while she played the piano for him. "I'm like, 'This is cool,' plus being close to your mother, at that age. It's just another connective tissue for me." When the time came for piano lessons, he watched as his sister tried and gave up. "But the little girl across the street, Marilyn Newell, was taking piano lessons. And my feeling, honestly, was that if she can do it, I want to do it."

Bill flunked his first instructor—that is, he decided that *she* was hitting too many wrong notes—so his parents found Ruth Newman, who stuck. When six year-old Billy brought in a Davy Crockett song, she broke it down for him, teaching him "the magic of C, D, E, the first notes that I read." He learned about the "happy notes" from his right hand, along with the left's "exotic, dark quality of the minor, and it just ignited this magical connection for me."

But she gave Bill (who's also called Billy) more than musical instruction. When he failed to prepare for his lessons, "she had a way of making me feel guilty without completely destroying me. But she was good about making sure I came to the lessons prepared, so I wasn't letting her down. Which was really important." Newman, young Billy decided, had become his "second mother."

He explored a couple of other instruments, clarinet and drums. In high school he even auditioned as a drummer for a band in Santa Maria. But he wound up where he belonged—at the keyboards, piano, and various organs with a band called the Debonaires. His first paid performance got him $5 and all the beer he could drink, which was none at all, as he was only sixteen or seventeen at the time.

But he hadn't decided on being a musician yet. As a kid in Ventura, he was a radio fan—following a DJ, Dick Shipley; calling in and winning contests; and even remembering some of the records he won, including *The Ghost of Billy Baloo* by Dorsey Burnett, whose big hit was "(There Was) a Tall Oak Tree" and whose brother was Johnny Burnett, who'd have a few hits of his own.

Watching TV, Billy also picked out music, whether from pop acts on the *Ed Sullivan Show* or the scores behind *The Maltese Falcon* or an Alfred Hitchcock movie. He absorbed it all.

After a short stint at college—a year and a half at Allan Hancock Jr. College in the Santa Barbara area and a few minutes at a school in

Ventura, covering 1967 and '68—Payne dropped out and lived on the streets for the first half of 1969. He slept in his car and dreamt about being in a rock band.

He visited Texas and, several times, San Francisco, where the Summer of Love had come and been long gone. Still, he thought of that city as the Paris of the late sixties: "the center of the music universe," a hotbed for live music. He met Bill Champlin, the talented singer and songwriter of the Sons of Champlin. But when he joined a band, Payne discovered that "they were basically drug dealers, and they had everything but talent." Next he met up with a group from Santa Maria in Southern California, where he'd gone to college. They were scufflers, telling Payne, "You have to sleep on the streets first." Payne had been there, done that. Just to prove himself, he hit the streets for a couple of weeks and then joined the band, called Wedge, for a gig—a Hell's Angels party—and promptly quit.

Payne was desperate, he says, to get any kind of work so as to avoid having to go to war in Vietnam. Back in his car away from home, Payne turned his attention back to Southern California. Since junior high school days he had been a fan of the Mothers of Invention. Now, he decided, he'd like to join them.

He knew about a deal Zappa had made with Warner Bros. Records for a label of his own—two, in fact. One was Bizarre, the other, Straight. Payne chose to try Bizarre, called the label several times, and was told that Zappa was in Europe. A secretary suggested Payne talk with Jeff Simmons, who was the guitarist with a band, Eureka, that was on Straight Records; Payne had seen them in a concert with Zappa and the GTOs. Simmons heard Payne play and was impressed enough to turn him away: "Jeff hears me play, and he goes, 'Whoa, I don't know if this is gonna work. I kinda play keyboards too, but I play guitar too." However, Simmons did give Payne a lead, saying, "There's a guy you ought to meet. His name is Lowell George." So Payne called the secretary at Bizarre again and asked if she knew a guy named Lowell George. He had just left the Mothers of Invention, Payne learned, and was forming a band.

As big a fan as he was of the Mothers—*Uncle Meat* had just been released, and, he says, "I fell in love with it"—Payne didn't know

Lowell George's name. No matter. He called him up and soon was driving, quite nervously, toward George's home in the Los Feliz area of Los Angeles. He felt hope, fear, and desperation, he recalled, and he found himself hugging the slow lane of the freeway. "I wanted to make sure I made it to my destination."

His memories of that day remain vivid. He showed up at George's home, on Ben Lomond Drive. "He lived in this little wooden house, next door to Liz, who eventually became Liz George," he recalled. "It's trees, the door's open, this blond-haired girl sitting cross-legged on the floor, listening to Eric Satie . . . she says, 'Oh, Lowell's expecting you, Bill, come on in. He'll be back in about four or five hours.' I go 'cool.' I'm here, with a nice girl. So I just started looking around. I'm checking out his books. He's got *Howl*. He's got Carl Sandburg's poetry. He's got *Last Exit to Brooklyn*—brutal book. . . . Those are some of the books I remember that he had. . . . His album collection consisted of *Om* by Coltrane, he's got one of Zappa's releases on Lenny Bruce, and there's the Smithsonian Blues Collection—"Join the Band" is on there . . . which we later used for *Waiting for Columbus*. So I'm noticing all this stuff. So he's got jazz, he's got blues, he's got Howlin' Wolf and Muddy Waters. Then up on the wall he's got a sitar . . . no, up on the wall he's got a Samurai sword. The sitar was in a corner, on another wall."

Having cased the joint pretty thoroughly, Payne waited several hours for George to return. "My reading on the meeting," he said, "was, it was like the first meeting between Castro and Che Guevara." The first time they met they talked about everything under the sun: "That's the way Lowell and I were. We talked about music, about goals, ideals, connections between things. I asked him about some of his books, the poetry and what not. We had a real connection." As Payne would later write, "What struck me most was his humor, his intelligence, and his innate ability to draw connections between disparate topics, musically or otherwise. He asked, did I want to join the band that he was forming? No, I wanted to meet Frank Zappa. He said, 'Well, it's really nice meeting you. Why don't we stay in touch, and maybe even try and write a couple of songs?'" George had a spinet piano, and they'd "traded musical quotes," with George on acoustic guitar.

George and Payne did more than keep in touch. Payne wound up staying at the house on occasion and, sometimes, sleeping outside—at his own peril.

As he recalls, "When Lowell got together with Patte, she brought a cat into the house. I'm allergic to cats, so I started sleeping out in Lowell's VW van, 'cause I didn't have any money to go anywhere. I would roll up the windows at night because the Lo Bianca family had been murdered a week or two before." Charlie Manson and six members of his own "family" had wreaked havoc at the home of the Lo Biancas, a husband and wife, on Waverly Drive in Los Feliz, just a few minutes drive from George's place on Ben Lomond Drive. "I was paranoid. I was sweating in a sweat box in this van, and I wound up a few years later writing 'Cat Fever,' which came out on the *Sailin' Shoes* record."

I won't let them get me 'cause they're demon figures that are after me . . .

Cat fever or not, Patte doesn't remember Payne living outside in a VW bus, van, or any kind of vehicle. "Jeez! Prior to Luke being born we had a second bedroom." And even with the baby's arrival, she noted, "There was a floor."

Payne did get to meet Zappa about a month later. "I realized that I wasn't in the league to play with Frank Zappa," he said. "I couldn't read well enough to do what he would require. I was also becoming more aware of Lowell's immense talents. I liked the guy."

As George himself recalled, "I took him up to Zappa's house to audition for the Mothers, but Frank was editing a trailer for *200 Motels* and didn't have time to talk to Bill. So we drove back to my house where he was staying and I said, 'Why don't you join a band?' He said, 'Okay, what the heck?' . . . "

Payne had been taken by George, by both his personality and talent. "I liked the guy. As a mentor, I thought, maybe I should just stick here. So he says, 'We got this band. I want you to play on this record with the Fraternity of Man.'"

That was the band that, thanks to its leader's drug issues, was having trouble with its second album. Payne had heard "Don't Bogart That Joint," and he knew that the band included ex-Factory hands Richie Hayward, Martin Kibbee, and Roy Estrada.

What he didn't know was that the band's founder and lead guitarist, Elliot Ingber, the former Mother who'd met George and Kibbee in Oregon, was falling apart. "Elliot Ingber, our fearless leader, cracked up," Kibbee said. "He was literally carried out on a stretcher. Lowell came in. A couple of tracks featured him."

As George himself recalled, "The guitar player was trying to play 'Rumble,' and on about take fifty-four they still couldn't get through the first verse, and the guitar player started talking to his amplifier. And then his amplifier started answering—it really did answer him. He spoke something to the amp and the amp spoke back, and it's on tape. Yeah, it was very strange."

Does Ingber remember any of this? I spoke with him one night around midnight by phone—Ingber, who's still making music, says the overnight hours are a force of habit. He did his best to recall the second album sessions: "At that point, where I was indulging to the point. . . . See, I'm not really a solidly based musician who was face to face with the reality of music . . . so it was kind of easy to blow me off my track, and by that time I was talking to my amplifier . . . and by that point the album was no longer viable."

I heard that the amplifier spoke back to you.

"I don't think anybody else was . . . "

You heard something, though, from the amplifier?

"When the early distortion device started buzzing and rattling away, it was nuts, really nuts."

The drug of choice, I suppose, was acid?

"No. It was the reefer, man. Reefer."

Somebody said you were also trying some PCP.

"That was my friend."

I see what you mean. . . . Lowell talked about the fact that you spoke to the amp, and Martin Kibbee said that you had to be carried out of the studio on a stretcher at one point . . .

"It wasn't a stretcher, but the guy was real far gone."

You.

"Yeah."

And so George came to the rescue, but not by himself. Lowell told Bill Payne that he should help out too. "You're gonna play on it," he said, "and then they'll disband, and we get Richie in our group."

Payne didn't get it. "So I'm gonna play with Richie Hayward's band, and they're gonna break up, and we're gonna start . . . I don't get that," he said to George. "He goes, 'Welcome to Hollywood.'"

Payne played on the album, which was produced by Tom Wilson, who'd worked with Bob Dylan, Simon & Garfunkel, and others. Sure enough, Fraternity of Man fell apart, and George began piecing together the band that would become Little Feat. He had Payne ready to go and wanted Hayward for drums. As for a bassist, Payne recalls trying out numerous musicians, including Paul Barrere, who, like George, was a graduate of Hollywood High. George graduated the year before Barrere entered, but Paul caught up with George, learning to play guitar, joining a couple of garage bands, and catching the Factory on occasion. George had also seen Barrere slinging guitar in his band, Led Enema. George invited him to try out on bass. "It's easy," he reasoned. "There's two less strings."

"Well, it's not," Barrere recalled. "It's a whole different animal." Barrere proved his point by failing the tryout.

As for Martin Kibbee, who'd played bass and written a few songs with George in the Factory, he was nowhere to be found. Actually, he said, he had married and was in Europe, where his wife had a good job. "I loved Paris," he said. "I wrote a lot of tunes, but I could never get a decent group together. So I came back." By then the band had filled its roster.

Kibbee must have been disappointed. But, he said, he was ambivalent about being part of a rock band again and having to deal with the turbulence that came with touring. "How about a van going through Arizona in a snowstorm with no heater," he said, "or stuck in a Chicago hotel when you can't reach your management company—literally 'Reluctant Management.'"

Tellingly, Kibbee also said that "When Little Feat came up, there came a time when I would have to more or less fight for my position as the bass player, and maybe I didn't have total confidence in my chops. I sort of shied away from the player part of it, since I was more interested in becoming a writer." Kibbee also knew he was no match for George's top choice: another Mother.

Roy Estrada never did many interviews after he was sent to a state prison in Texas in 2012 for life—and beyond, if that were possible. That's because he was found guilty of "continuous sexual abuse of a child" and sentenced, at age sixty-eight, to twenty-five years without possibility of parole.

For decades he merited only a paragraph or two in histories of the Mothers or Little Feat. His biography consisted of his membership in a couple of L.A. soul bands before he became part of the Mothers and, then, Little Feat.

From Fort Stockton state penitentiary in Pecos County in western Texas, he phoned (collect) in response to a request for an interview. He spoke in a quiet voice. He was doing alright, he said, "considering the circumstances."

We got down to business, and he told me about his childhood.

Estrada was born in 1943 in Santa Ana, famed for its offshore winds. His family wasn't particularly musical, although his father played a one-string violin. At age ten he was taking accordion lessons, but the squeezebox failed to fire his imagination. He was more taken by a local band he heard practicing down the block from his family home.

"I'd walk in and listen," he said. "It was not Lawrence Welk and 'Lady of Spain'—it was R&B and rock and roll."

In the midfifties rock and roll was just beginning there, and young Estrada, who also liked R&B and jazz on the radio, found himself drawn to the guitar. Soon he was playing the instrument with a friend, but after a while his ear told him that they could do better than twin guitars. "I said, 'Why don't I purchase a bass?' Fender had just come out with bass guitars in the late fifties, and I got a Precision bass."

Although in a rock band the bass is less glamorous than a lead guitar, Estrada had his reasons for switching. "It sounds more comfortable," he said. As with the guitar, he taught himself to play.

From his duo with his buddy, he moved on to a much larger band, the Viscounts, who, beyond the basic instruments, included four saxophones. The Viscounts played dances and weddings—wherever they were invited.

In between he was a bass guitarist who worked in several R&B bands around Los Angeles, bands with names like the Debonairs, and fronted one: Roy Estrada and the Rocketeers.

While playing with the Soul Giants he met Frank Zappa, who joined the band to replace their guitarist for a weekend. In turn he joined Zappa when the latter formed the Mothers, later known as the Mothers of Invention. He played bass and sang, notably doing the high parts on the song "Oh in the Sky" on a TV special called *Color Me Pop* in 1968.

He played on the first Mothers albums. On *Weasels Ripped My Flesh*, Estrada's big turn was on "Prelude to the Afternoon of a Sexually Aroused Gas Mask," a Zappa nod to Debussy's ballet *Prelude to the Afternoon of a Faun*. Estrada is credited with the vocals, which went from falsetto moans to mock opera to self-conscious laughter to a chorus of a cappella yowling and some animalistic growls and barks. No gas masks appeared to have been harmed in the song's production.

It was as a Mother that he met Lowell George. "In '69," he recalled, "the last tour that I did with them, Lowell was with us, and that's how I met Lowell."

When Little Feat was being put together, George and his first picks—Payne on keyboards and Hayward on drums—thought Estrada would be their bass player. But Estrada, already seasoned by stints with various local bands, wasn't certain about the new venture, so they went through their parade of auditions. "He was being coy," said Payne, "and wisely so, 'til we either had a record deal or something he felt was substantial enough to commit to playing with us."

Actually, Estrada told me that at the beginning of 1970 "I was trying to get a group put together, in the area of Blood, Sweat & Tears, that kinda style, and I met this Lenny Capizi, who had wrote a few songs, and he was a singer in about an eight-piece group, kinda like Blood, Sweat & Tears, and we rehearsed a few songs in my living room."

Those sessions went nowhere, however, and when George called, Estrada was responsive. "He asked me what I was doing. I told him

I had just finished doing that big group, and he said, 'How about getting together?'

"After the stuff I had been doing with Frank," he said, "he was way different. He was southern rock music. He definitely had his own music. That's what drew me into it, 'cause I figured that this was a guy who had something going."

Estrada was officially in. Martin Kibbee would make several major contributions, helping George to write the songs "Dixie Chicken," "Easy to Slip," and "Rock and Roll Doctor." But he missed out on the first album, where the songs were by George himself, by Payne, and by the two together. After four cowriting credits with the Factory and four more on three Little Feat albums (the fourth song was "Feets Don't Fail Me Now"), Kibbee faded from the scene.

In late 1969 the group began with some demos. Several of them would appear, almost twenty-five years later, on an album called *Lightning-Rod Man* and would be credited to "Lowell George & the Factory." The fifteen-track album was clearly a money-making effort by Herb Cohen, who, with Frank Zappa, had auditioned the Factory. The four Feat demos, one of which is labeled "For Herb Cohen," indicate that he had an interest in George's new band.

Three of them would wind up, in different forms, on three Feat albums: "Crack in Your Door" on their debut, "Teenage Nervous Breakdown" on *Sailin' Shoes*, and "Juliet" (respelled "Juliette") on *Dixie Chicken*. The fourth, "Framed," by the legendary songwriting team of Jerry Leiber and Mike Stoller, recorded in 1954 by the Coasters (when they were still the Robins), did not get past the demo stage. The four soon-to-be Feats had a couple of guests on the sessions, including Elliot Ingber, then apparently recovered from the demise of Fraternity of Man, and Ian Underwood, yet another Mother alumnus, on sax on "Juliet."

Legend (and a Warner Bros. press release) has it that the band name, Little Feat, came from a wisecrack from the Mothers' Jimmy Carl Black, who identified himself as "the Indian drummer." As the story goes, Black was backstage at a Mothers rehearsal with George one evening, took a look at George's feet (size eight and a half, reportedly), and said, "You sure got little feet." "Everybody who knew

Lowell teased him about his feet," says Paul Barrere. "I used to call them earth pads, because they were as wide as they were long. So Jimmy looked at them one day and said, 'You got really ugly little feet.'" Rick Harper, the late road manager, said it happened at the Shrine Auditorium, at the end of a Mothers concert, when Black pointed to George's feet and uttered, "Little Feet." Harper took credit for spelling it F-E-A-T.

Black, who died in 2008, naturally had his own version: "When Lowell George was in the Mothers he used to room with Roy Estrada and myself. He feet were short and wide, so I told him that if he ever started a band, he should call it Little Feet." And, according to Hayward, "Feet" became "Feat" as a salute to the Beatles.

At least one thing is certain: Jimmy Carl Black gave the band its name.

Or did he? Patte Stahlbaum, of Price sisters and Mrs. Lowell George the First fame, has a different take on the naming: "The band was over at Lowell's and my house, and they didn't have a name yet . . . and they were rehearsing and talking about stuff, and one of everybody's good friends, because she was also the marijuana dealer, her name was Leslie Krasnow. And she looked at all of the guys at the time, and she said, 'Wow, you guys all have such little feet.' And Lowell said . . . 'Little Feet. And we should spell it Little Feat.'"

Wait—no Jimmy Carl Black? Was she sure? "I was the sober one," she said. "I was about to be a mother, so I was the sober one."

Of course, Black already *was* a Mother, and others back his account, albeit with varying details. At least all of them were in agreement on one thing: Lowell George had short, wide feet.

Chapter 4

FEAT'S FIRST

With Billy Payne, Richie Hayward, and Roy Estrada on board, George had a band. They had a name. They had begun work on some demos. Now all they needed was a recording contract.

While they mulled the possibilities and began composing and practicing songs, George tried out a couple of fairly new hats: record producer and session player. He'd done a couple of tracks with the GTOs and had seen the insides of a couple of other studios while working with the Factory and Fraternity of Man. Now he wanted to do more.

Shortly after the Fraternity party ended he took on a job for Peter Tork of the Monkees. Tork quit the group early in 1969, was doing some teaching, formed a production company, and managed a folk singer, Judy Mayhan. One of his students was a cousin of Lowell's, and Peter gave him a call, inviting him to help with the music for a demo for Atlantic Records. Mayhan got the deal, and although Tork was soon out of the picture, George, along with Hayward and Klein, played on her 1970 album, *Moments*. George played guitar and flute, Klein played his sitar, and Hayward, of course, was on drums.

By then George was also working with Ivan Ulz, who knew

George from his high school days. Like Patte, he went to North Hollywood High, but Ulz had an occasion, in 1961, to work with Lowell on a music project—"recording a couple of sisters in high school." After high school Ulz disappeared, but he returned in mid-1969. He was now a songwriter, had a contract, and, when he visited his schoolmate Patte, discovered that she was living with Lowell George. They talked some music, and Ulz mentioned that the previous night he'd been at the Troubadour and caught the Sunshine Company, a folk-rock group in the mold of the Mamas and the Papas. A couple years before, they'd had a Top 40 hit, "Back on the Street Again." "They introduced a song that was incredible," he said. "The hook was . . . 'Weed, whites, and wine.' Lowell's jaw dropped. He said, 'That's *my* song!' And we became friends."

When Ulz, who had a publishing and recording contract with Rod McKuen, the poet famed for *Stanyan Street*, went into the studio to make his debut album, he called in George and a few other friends, including the songwriting phenom Jackson Browne, who had yet to make his own debut. (George and Browne would become close friends.) Payne and Hayward also chipped in, and although the result, *Ivan, the Ice Cream Man*, didn't sell, Ulz would stay in the music business, and in touch with George—in a significant way.

George's juggling of session and production work, along with the work of putting a band together, didn't surprise his friends. Martin Kibbee says George learned from watching Zappa in the recording studio. "I think that was a very important and formative experience for Lowell," he said. "Frank became his role model in many respects." George picked up on Frank Zappa's work ethic—make that workaholic ethic. Before long, George was working day and night in recording studios. The first in line to sign Little Feat were his old boss, Frank Zappa, and the Mothers' manager, Herb Cohen, who had already spent some time with the guys in a studio.

Zappa, who'd encouraged George to form his own band even while letting him go, wanted him for his Straight label. Another producer, Gabriel Meckler, who'd had hits with Steppenwolf and Three Dog Night, courted the band for a label he was starting up, called

Lizard Records. So did Terry Melcher, a producer who'd worked with the Byrds and the Beach Boys.

Bill Payne remembers a meeting with Ahmet Ertegun, head of Atlantic Records, which began as a jazz and R&B label but had extended into rock. "The first stuff we wrote, we took to Ahmet Ertegun, and we played it for him, and he goes, 'Boys, it's too *diverse.*' So we go back to the drawing board. Now we're coming up with 'Brides of Jesus,' 'Hamburger Midnight,' 'Strawberry Flats,' and 'Gunboat Willie,' which is completely eclectic and off-the-wall music. So you can only imagine how eclectic and off the wall we were before."

Ultimately it was a friendship George had with Russ Titelman that tilted the Feats to Warner Bros. Records. Titelman, a singer-songwriter-musician, dated back to the early years of Phil Spector, before his multilayered "Wall of Sound." He began with what might be called light rock with his Teddy Bears. Titelman was part of Spector's second group, the Spectors Three, and played guitar and sang on his 1961 production of the Paris Sisters' big hit, "I Love How You Love Me."

Through Spector, Titelman met the composer and arranger Jack Nitzsche, of "Lonely Surfer" fame, and worked with him on various film scores and recordings. When Nitzsche began scoring *Performance*, Mick Jagger's first acting vehicle, in 1969, he called Titelman to help out. Together the two wound up writing "Gone Dead Train," which would include Ry Cooder on slide guitar and Randy Newman on vocals.

Titelman knew George from Ravi Shankar's school. "I couldn't play sitar that well," Titelman said, "but Lowell could." Nitzsche was open to different sounds for *Performance*, so after "borrowing" a tamboura (a fretless lute) and veena (a plucked string instrument) from the Kinnara school, Titelman invited George to a session. "Lowell was amazingly talented," he said. "He was a flute player, and he knew how to play Japanese shakuhachi flute. Anything he picked up he could figure out. And, of course, he was a truly great guitar player."

Although George appears in the credits for the film, Titelman isn't sure what he contributed. "I don't think he played guitar," he managed. "He played odd instruments."

"Lowell and I got close," he said, "and drove around all the time in this Morgan car he had, taking LSD and mescaline." They also wrote some songs together, "and we actually got signed to Koppleman and Rubin's Publishing Company." Those two names were becoming known for its catalog of Lovin' Spoonful songs.

In 1969 George was still wrapping things up with the Mothers. As George recalled, "Russ Titelman was starting a publishing company, and he asked me if I wanted to copublish the tune ['Willin''] with him and see what he could do with it." George and Kibbee had formed their own Naked Snake Music years before, when they began writing together, but George agreed to a deal with Titelman. "So I recorded it and went on the road the same day with the Mothers and was gone for about five weeks. . . . Somehow a demo of the tape got out, and it was the rage of the Troubador. People like Linda Ronstadt heard it and the Sunshine Company. All these people heard the tune and cut it. Then we did 'Truck Stop Girl' at some sessions, and Clarence White covered that, and I thought he did a fantastic job."

Titelman had also done his job, sending the demos out. He and George produced a couple of other tracks, but "Willin'" (by George) and "Truck Stop Girl" (by George and his occasional house guest Bill Payne) clearly stood out. Other artists were soon picking up both songs. The Byrds recorded them for their album titled *(Untitled)*, released in 1970. ("Willin'," however, was left off the album and would appear years later as a bonus cut on a reissue.) "Willin'," besides getting performed by the Sunshine Company at the Troub, was recorded by country artist Johnny Darrell, the spacey country rockers Commander Cody and his Lost Planet Airmen, and the jazz-rock ensemble Seatrain. The publishing deal with Titelman appeared to be paying off.

When George told Russ that Little Feat were entertaining an offer from Lizard Records, Titelman made his own proposal. Through his work in the record business, he was buddies with several of the young execs, producers, and musicians who were beginning to convene at Warner Bros. Records, a company that in the early sixties was beginning to move from soundtracks, middle-of-the-road music, and comedians to pop artists—and rock. By 1968, between its own A&R

staff (talent scouts) and deals with European labels, Warners and its sister, Reprise, had Jimi Hendrix, Joni Mitchell, the Grateful Dead, the Fugs, and Tiny Tim in their stable.

One of Titelman's pals there was Lenny Waronker, an A&R man who'd already worked with Randy Newman and Ry Cooder. "And I said to him [George]," Titelman recalled, "maybe Lizard Records was not the best idea. Why don't we just go and talk to Lenny at Warner Bros. Records?

"So we went. Me, Lowell, and Billy Payne went over to Lenny's office in Burbank, at the old office building, which was like a bunker. He had a spinet piano, and Billy played piano, Lowell played guitar, and they played about three songs: 'Willin',' 'Truck Stop Girl,' 'Brides of Jesus,' and maybe another one." Payne believes they played "somewhere between seven and nine songs, and we were signed on the strength of those tunes."

Titelman agrees: "Lenny said, 'That's really great. Go upstairs and make a deal with Mo.' 'Go make a record.' That's how that happened."

Upstairs, according to Carl Scott, who was doing some booking and management work for the label, he met with Mo Ostin, president of Warner Bros. Records, and relayed George's request for a $15,000 advance. "Mo gave me a look, and I thought I'd die. But he got it, and that was pretty much the end of that."

In 1969 Warner Bros. was young and loose enough that Titelman, who'd never produced a record before, got the assignment to oversee Little Feat's debut album.

At United-Western Recorders on Sunset in the heart of Hollywood, Little Feat got down to work on their album. As it turned out, they had a head start. Four of the demos that Titelman had recorded with George and various musicians wound up on *Little Feat*: "Willin'," with little more than George on vocals and guitar and Cooder on bottleneck; "Truck Stop Girl"; "I've Been the One"; and "Crazy Captain Gunboat Willie." Only "Crazy Captain," which includes a sly reference to George's newborn son, Luke (as "Luke the rat"), was embellished during the album sessions. "I think we added some orchestration to it," he recalls.

Titelman began with a lofty goal: "I wanted it to be like a Band album. I idolized those two records [*Music from Big Pink* and the then-brand new *The Band*]. To this day I think those are two of the greatest records ever made. And it [*Little Feat*] was, in a way, kind of like it, but the writing wasn't like it." Little Feat was more into the blues than the Band, he said. "We cut 'Forty Four Blues' and 'How Many More Years', and they [The Band] never did anything like that."

The medley of songs by Howlin' Wolf was George's salute to one of his musical heroes; his vocals on originals like "Snakes on Everything" and "Crack in Your Door" echoed Mick Jagger, and songs like "Willin'," "Truck Stop Girl," and "I've Been the One" made it clear that Little Feat had country inclinations as well. George and/or Payne wrote most of the songs. George teamed with bassist Estrada for one tune, "Hamburger Midnight"—yet another song with a vehicle theme ("I got red hot tires, my tires are smokin'")—that would be the band's first single. "I wrote some of the lyrics with Lowell," Estrada told me. "I shoulda done more of the writing together, but I figured Lowell was doing most of the writing, so I just let him do it."

Estrada diminished Titelman's role as producer: "We produced it on our own. Russ was there with us . . . he never produced us."

But he did. Titelman agrees that he collaborated with George and the band. More specifically, "Between the two of us," he said, "we decided which songs we were going to record, and the approach. I recommended orchestration ideas, strings and things like that. And it became rather contentious toward the end. I think Lowell . . . saw it differently and wanted it to be a different record. Close to the end, we were fighting."

Although others have said that the fight was over the publishing rights to "Willin'," which appears on the album associated only with Titelman's publishing company, Titelman says it was over money, creative differences, and control. "We didn't have a big budget, and I think we went over budget," he said. "You know, it was my first production, so I was concerned. I didn't want to lose control and have to start going back and rerecord stuff. So we got in big fights."

Payne witnessed it all, stating, "I was just appalled at the fact that two guys that really liked each other now really hated each other."

The sessions came to a halt after George had an accident that caused a hand injury and greatly affected his guitar playing. One of his hobbies, from childhood, was model airplanes. As Kibbee recalls, "He had a scheme to drop dog shit on [then mayor of Los Angeles, Sam] Yorty out of his model airplane. But one day he stuck his hand in the propeller, and it was his chording hand."

Actually, says Payne, George got injured by making a defensive move. "Lowell was going down to Griffith Park and letting these airplanes fly. Everybody else had a remote control; Lowell would simply let the plane take off. It would run out of gas; it'd miss a car by about *that* much." One day he was in the kitchen at his home on Ben Lomond, with Rick Harper watching TV in the living room. "So he was working on a model airplane, just the engine of it," says Payne. "And it flew off. He was, I think, a brown belt in karate, and he put his hand up, and it smashed into his hand." As Harper told writer Bud Scoppa: "All of a sudden, I see him turn around and he's got the engine in his hand with the prop broken. He takes the engine—which is now burning hot—pulls it off, and the palm of his left hand is nothing but hamburger meat. I almost threw up. He had I don't know how many stitches."

Within a month George was back, and recording resumed. He wasn't at full speed but, according to Harper, didn't tell anyone that. "He'd lost the feeling in two or three of his fingers," said the roadie. "He said at first it was like marshmallow and he couldn't tell how much pressure to put on the strings. Could you ever find a guy who could do more by playing two notes in some rhythmic way?"

But George didn't fool everybody. For the Howlin' Wolf blues medley, Titelman waved in some help—support that was conveniently nearby.

Ry Cooder, who could play more than a little slide guitar and had by now worked with the Stones, Randy Newman, Arlo Guthrie, and others, was at Western. He was recording his own debut album for Warners, with Van Dyke Parks on keyboards and Richie Hayward doing some session work. Cooder agreed to help out. "So we're doing 'How Many More Years' and '44 Blues'," said Payne, "Ry's out there, and Lowell says, 'Fuck this, I'm gonna go out there and play.'

So he does, and he's bleeding all over his guitar, but it was wonderful. It sounded great, and it was actually one of the high points of the record."

Parks watched what amounted to a slightly bloody duel. "There was nobody allowed to play bottleneck around Cooder," he told Scoppa. "Lowell had to play bottleneck, but in fact Lowell did it in spite of this problem, and it pissed off a lot of people. It was a Mexican stand-off, at best. It was sibling rivalry. It was eat-or-be-eaten time. They put it on that level, which improved their competitive edge."

By the time Little Feat were doing their first recording sessions, George had been playing bottleneck—or slide—guitar for a couple of years. Instead of the usual devices—the neck of a wine bottle, a length of tubing, or a medicine bottle—he used a sparkplug puller. Said Harper: "The whole reason he got heavy with the sparkplug puller, which he'd already come up with, was because, well, part of that was that accident. It was always something with him, man."

Little Feat completed the recording, adding several session players, including pedal steel guitarist "Sneaky Pete" Kleinow and Titelman himself, on piano, on the demo, "I've Been the One." Titelman then oversaw the mixing of the tracks. More problems ensued.

Titelman reportedly made the control room off-limits to George and the band. He says he doesn't remember doing that, but "it could be true. It was so contentious. I think some of the time, Billy came, but Lowell and I were at each other's throats, so it would have been kind of impossible."

Payne fretted about both the album and the band he'd joined, stating, "I was so new to it, I wasn't really sure, I thought because of all the mental turmoil that was going on, I thought, *Oh my God, this is so chaotic. Russ and Lowell are at each other's throats.* There's the Vietnam War going on, there are riots, Kennedy and Martin Luther King Jr. were murdered. Those kind of things affect everyone, but they especially affect artists, because what do we share with people? What we're going through, what are we writing about—so our music was all over the map for a lot of reasons because there was so much chaos in the air."

Despite Payne's concerns, *Little Feat* got a warm reception from rock critics. When Andy Childs, editor of *Zigzag* in London, heard the band, courtesy of DJ John Peel playing "Hamburger Midnight," he thought, "It sounded glorious. A real moody, sizzling rocker with some fabulous guitar playing." When he got the album, he could hardly believe it was the band's first time out, writing, "The maturity and variety of styles it displays is impressive, to say the least."

Even before the album was released, *Rolling Stone* published a rave for the first single, "Hamburger Midnight," which Warners had released early, hoping for some radio exposure. On the B side of the 45 was "Strawberry Flats."

Reviewer Ed Ward flipped over the single. "This is the masterpiece," he began. "It is perhaps the best record I've heard in several months." He particularly liked "Strawberry Flats," which he called "one of the definitive statements of where youth is at today." Although George's vocals could evoke Mick Jagger, Ward heard another group. "The music sounds like the Band taken one step further," he said of "Strawberry," "and it is difficult to believe that they generate so much excitement in two minutes and 21 seconds." The song, he said, deserved to be played "on every radio station in the country."

But Little Feat would have settled for just a few.

As they took off on their first tour, they discovered that Warner Bros. had yet to release their album, so they would be playing for people who could not buy their music and, in some cases, people who just didn't care.

"It was odd," said Payne. "Our first date was in Cincinnati, we're freezing our asses off, it was Christmas Day, it was a club called the Reflections, and we did two shows. We get in there—it holds about a thousand people, and people are singing Ohio football songs. Woody Hayes was their coach—they were going to the Rose Bowl, [so] they didn't care about us."

One member of the audience, Craig Fuller, concurred. He and his band, Pure Prairie League, lived in Cincy and knew the club. "It was a disco place where guys went to pick up girls and not to appreciate music."

Through record industry friends, he'd gotten a copy of Feats' album, liked it, and showed up for the second night. "I remember they took a break, and Richie went across the street to a 7–11 and bought a pepperoni. He had it inside his pants."

Payne remembers Hayward asking if he could introduce the band. "So he goes up, he takes a sausage out of his pants, cuts the tip of it off, takes a bite of it. 'Ladies and gentlemen . . . Little Feat.' Nothing. No response. He walks back to the drums, goes, 'One, two, three, four . . . ' and we're playing. . . . He was pissed."

Fuller recalls Hayward chewing his pepperoni and snarling, "This is for you, all you *Cincinnatians*."

Payne also was less than thrilled about his first leg of his first-ever rock-and-road trip. "I'm having a tough time sleeping, adjusting to the water—I was just a fragile guy. I said, 'I don't dig this shit.'"

Next, just after New Year's Day, the band hit New York City. "This is supposed to be Little Feat's big splash," said Payne. "We play a place called Ungano's. It's not a good time to be playing, 'cause everybody's still blown out. . . . Well, we play this gig, there are two paying customers. It's like a Fellini movie. They're dressed in full ballroom regalia, they're dancing ballroom style to 'Hamburger Midnight,' to 'Strawberry Flats.' But we had five or six people there, several of the higher level of the Warners crew. I had this thought that they were purposely trying to break us up by embarrassing us so they could get Richie into Ry Cooder's band, 'cause Ry was their darling."

Payne was just being paranoid. He had reasons to disbelieve: he'd been sent to the Fraternity of Man, then enlisted into Little Feat. A rookie in the biz, he'd already found it "chaotic and cutthroat." "So it's not out of the realm of reason that they would do this," he said. "Our music is not commercial—far from it. But no, it was just idiotic planning."

Things brightened considerably a couple of weeks later when, after a short break, Little Feat hit Houston for three nights. The first night in town Payne had lunch with an uncle who lived there. He got to his hotel to be greeted by Rick Harper, now on board as Little Feat's road manager. "There's this group of girls here, about five of them," Harper said. "'I'll take the one that's maybe not as good looking as the other girls, and this leaves four . . . you got your pick. Go on up and see what you want . . . who you want.' And they are all gorgeous. I pick this girl, and it's Andrea. And I wind up knowing Andrea for many years. But they were a part of a thing called the Houston Welcoming Committee. After that experience not only did we write a song about it; Lowell wrote a song about it. I think it was on the second album, called 'Texas Rose Café.'"

. . . Then this dancer grabbed me down by the bus stop
And she said I'm takin' you with me . . .

Not bad. Cowgirl companionship—and inspirations for new songs. "And what it did for me, other than the obvious, releasing all this tension—I went the completely opposite way. . . . I love touring now. I want to tour again. That was it."

Chapter 5

EASY TO SLIP

DESPITE EARNING MOSTLY POSITIVE REVIEWS, LITTLE FEAT'S FIRST album tanked. It sold about eleven thousand copies.

In 1971 Warner Bros. was already known for nurturing its artists, for giving them a longer-than-usual leash. As Titelman noted, the band had plenty of supporters in the label's Burbank offices. "People who worked at the company loved the record," he recalled. Still, in a year in which the label scored major hits with Van Morrison (*Tupelo Honey*), James Taylor (*Mud Slide Slim and the Blue Horizon*), Black Sabbath (*Paranoid*), and the Faces (*A Nod Is as Good as a Wink . . . to a Blind Horse*), the Feats were little, indeed.

Titelman and George would see each other again, but never became friends again. "I don't think we ever sat down at a table and reconciled," the producer said, "but we worked together later. He played on *Gorilla* [a James Taylor album produced in 1975 by Titelman, who would also work with Eric Clapton, Rickie Lee Jones, Randy Newman, George Harrison, Cyndi Lauper and others]. We saw each other. He would show up at Warner Bros., and it was okay. After a long time."

Obviously Little Feat would have a different producer for its second album—if they got to do a second album. "Warner Bros. made no commitment after the first record and refused to finance a second one," Van Dyke Parks told me. Parks, besides being an artist and producer-at-large at Warners, was close to the powers that be, and despite a way with words that often left his listeners speechless (label head Joe Smith once told me that "Van Dyke has a difficult time going from A to B. He likes to stop off at F and G"), he had the ears of people who counted.

Parks, a composer, vocalist, multi-instrumentalist, arranger, and producer, was famed for his work with the Beach Boys (he wrote "Surf's Up") and his eccentric, eclectic solo albums. What's more, he traveled some of the same roads various members of Little Feat did. In 1965 he played briefly with the Mothers of Invention; he had a hand in the sessions for the second Fraternity of Man album. And that's where he met Lowell George, who struck him as a kindred spirit, "somebody to admire."

He found Lowell "very smart and very musical. And to me, that can't be illustrated more tersely than by noting that he picked up the piccolo in the band [at Hollywood High]. You might be wondering why a man would want to do that . . . a 'manly man' like Lowell. In fact, he told me, it was because it was the lightest instrument in the orchestra." Parks related this, in part, because his own first instrument, when he was a boy in Lake Charles, Louisiana, was a clarinet.

"And I'll tell you several things that interested both Lowell and me," he continued. "I preceded Lowell in the Mothers of Invention. I was 'Pinocchio' [in 1965]. Roy Estrada was 'Teflon-Man.' There's a corroborative force in all of that. And we shared an interest in Howlin' Wolf, who was my favorite blues singer, and happened to be Lowell's. There were things, too, that I loved and that he understood . . . like the cartoon consciousness . . . the Mexican comic book where the lipstick would be on the cheek and the dye from her hair would be on the lovers' arm. Lowell and I both appreciated cartoon consciousness . . . that's what we called it."

There was also something they called "*droite gauche*." Their translation: something that should not be done. And they would do it.

"It is a French *non sequitur*," said Parks. "'Droite' as in right, 'gauche' as in left. It became our mantra. That's what we would do in life." If something was "right," they had the right to go left, without concern for what others might think.

That was the attitude he took into executive meetings at Warner Bros., with his frère in mind. "I was going to an A&R meeting every Monday morning," he recalled. "And we would sit there and discuss the finances of record projects and stuff like that." One of his goals was to protect George's and Little Feat's interests. Mo Ostin, he noted, came from Reprise Records, a label Frank Sinatra partly owned. Ostin began in bookkeeping and worked his way up. "The man trained as a CPA," said Parks. "Little Feat represented a redundancy. . . . They didn't even know how to sell Ry Cooder or Randy Newman—they didn't know."

Parks says he knew. "I was his inside job. And I'll tell you why—it was very important to me. . . . I couldn't afford, psychologically, to lose with Lowell. . . . He meant too much to me. And I wanted so much to find celebration in his survival."

One way he helped George and the band to get a second chance, he says, was with "Sailin' Shoes," the song that would become the title of their second album. Parks and George created the song during a session for Parks's own second album, *Discover America*, and he included it, hoping to raise the song's—and George's—profile at the label. Parks says he came up with the title, and the two made up the tune. George had an entirely different recollection of the song's creation: "I had some verses and pieces of a chorus, but nothing was happening with it, and Van Dyke came into a room and said, 'Okay, let's play it.' And we sat down, with him at the piano, and I had a guitar, and he said something, and there was a flash of light, and I had it. It was a Zen experience."

Parks said it was not that way. But no matter. "It was all he needed to get another record," he said. While they worked on Parks's album at Sunset Sound, they scored a strange, if not exactly Zen-like side gig. "I remember we didn't want anybody to enter the studio, probably because we might be smoking grass," Parks said. "It was a closed session is what it was called. . . . All of a sudden I looked up from the studio and I saw seven men standing there. In the control room. I was in a rage. I felt violated, and probably because I would rather fight than go in flight." Parks laughed. "They all bowed, because they were from Japan. There were four boys trying to look like Beatles. And there was a producer and an interpreter. Anyway, no way, and they said, 'Mr. Parks, we want you to make us an album of the California Sound.' These are the first Japanese I've seen since I put down a *Life* magazine article probably in 1948 and saw what the Japs did to the Yanks. Well, I mean, it was a transformation. At close range, possibly emotive, Japanese American event."

One of the men opened his briefcase and handed Parks a pearl—a peace offering, of sorts. "And I left the room to cry," Parks recalled. "I was so ashamed that I'd been mad at them. And so I took the encased pearl to study it in the next room . . . and pulled myself together, and when I walked back in the control room Lowell was standing there, with the briefcase open, and it was filled with twenty-dollar, maybe fifty-dollar bills. And Lowell was embracing it and smiling broadly, and he said, 'I think we can make music out of this.'

"So the way it shook down: I said, 'No, you can't do it,' I don't want Mo Ostin to put a horse's head on my pillow tomorrow morning—I'm supposed to deliver this product. So the guy said, 'Can you make us a California Sound with this group, called Happy End?' And, right on the spot we incorporated a tune, with Lowell playing— we're playing for the group, we are the group, it's a song Lowell and I made up and, as I understand it, became 'Number One Hit in Japan.' It went, 'Sayonara, America, sayonara-Nippon.'" (Parks sang it, "Say-YOR-nara")

"It was like a chant, and the chorus was 'Bye, bye . . . bye, bye' . . . and a bottleneck . . . 'Sayonara' . . . it was so far out . . . and it became number one in Japan. . . . And that album had a seminal effect on the Japanese populace. Really big time. Sort of like being a flywheel on the Rolling Stones to learn so much from Lowell." Horse's head be damned, Parks went ahead and produced Happy End's album, adding to the Japanese quartet Bill Payne, saxophonist Tom Scott, and three additional horn players.

Although Parks said that "Sailin' Shoes" gave Little Feat new life at Warner Bros., others say that the savior of the band was another song, "Easy to Slip," which George came up with in a direct attempt to score a hit single. "So Lowell takes it upon himself, rightly upon himself, to write the hits," says Bill Payne. "I was not super-happy about it. But he comes up with a beauty of a song. I thought, *Man, that's really cool.*"

Actually, George didn't try to write a hit record by himself. Kibbee claims he wrote most of it after his wife left him in Paris. "I came back just as they were starting up with their second album," he recalled, "and they had a problem. The label was dubious, and I had this song." Lowell, he says, added the guitar solo in the middle of the song. "'Easy to Slip,'" he says, demonstrated to Warners "that we could write."

Parks and Kibbee both may be overstating their roles in saving Little Feat's neck. After all, they were by no means the band's only champions. Carl Scott, the in-house manager who helped book Warner Bros. acts into nightclubs and on tours, says he and Bob Regehr, a hip and wily public relations guy, also pushed for the band. And, Scott says, Little Feat had support at the very top. Vice president Joe Smith, a former DJ in Boston who would rise to the presidency at Warners and other companies, compared Little Feat with such artists as Parks, Captain Beefheart, Ry Cooder, Bonnie Raitt, and Randy Newman.

The Feats, he said, weren't quite as esoteric as a Beefheart, Parks, or Cooder, adding, "They were in there, but they were less esoteric . . . they were a rock 'n' roll band, and the FM stations loved them, but they were still not in our top ten or fifteen best-selling artists at any point. But in the company they had a great following of people who loved them. Bob Regehr, he was their Rabbi, and Carl Scott was very close with them too, and so whenever a conversation started about what we could do for a band, Little Feat was always one of the bands."

So Little Feat lived to see another album. With Titelman out of the picture, they needed another producer. The Warners execs tapped another musician with an interest in production work: Ted Templeman. Only four years before, in 1967, he had hit the charts with his group, Harper's Bizarre, with a cover of Simon & Garfunkel's "The 59th Street Bridge Song (Feelin' Groovy)."

Harper's Bizarre, from the San Francisco Bay Area, had been the Tikis when Warner Bros. purchased the indie label they were on, Autumn Records. (The Beau Brummels were the prize of the label, and its small staff included booking agent Carl Scott.) Lenny Waronker produced the Bizarre and brought in musician friends of his, including Cooder, Glen Campbell, Randy Newman, drummer Jim Gordon, and Leon Russell, who did the arrangement on the hit single.

Templeman was the band's drummer, but he deferred to Gordon and just sang. He wasn't very good, he admitted, but he was richly rewarded. He made a connection with Warner Bros. Records, and after tiring of touring, he decided he wanted to go behind the scenes and work with other artists. He talked Waronker into hiring him for something like $50 or $60 a week and began hanging out at sessions. Templeman soon began earning his salary—and then some. He and Waronker encouraged Warners to sign a rock band out of San Jose with a stoners' name: the Doobie Brothers. Templeman and Waronker jointly produced their first effort (not a hit), but Templeman would go on to score successes with the Doobies, Carly Simon, Van Morrison, and many others.

As a musician, a fledgling producer, and part-time talent scout, he was aware of Little Feat. "I heard 'Hamburger Midnight' and I went crazy," he recalled. "I used to go and watch their shows, 'cause I never quite heard a drummer play like Richie. It was just a killer. And I wanted to produce them."

When he got his wish, it was a dream come true. "I was a drummer myself," he said, "and when you hear a drummer like Richie, plus the tunes. I think I was assigned to it, but at Warners, nobody was assigned anything. 'If you want it, fine . . . ' But I was jumpin' at it 'cause I had been doing the Doobie Brothers and working with Van Morrison all at once. And these guys were monsters in terms of musicians."

With Templeman in the studios, *Sailin' Shoes* presented a more fully realized version of Little Feat than the relatively sparse first album.

"Willin'" was showcased with the entire band—enhanced, even, with some steel from "Sneaky Pete." Where vocals on the debut effort generally were undermixed, *Sailin'* sounded brighter, and the numerous rock tunes rocked harder.

Templeman looked back to the sessions with fondness. "I went to their rehearsals," he said. "I rehearsed them in the sound stages at Warner Bros., and Richie was a killer. They used to compare him to Levon Helm, and I've used Levon in the studio, and Richie was just an incredible drummer. And Billy—Holy God, he was just amazing. There's so many things that Billy would do. There was this song I loved, 'Texas Rose Café,' and in the middle of that thing he took it to Mars. . . . And that was Lowell letting him do it."

Templeman thought for certain that "Easy to Slip," the George-Kibbee composition, would be a hit record. But, he said, "I think I put too much limiting on the guitars. I liked it a lot. It had all the makings of a hit, but in retrospect it kind of wandered around a little bit."

In the sessions George was the main idea man, Templeman said. "Lowell was something else," he recalled. "On 'Sailin' Shoes'—I loved it . . . he played the brushes on that [a snare drum]—and the brushes are off, it's not with the groove at all . . . and I was telling him, and he said, 'No, I want it this way . . . ' He wanted it to be a little wacky . . . And then I knew, with another one that was on that album, called [he sings] 'Turn your clock back, woman, when you see me comin' down . . . 'Cause my feet don't even touch the ground . . . ' 'Cold Cold Cold.' He was talking about being high! That stuck in my mind.'

"'Cold Cold Cold,'" he recalled, "was where we put the drums up on a riser, at Sunset Sound, which was like a [meat] locker with parallel surfaces and horrible sound. We miked it from far away and up close and used every limiter we could get in town to get the sound of the drums on that thing, And then Lowell, we had him sing on 'Cold Cold Cold' into a microphone, then we ran it through an amp and put it in the bathroom at Amigo [a recording studio owned by Warners], then we miked that so that his voice was going into the amp, coming out of the bathroom so it would sound cold.

"I was lucky to have an inventive group," the producer said. "Richie was great, 'cause I'd put him in the corner at Sunset Sound

Studios, and I'd have some ideas—he knew what I wanted, and he'd play them . . . the rapport was great. When you have an artist like that there's not much for a producer to do except listen to them. Lowell was great because we had a personal relationship, and he would ask my opinion all the time. He wasn't one of those guys who thought he was in charge . . . he was a very humble cat."

As he did during the sessions for the first Feats album, George wanted to participate in the mixing, but he was kept out. "That's one thing I didn't dig," said Templeman. "I always mix myself . . . with Donn Landee, my engineer. The guy's a genius, and we were a team."

Aside from keeping the band out of the mixing process, Templeman said, "I never had any arguments. I always got along with all my guys. I was in a band, and I always approached it like 'we're in this together.'"

There was much to love about *Sailin' Shoes*, from "Easy to Slip's" chiming guitars (we'd hear something similar months later in the Eagles' "Take It Easy") and ringing harmonies (with George and his brother-in-law Hayward vocalizing together) to more Howlin' blues ("A Apolitical Blues" and Payne's piano-and-Leon-Russell-driven "Cat Fever"). There are raucous celebrations of the rock 'n' roll life, including "Teenage Nervous Breakdown," resurrected from the pre-Feat demos done for Herb Cohen.

Groupies, first encountered in Houston, were saluted not only in the honky-tonk women-populated "Texas Rose Café" (by George) but also in "Tripe Face Boogie" (by Payne and Hayward): "Buffalo'd in Buffalo and entertained in Houston . . . "

Elizabeth George believes three of the album's songs were composed with her in mind: "Cold, Cold, Cold," "Trouble," and "Sailin' Shoes." George, who wrote all three songs (with help on "Sailin'"), expresses longing in "Cold," sympathy in "Trouble," and optimism in "Sailin'" (with a nod to Liz's son Jed—"Jedidiah" in the song).

If so, George had nerve. In 1971, when Little Feat were at work on the album, he was still married to Patte, who had delivered their son, Luke, just a year before.

But Patte, having known Lowell since childhood, came to understand that he would not be a one-woman man, and he soon moved out. They would remain technically married until about 1974, but George's shoes had sailed away long before.

Patte had firsthand knowledge about the inspiration for at least one song, George's greatest musical achievement: "Willin'." It's a truck driver's melodic survey of his landscape—physical, mental, and romantic. It's cast with vivid names ("Dallas Alice"), phrases ("Had my head stoved in"), and imagery ("I smuggled some smokes and folks from Mexico, baked by the sun almost every time I go . . . "). It doesn't sound like the product of a child of Hollywood.

Richie Hayward, who was living with wife, Pam, and her sisters, Patte and Prissy, had a major role in the birth of the song. Paul Barrere heard it this way: "They were all sittin' around when Richie lived on Fountain during the Factory time, talking about some rocking chair that had been left out in the rain, and he goes, 'It's all warped by the rain.' It went right into the lyric. Lowell was great at seeing, hearing, being around, and capturing things that go on in everyday life that just kind of hit you."

Patte recalls that evening entirely differently. "We always cooked together, ate together," she says. "I remember us sitting down at the dining room table and writing 'Willin'.' And Prissy worked at a pre-school, and I remember her telling us how the chairs at the school had been warped by the rain. And I remember Lowell saying, 'Warped by the rain . . . ' And away it went. And we all threw in lines." (Kibbee says that George sent royalty checks to Prissy for years, but Patte believes that her sister received just one check, for $100.)

George himself had varying explanations for the song. The most relevant was a blend of the other recollections. He was talking with Paul Kendall of *Zigzag* magazine in 1976: "I remember that I wrote it at Richie's house, where a guy was talking about the 'three wicked W's,' which were weed, whites, and wine, and I went, 'Oh, that's it.' Then Richie's sister-in-law walked into the room and said, 'Oh, look at that chair: it's been warped by the rain,' and I thought, 'I'd better start making some notes here.' So I scribbled various things down and bashed it into shape, and it all seemed to come together with a tune I'd written the previous day . . . some music without words that I'd started. The song just happened . . . and I feel that those songs . . .

are subsequently the ones which have been the most successful . . . in terms of a song having substance and quality."

Kendall asked whether songs often came "almost accidentally." George, no doubt smiling, responded, "Very occasionally, when the moon is in Asparagus, and the planets are aligned."

As for the country roads feel of the song, in 1973 he told David Rensin, writing for *Crawdaddy!*: "I did a lot of driving, and I went through places like Bakersfield every once in a while. I'd stop for a bit and I'd see these juicers putting on 'Harper Valley PTA'-type songs three in a row and really dig it. Now I love that kind of music; the whole scene is truly American. It's a trucker's world, so I wrote about it."

Then, in an interview in 1978 on Australian Broadcasting Commission FM, he said, "I worked in a gas station for a long time when I was in college and got a lot of inspiration from the characters I saw come through there."

"I admit I have a thing about truck drivers," George said that same year to writer Mark Leviton. "After all, they're stuck like the rest of us. He might enjoy himself, the freedom of the road, but he's been through Hell, too."

Whatever the inspiration, George took it to levels that stunned friends who got to hear it up close and personal. On a commercial level the song, with its references to drugs, had no chance in the early 1970s, when the FCC and other watchdogs, including publishers of radio tip sheets like the *Gavin Report*, were warning stations to censor songs that might be deemed to be pro-drugs. "Willin'" had no chance at wide airplay and was never released as a single. But when George sang it, people were captivated.

June Millington, who, with sister Jean, formed the all-female rock band Fanny, had just signed with Warner Bros.' sister label, Reprise, when she met George at a jam session in 1969. The two became close, and, she said, "Our intimacy stretched beyond the purely musical." Millington, who was writing a memoir when we spoke, let me see what she'd written about George, including these excerpts.

We had a rehearsal space in the basement of this Spanish-style mansion a few blocks up from the Chateau Marmont and could play 24/7 and no one bothered us. Supposedly it had been Hedy Lamar's house. . . . Mostly we played each other songs-in-progress and there was one phase in which he was so pleased with a song he'd just written that he played it over and over again, for weeks. I liked it a lot too; it had a catchy phrase about "weeds, whites and wine." But what he was especially pleased about was the use of the names of some towns in Arizona he'd hitchhiked through: Tucumcari, Tehatchapie and Tonopah. He'd passed through those towns and loved the rhythm of the names, and couldn't believe he'd actually used them successfully in a song.

What joy the song brought: it was the stark, spare and beautiful. . . . We were stupefied with awe and respect at the song. And he was the only one who could play and sing it just like that, believe me. The first part, half-spoken, half-sung, and then he'd break out in his clear voice: "And if you give me . . . weed, whites, and wine, and you give me a sign, I'll be willin'." Damn. That was one great song. There we sat in the moonlight in Hedy Lamar's house, on an ornate yet stylishly-rococo sofa we'd found at a yard sale, and it was perfection. When the last note rang out, the silence was holy. And then he'd start again.

Linda Ronstadt covered "Willin'" on her 1975 album, *Heart Like a Wheel*, which topped the *Billboard* album charts and, no doubt, gave George's song substantial airplay, no matter that she was wailing about "weed, whites, and wine."

Trying to explain her attraction to the song, she began with a faint recollection of when or where she and George first met. It might have been at a small music festival in Topanga, where George and his family lived. "I was living out there, and I just barely remember it because . . . I can't drink." She's allergic to alcohol. On occasion, however, she would relent in the face, say, of a taste of Sauza Conmemorativo, the Tequila of the rock stars in the early seventies. Meeting George may have been one of those occasions. "I think that was the first time I ever met him, but don't remember if he was the person with the tequila."

Ronstadt added that she might have run across George years earlier. Her band, the Stone Poneys, who had the hit "Different

Drum" in 1968, used to open for the Mothers of Invention because they shared Herb Cohen as their manager: "So, 'Hey, the Mothers need an opening act.' It was like putting *Bambi* and *Deep Throat* on a double bill!"

But she believes George had left the Mothers by then. Their real first meeting may have been in 1973, when the Topanga Days celebration, including a music fest, was staged for the first time. "He had 'Willin'' then, and he played me part of that, and I thought it was real good. Then I saw him playing it in Atlanta [Little Feat performed there in September 1973] and had forgotten about it in between times, so when I heard 'Willin'' it sounded familiar, and I asked him to help me learn it."

"It was just such a compelling song," she said. "I loved the story and its odd structure. He wrote oddly structured songs, but they were very strong."

On the first two Little Feat albums, "Willin'" was structured, arranged, and performed differently on each. The demo with Ry Cooder was spare and sparse, sung in a consistent midtempo. With the full band—and "Sneaky Pete" on steel—George sang in a higher key, showed things down before the "weed, whites, and wine" lines, and added rich harmonies. "I wanted to do a group version," he explained during a radio interview in 1973.

The liner notes, which George wrote with a winking archness (he included the estranged Russ Titelman in his acknowledgments with a "russ t., may he remain calm . . . "), noted, "the real name of this album is *Thank You! I'll eat it here!*"

That, if anything, could explain the cover. For their debut, Little Feat were barely visible, standing, spaced apart, in front of a mural of a storefront on a snow-covered street. For *Sailin' Shoes*, the cover was a painting by Neon Park of a cake on a swing, with pink frosting hairdo, made up eyes, high heels, and one slice missing, kicking off a shoe—a sailin' shoe, if you will—in front of a gigantic snail, while behind her stood a figure out of an eighteenth-century French painting.

Talk about cartoon consciousness. Park, born Martin Muller, was an artist who'd been in San Francisco, drawing posters for the Family Dog, which, along with Bill Graham, put on dance concerts. Frank

Zappa saw his work and hired him to come up with a cover for the album *Weasels Ripped My Flesh*. Park found an advertisement in a *Life* magazine from the fifties in which a businessman, shaving with an electric razor, was drawing blood. Park replaced the razor with a weasel. Warner Bros. execs fought with Zappa over the cover, but the Mother won out. Everyone loved the cover—except the record company. In the process Park earned a new fan: Lowell George.

One night, not long after that brouhaha, Ivan Ulz, friend of Patte and Lowell, was hitchhiking. "I was on Sunset Boulevard," Ulz recalled, "and I was clutching my guitar in the rain. Neon pulled over and I got in. I said, 'Where're you going?' He says, 'I don't know. Where're *you* going?' I looked in the backseat and saw the covers for *Weasels*. He said he'd done that work. I said, 'Listen, if you got nothing to do, come with me and I'll introduce you to this guy.' We went to Lowell's house, and a couple of GTOs were just coming out of the house, and we went in, and the two of them hit it off." Said George: "I admired his cover of *Weasels Ripped My Flesh*. I mean, an electric weasel—whatever next! So we began a friendship and also a business relationship, in that I would say, 'Give me a cover.'"

The cake cover drew plenty of notice, and the album earned another round of rave reviews. Bud Scoppa, writing in *Rolling Stone*, praised Payne and George's songwriting for not being simple or literal and for flashing "a myriad of fleeting, haunting images." As for the playing, he raved, "Lowell George and Bill Payne don't stop at being the writers of virile, touching songs—they're also masterful musicians. Payne plays a cool, elegant piano and a hot, whirring organ. George makes his slide guitar howl and roar like a tractor trailer in the midst of a steep, mountainous descent. George illustrates the muscular mating of men and their machines, while Payne celebrates it. Together with former Mother Roy Estrada on bass and Richard Hayward on drums, they compose one super rock & roll band."

In England Barney Hoskyns, the British rock journalist and critic, noted, *Sailin' Shoes* became "something of a cult album." On Hoskyns's archival site, Rock's Backpages, one can find a 1975 cover story from *ZigZag* magazine in which editor Andy Childs writes, "If [their] first album alone established Little Feat as one of America's top bands, then their second album, *Sailin' Shoes*, confirmed their status beyond any shadow of a doubt." He continued: "If you haven't already got *Sailin' Shoes*, don't wait a minute longer; it's definitely one of the best records from any American band ever!"

Yet *Sailin' Shoes* didn't sell much better than the debut, *Little Feat*. "Something seemed to jinx the band," Hoskyns wrote in *MOJO* magazine in 1994 in an essay entitled, "Little Feat: The One That Got Away." Perhaps, he said, George "eschewed the kind of accessible Californian rock which helped the Doobies and The Eagles go platinum. There was always something gritty and knotty about the best Little Feat songs—invariably those written by George—which ruled out the possibility of major commercial success."

But George did not sit around worrying about record sales. He kept busy, appearing as a session musician on various albums. In early 1972 he played guitar with the inventive, time-warping singer and composer Nilsson for the album *Son of Schmilsson*, a follow-up to *Nilsson Schmilsson*. George enjoyed working with producer Richard Perry but recalled that he didn't get paid for his work until he spoke with Van Dyke about it. Parks suggested that George send Nilsson a telegram saying, "Pay me, schmay me." He did, and he got paid, if not schmaid.

Chapter 6

TWO TRAINS

It crushed me that *Sailin' Shoes* didn't do better.
—TED TEMPLEMAN, PRODUCER

WITH *SAILIN' SHOES*, LITTLE FEAT HAD GOTTEN A SECOND CHANCE from Warner Bros. But despite the solid reviews, the adulation from Britain, the weary yet sheer beauty of "Willin'," the hit-like "Easy to Slip," and the excellent, adventurous production, the album sold only thirteen thousand units in its initial release.

Nonetheless, Feat were unfazed. If they got a third swing from Warners, they'd take it—well, most of them, anyway. After a tour to push the album, one member quit.

On February 13, 1972, Little Feat was the opening act for one of George's peers and heroes, Don Van Vliet and his band, Captain Beefheart and His Magic Band. They were at the Cincinnati Music Hall in Ohio.

With regret in his voice, Bill Payne recalled that wintry day: "So here we are. It's a really nice venue too. And the sound system goes off. We hear, 'It could take two hours to fix this.' And Lowell goes, 'I want to go ice skating.' I go, 'No, you're playing, man.'" When

George insisted, Payne decided to go with him, despite a fear that the system might be fixed in fifteen minutes.

"We're gone about an hour, an hour and a half, and finally I'm going, 'Lowell, please get off the rink. We've gotta get back.' We jump into a cab, the cab driver can't find the venue, we go, 'No, there it is! Right there!' We throw the money at him, we run as gingerly as we can into the venue, we walk in, and there is a line of people looking at us. Including Don Van Vliet, although I don't think he was really that upset. They had fixed the sound about fifteen minutes after we left. We'd been gone for an hour and a half."

However, Roy Estrada, Little Feat's bassist, was upset. "Roy was furious," Payne said, "and he was gone. He quit the band right after that." In fact, he joined Captain Beefheart.

As Richie Hayward recalled to Bud Scoppa: "Van Vliet made Roy an offer he couldn't refuse, like $500 a week. He left Little Feat to join Beefheart for security, which I find funnier than hell."

It's true that Estrada took his time deciding whether to join Little Feat because he was uncertain of its commercial potential. But, he told me, he had an entirely different reason for leaving. Listening to my list of other people's explanations for his departure—the Cincy screw-up, his longing for financial security, Captain Beefheart's humongous salary offer, Lowell's theory that Beefheart's music was "more in the concept he was accustomed to," and, from out of left field, an interest in becoming a computer programmer, Estrada said it was none of the above. He left, he said, for his health.

Zappa had once described him as "an asthmatic Pachuko." When I told him this, Estrada laughed. It was true. And he added, "The reason I left was that I have asthma. At that time we were living in Los Angeles, there was smog real bad, and I was approached by Captain Beefheart, who lived way up in Northern California, above Eureka. I thought that would be good for me, to live up there."

Was he thinking about switching from music to computers? "I thought about it," he said, "but didn't try it, didn't go all the way there."

With Estrada gone, the band in a lull, and its future with Warner Bros. again uncertain, Little Feat fell into disarray. Payne took his keyboards to work with the Doobie Brothers and, along with George, played on Carly Simon's *No Secrets*. At this point Little Feat was being managed by Bob Cavallo and Joe Ruffalo, whose client list included the Lovin' Spoonful and, since their breakup, the band's lead vocalist and songwriter, John Sebastian.

Soon backstage forces were at work for a possible new ensemble centered around George—not merely an ensemble but, in the parlance of the seventies, a supergroup. It would consist of George, Sebastian, and Phil Everly of the fifties and sixties stars the Everly Brothers. As a matter of musical, historical fact, George would be dwarfed by Sebastian—he of the Lovin' Spoonful and a solo album, *John B. Sebastian*, which had charted in 1970. But Cavallo gave Sebastian a copy of the first Little Feat album, and Sebastian was pretty impressed. The next day, he told Cavallo that "This is the next Elvis. This is the guy we gotta keep track of." In his effusiveness Sebastian fell into step with Parks, who once declared George to be "the King of Rock and Roll."

Sebastian soon met George, and they wound up producing a song, "Face of Appalachia," which Sebastian would record for his 1974 album, *Tarzana Kid*. After that, Sebastian stayed in touch with George, and after Estrada left, he says, George contacted him. "I never would have come up with this by myself, ever," he said. "But the sequence goes like this. I helped Paul Rothschild make an album with the Everly Brothers, called *Stories We Could Tell* . . . and out of it grew a musical friendship between Phil and I."

Beginning work on a new album of his own, Sebastian had Everly over while he was trying out a couple of songs. "What came out was really nice," he recalled, "so that got me thinking, 'Well, okay, now we're gonna do something where I'm the guy who sings under.' . . . And so, out of that, I'd say we even had a gig or two someplace not too conspicuous, where we were experimenting with how healthy that was. . . . And somewhere in there Lowell just might have caught the show, and that might have been where the idea came from. . . . It was a difficult time for Little Feat. . . . I'm not on the inside of that, but I could sense that I wasn't sure whether this was the indicator that he was gonna become a solo artist or that the band was gonna shift personnel. . . . I really was not on the inside. . . . Then he actually called a rehearsal that included Phil and I, and so we went to this rehearsal and we sang along. . . . But I think it was very clear to us that, especially with the rest of the guys in the band, they were playing their asses off that afternoon, they wanted us to know that this unit was perfectly healthy and complete just as it was. . . . And the other guitarist, Paul Barrere, I've never talked to Paul about it, but I know he'd be blisteringly frank."

Actually, Barrere was blisteringly vague. He didn't recall such a rehearsal and thought that it took place before he joined the band. (Payne's recollection is that it was just George and him with Sebastian and Everly. And, he adds, "I wasn't thrilled about a 'superband.' Lowell thought of it as a temporary thing.")

Regardless of who was there, the attitude, Sebastian says, was "to make sure we knew that we weren't needed. You know, it wasn't the 'go away' thing, it was . . . 'Hey, we're already here.' And we tried a number of things. I remember we played 'Dixie Chicken'—that was amazing to hear that in a room . . . unbelievably exciting." George agreed—to an extent. "We had one get-together which was really nice," he said. "Real great three-part harmony, with John on the bottom, Phil on the top, and me in the middle . . . but it could never have come to fruition, not in a million years. We were just not aligned . . . human chemistry ruled out any chance of a workable unit."

He was talking about a generational divide, he being a seventies kind of a guy, whereas Everly was rooted in the fifties and sixties. Or, as he flippantly put it: "I don't think that Phil Everly and I could share a stage. I mean, I'm twenty pounds overweight and he's twenty pounds, er, over the hill." He praised Everly's singing but added, "He's been doing what he's done for so long that I don't think he'd be prepared for anything I'd want to lay on him."

George was also wary about the foundation on which other so-called supergroups had been mounted. "Money was the prime motivation for that little scene, and I don't think I could have handled it," he said. "Money moves me, but it doesn't move me that far. I think of all those pop groups who hate each other, making fortunes every night, and I can't imagine doing that."

George did, however, have a musical flirtation with Jackson Browne, who approached him about forming a band. George told *Zigzag* magazine in 1975 that Browne had invited him "to join a group with him . . . folks from L.A. that had had a hard time of it." The timing was wrong, he said. "But he's one of my favorites. He really is Mr. L.A."

Later, in an interview with Bill Flanagan of *Musician* magazine in 1983, Browne recalled, "I put myself in Lowell's hands for a while and made him my tutor, and he very good naturedly accepted. Since he had studied with a lot of Orientals [I'm sure he meant "Asians"], both musically and in the martial arts, he adopted that sort of big, mean approach: 'Okay, if you want to know what I know, you've got to do that and that . . . and when you're through, we'll talk about it.' He called me the student prince because I was so willing to learn." But George and his grasshopper never did form a band.

After George had exhausted his various options for non-Feat ensembles, he and Payne, along with Hayward began considering a replacement for bassist Estrada. True to its warped way of doing things, the band invited Paul Barrere to try out again. Barrere had to remind them that he was, just as he was the first time around, a guitarist.

George and Payne then hired a proper bass man, Kenny Gradney, then added a conga player, Sam Clayton, and—why not—Barrere, where he belonged: on guitar.

Rick Harper, the late road manager for the Feats, said he persuaded the band to hire Barrere. "So they said, 'You go get Paul and go to your place, and you have him learn all Lowell's rhythm guitar lines.' So Paul shows up and says, 'Gee, man, I don't know.' I say, 'What do you mean, you don't know? You can cop all these lines. You can do this shit in your sleep.' We started in the beginning and went through every single album, and he copped every single lick just perfect, all the rhythm parts. Just to make sure, he learned some of the lead stuff as well. We were rehearsing out at Warner Bros. on Soundstage 24, and there it was. He was in."

Barrere himself remembers it differently. After his first audition as a bassist in 1971, he says, he told George: "If you ever need a second guitarist, call me." After Estrada left and after failing his second tryout on bass, he says, "Lowell came to me and said, 'If you really want to be the second guitarist, here's this record, *Sailin' Shoes*. If you can learn the intro to "Cold, Cold, Cold," you can be in the band. And by the way, learn all the rest of the songs too.' So I showed up and played 'Cold, Cold, Cold' for him, and he went, 'You're in.'"

Barrere acknowledged that Harper was a factor, if only in his friendships with various band members. He and Harper had known each other since they were five or six, he says. But he'd also known George—or at least knew of him—since high school. Born in Burbank and raised in Hollywood, Barrere was three years younger than George, but his two older brothers attended Hollywood High with his future bandmate.

"There's a funny thing," Barrere begins, the thought of common bonds still in the air. "My grandfather, George Barrere, was brought to the United States by Walter Damrosch, to be first chair in the New York Symphony before it became the Philharmonic. And he later went on to teach at Julliard. He had a bunch of students, and evidently, one of his students was Lowell's flute teacher. Out here . . . it doesn't get any weirder than that."

Music was in his blood. "I have two older brothers, so we all took piano lessons. I took them from the age of six to eleven, but I had a really good ear and sort of faked my way through, showing the teacher that maybe I was reading, but I wasn't. I knew the notes. I can't play and read 'em at the same time, but I can go through 'em." He learned mostly show tunes, and for his final recital he performed "Rhapsody in Blue." He was eleven.

And he was tired of the piano. After watching *The Benny Goodman Story*, with Steve Allen playing his clarinet outside on a fire escape, he decided portability was hip. At a party the thirteen-year-old Paul watched as girls gathered around a kid who was playing some Jimmy Reed blues on a Gibson guitar and, at thirteen, picked up a guitar. "I said, 'That's it. That must be the deal.' That and the Beach Boys." He quickly got to work on songs by those babe magnets, Jimmy Reed and the Rolling Stones.

He recalled that "I always thought the act of playing music was kind of spiritual." But he also loved baseball and, as a teenager, aspired to play the game on a serious level. "But then pot and surfing got in the way."

Barrere played in a couple of garage bands. "One was called Dick Butter, which is a term for the juice of a female orgasm. And then the one that I got serious with was a band that had the name Led Enema, a garage band in Laurel Canyon." This was around 1967 or '68, in case that helps explain the names.

Lowell George, who'd been friends with Paul's older siblings, became a fan. "He heard the band quite a few times and thought, *These guys are crazy*." said Barrere. "'Cause it was myself on guitar, another guitarist who had a solid-body National, tuned it way down to a C# minor tuning, a harmonica player, and a drummer. We had a bass between us, and the other guitar player and myself would occasionally play bass on one of the songs. But usually it was just the two guitars, harmonica, and drums."

As for those songs, which Barrere helped write, the repertoire included "A Very Careful Fly in Anybody's Ointment," "The Vermilion Antagonist," and "The Whisky Stealin' Indian," "about an old white guy pissed off that the Indian was stealing his whisky, not knowing that we'd stolen the country from them.

"We had a song called 'Cheese Street,' which was a takeoff on a gospel song that morphed into a John Lee Hooker kind of shuffle," Barrere recalled. "The lyric went, 'Cheese is three-dimensional Christ, what are you doing on Cheese Street.' . . . Lowell really liked that." In turn, Barrere went to see George and his band, the Factory, numerous times at Bito Lito's.

He also maintained friendships with the other guys in the Factory, participating in blues jams with Hayward in a club downtown—"one of those typical forty-minute blues jams with a thirty-minute ending," he said.

Now, two and a half years since his failed audition as a bassist for Little Feat and after reminding the band that he still wasn't a bass player, George came calling again. This time he was in the market for a supporting guitarist. "I asked him if he wanted to play," said George. "In terms of guitarists, I needed a place keeper. I'd be lost most of the time trying to find out where I was in relation to the rhythm section, so Paul was helpful in that he covered a lot of the guitar parts that I used to play . . . or didn't . . . enhancing them in his own way, which left me to play some lead."

With Barrere in place, George, Payne, and Hayward still needed a bass player. They found a solid musician who'd heard about the opening through a rehearsal facility used by many artists. The musician was interested, even though he'd never heard of Little Feat.

IF NOT FOR THE KU KLUX KLAN, Kenny Gradney could've been a Texan. But just before he was born, he says, the KKK ran his father, a native Texan, out of Houston. The burgeoning Gradney family (there'd be eleven kids in all) moved to New Orleans briefly—long enough, anyway, for Kenny to be born in 1950—and then, defiantly, back to Houston.

Baby Kenny wasn't long for the Lone Star State. By the time he was ten months old he was packed up again, this time for Los Angeles, where his family settled into the south central part of the city.

But the Bayou was still in his blood. "I'm Creole," he says. "I am Italian, French, American Indian, part German. I wouldn't say African American, but I'd say Haitian. If you'd see my mom, you'd see the Haitian." He appears happy to embrace it all.

Although he grew up in southern California, much of his music was from Louisiana. "My mom was always dancin', party," he says. "That's what they played. Having seven sisters and three brothers, there was a huge, vast array of music that we listened to." His father was in the music business, managing and producing pop and blues artists like Bobby Day, who clicked with "Rockin' Robin" in 1958, Eddie "Cleanhead" Vinson, and Charles Brown ("Merry Christmas Baby").

Living in the Crenshaw district, he and his siblings expressed their love of music in any number of ways, such as singing doo-wop in school and wherever they could get together. "We had stacks of 45s at my house," Gradney recalls. "We would just stack them on the stereo. The first person in the house turned the stereo on, until the last person. And we'd all be dancing. My mom would be in the kitchen, cookin' and dancin'. We would dance all the time. It was pretty cool."

He continued: "If it was raining, we would get the stereo in the bedroom, and my sisters would make Kool-Aid, and we would wear my mom's clothes—we were kids! We would put on Ramsey Lewis. Everyone would pick songs, and we would all lip sync, except my sister Marie—she sang so damn good, she sang along with the track. I would lip sync."

But he could also play. By age ten he was picking up instruments. "When I was twelve years old, and 'cause my friends Ernesto and Roland played guitar, I started playing bass. [Roland Bautista would wind up with Earth, Wind and Fire.] It just fit me. I wanted to play percussion, and I just knew the bass was perfect for me. I was in love with James Jamerson from listening to Motown and what he played, and I just got every Motown record I could get. 'Signed, Sealed, Delivered' just had me. I had to learn every note on that album. It drove me crazy."

Along with Roland and Ernesto as well as a cousin, Kenny found himself in a band, the Royal Mixtures. He was thirteen or fourteen, he figures, and the band played casual family gatherings. With the addition of a drummer, the band began to rock. "We started learning everything from the Beatles to Jimi Hendrix." And, of course, Motown.

In high school, around 1964, 1965, Gradney's Royal Mixtures became the Turbans (not the midfifties Turbans, who had the hit "When You Dance"). This was Gradney's musical education, playing at parties and at under-twenty-one clubs. "They taught you how to put a band together and make a show. We played everything. We ended up on the Pepsi Boss Battles, on the *Sam Riddle Show*." He was a big DJ on Channel 9 [and on one of Los Angeles' Top 40 radio stations].The Turbans did Smokey and the Miracles' "Ooh Baby Baby" and got second prize, good enough for $1,500 in savings bonds and another $1,500 in musical equipment from Fender.

By age sixteen Gradney had landed a gig with the very adult Ike & Tina Turner show. "A friend of mine played in their band and called me and said, 'Come down here and play bass.' And I did, and I got the gig. I played with them for the summer of '66."

By then Gradney had his own band, called One Flight Up, playing clubs around LA. Life was good . . . enough. But things picked up a couple of years later, thanks to one of his brothers.

In 1969 Gabe Gradney started S.I.R. (Studio Instrument Rentals, which would grow to set industry standards in rehearsal spaces), with Ken Berry and Dolph Rempp, who'd known Kenny Gradney since he was fourteen. Gabe became friends with the manager of the blues-rock ensemble, Delaney and Bonnie, and got a gig as a road manager for the band. One day, late in 1969, as Gradney recalls, Gabe handed him a piece of paper. "He said, 'Call this number.' Bonnie [Bramlett, Delaney's wife] answered. I talked to her awhile. The next day I go and audition and get the gig. I played with them for three and a half years, until '72."

Delaney and Bonnie had just lost most of the band that had recently done a triumphant tour of Britain with Eric Clapton. Leon Russell, a friend of Bramlett's who'd played keyboards and guitar on their first recordings, poached drummer Jim Keltner, horn players Jim Price and Bobby Keys, bassist Carl Radle, and singer Rita Coolidge to join him on the Joe Cocker-fronted Mad Dogs and Englishmen tour. Suddenly, a powerhouse band, Delaney & Bonnie & Friends, was down to Delaney, Bonnie, and organist Bobby Whitlock. The Bramletts assembled a new crew, including guitarist Duane Allman, conga player Sam Clayton, and, from Elvis Presley's band, bassist Jerry Scheff and drummer Ron Tutt. Gradney says he was part of the new band, played on the albums *To Bonnie from Delaney* and *Motel Shot*, and left around 1972 when "the band started coming apart." The Bramletts were splitting up, and Gradney was out of work.

Once again it was Gradney's connections to his brother that led to a new gig: "Dolph Rempp called me up one day from S.I.R.'s practice studios. 'Hey, there's a band over here called Little Feat,' he said, 'and I think you'd be perfect . . . you should come and audition.'"

Gradney didn't know who Little Feat were, but he made a couple of phone calls and reached Payne, who invited him in for an audition. He arrived and surmised that the keyboardist "had been going through bass players like crazy. So I sat down next to him, I tuned my bass, and he said, 'You don't need to audition. Why don't you just come up later today?' I went to Warner Bros.' lot. They were on one of the big stages there. It's where Bill Cosby used to do his Crest commercials. I walk in this big empty stage where there's this giant toothpaste tube on top of these giant teeth, and I said, 'Holy Moly, where am I?' Over in the corner was the band . . . So I went and met Lowell, met the guys—it's like noon—and we just jammed till about five, and we went through all their tunes. I played everything, and they said, 'Are you up for it?' I said, 'Sure. I'm looking for a gig.' He said, 'You got one.' And that was it."

Just one more thing: Gradney proposed that they give a listen to his buddy, Sam Clayton. Not that Little Feat was looking to add another percussionist, but, Gradney reasoned, "He was my partner. We had just left Delaney & Bonnie together. And I said, 'I'll get us another band, don't worry.'"

SAM CLAYTON IS the low-key man on the Little Feat totem pole.

I've had reticent interview subjects before, but Clayton is ridiculous. He's driven up from San Diego for our session in L.A., he knows this is for a book about his band and that the band and management, though they have been given no promises about how the book might turn out, has offered to cooperate.

But Clayton looks suspicious from the get-go. He sits down in the interviews room, looking as though I'd be so intrusive as to want to know the basics of his background, like where and when he was born.

"Does that have to be in there?" he asks about his birth year (1946).

I just want to know, I reply, so I can trace his musical chronology, how young or old he was when certain artists came to the fore: the Beatles, Hendrix, Santana, the original Little Feat.

He nods. He knows he's expected to be one of the boys in the band and to play along, so he provides answers—incomplete and sometimes involuntary answers, but answers, nonetheless. And given his pivotal role as part of Little Feat's percussive rhythm section, these answers will do.

He was born in Colfax, Louisiana, about twenty miles north, he says, of Alexandria. His father sold clothing and his mother was a nurse. He had one brother and three sisters, one of whom, Merry

Clayton, became famous in the seventies as a backup vocalist with the Rolling Stones ("Gimme Shelter," anybody?) and recorded albums of her own.

As for Sam's musical interests: mostly conga drums. "My Dad was a clothing salesman and Mom was a registered nurse," he said. "I grew up with one brother and three sisters . . . and I always wanted to be a conga player."

But why the congas? In the twelfth grade he had a girlfriend who was in the Lester Horton Dance Group. Once, she performed in a production of *The King and I* and took Sam to a rehearsal. "I saw this guy playing these drums, and it was phenomenal. I couldn't believe it."

He actually fell in love with drumming as a kid and says his first instruments were oatmeal boxes and pots and pans. By the time he was in seventh grade he wanted to take drumming lessons, but he switched to congas. "I said, 'This is more natural, when it comes to playing the conga drums. It's your body and that other body, like you're playing skin on skin. And it just sounds so great.'"

After further inspiration from the Lester Horton Dance Group's drummer, Sam played drums at his home in Watts to records by Mongo "Watermelon Man" Santamaria, vibraphonist and bandleader Cal Tjader, and, frankly, anyone who had a beat. "I could play congas to country music," he said. "If it's got good rhythms, you gravitate toward it."

Outside his home—in the neighborhood, around town, and on the beach—Clayton began participating in jam sessions. "Somebody would have a flute," he said, "or somebody would have a cowbell, that's how I started playing."

Clayton, who'd served his time in the US Army as a military policeman in Japan, was working as an electromechanical engineer at Douglas Aircraft. When the time came for a number of workers, including Clayton, to be laid off, he attended a "termination party." "It was at a place called Rochelle's in Long Beach," he recalled. "We get out there, we're gettin' ready to get laid off, and we had this party. There was some congas up there, and my buddies say, 'Hey, man, you said you could play . . . why don't you?' and this and that." One of his pals asked a member of the band if Sam could play with them. "The guy says okay, 'cause you figure all those guys are drunk. I didn't drink. He said, 'You can play one song.' And I played, and he came over and said, 'You wanna finish the set with us tonight? Play as long as you want to play.' 'Yeah, man, sure.' It was great."

The band was called Formula Five, and its leader, Brent Seewell, would figure greatly in Clayton's future. After Sam had joined the band, Seewell, assessing his skills, told him, "You should go on tour." A guitarist in Formula Five introduced him to Delaney Bramlett, and Sam wound up playing congas in a movie. It was *Vanishing Point*, a car chase extravaganza released in 1971 that starred Barry Newman, Dean Jagger, Cleavon Little (as a blind DJ), and a nude woman on a motorcycle.

Delaney and Bonnie were hired to portray members of a traveling "religious cult band," as Clayton called it, along with David Gates (later of Bread), Claudia Lennear of the Ikettes, and Rita Coolidge. Sam, in denim overalls, stood behind them on a truck bed platform stage, providing percussion for the "J. Hovah Singers." (The film also featured a song by Longbranch/Pennywhistle, a folk-rock duo comprised of J. D. Souther and future Eagles cofounder Glenn Frey.)

After appearing in the film, Clayton joined Delaney and Bonnie's post–Leon Russell band, and that's where he met Kenny Gradney. A year or so later Gradney heard about an opening in Little Feat and landed the gig as Roy Estrada's replacement on bass. He brought Clayton in to meet the band, which had already added Paul Barrere on guitar. There was not a need for additional percussion.

"There wasn't," said Gradney. But, he added, "He was my partner."

Clayton, with a little prompting, recalled what happened. He had hurt himself playing basketball: "I blew out my knee, had a ruptured patella tendon. So [Delaney] got this pro wrestler, Jay York, who was, like, the security guy around the band. He wanted to play congas and wanted me to teach him, and I was showing him stuff. Anyway, he hired that guy, and Kenny was angry, so he split."

Gradney remembers Clayton injuring both of his knees in about a year's span and getting fired after the second offense. "I called Delaney's brother, who was managing him at the time, 'cause I wanted a raise. He said 'No.' I said, 'You fired Sam. I quit.' I hung up the phone and said, 'Don't worry, Sam. I'll get us a gig.'"

Gradney believes that, after Delaney & Bonnie, Clayton was thinking of assembling a band including Claudia Lennear and Bonnie Bramlett. As he told the writer Bud Scoppa: "Sam had a bunch of girl singers, and he was going to start a band with them. I said, 'You're not going to start a band with the girls—you're gonna start an orgy with the girls." Clayton, asked about this, said he doesn't recall any such idea.

When Gradney landed with Little Feat, however, he suggested that the band add Clayton. "I got him to come and sit in with Lowell, and he loved him. He was rockin' . . . "

Clayton was less than thrilled about joining a band he'd never heard of. "I didn't want to come with them," he admits. "I was trying to get with Chicago, one of the bigger bands." In fact, while he was working out his Little Feat deal, he says, he got an offer from the Doobie Brothers. "Bobby LaKind, their road guy, started playing congas with them. Then something happened, and they had me come in. They were playing at the Greek and said, could I do the gig? I played it, they said, 'Yeah, fine.' And then the guy wants his gig back." Clayton had lasted about as long as one good toke of a doobie.

Still, when Lowell George extended his job offer, Gradney remembers Clayton hesitating again. George then let them know that time was short, that the band had a gig in Honolulu at the Sunshine Festival at the Crater in Diamond Head, home of the annual Crater Festival. "Really?!" Clayton replied. "I'll go to Hawaii!"

As Gradney recalled, "We got up in the Crater for our first show, and it was forty thousand people. We killed 'em. I got to see Lowell work the audience. He did his job. He was awesome. It was Lowell's persona. I just knew I'd get rich with this guy. So Sam and I said the same thing: 'I'm not leaving this band.'"

Among others who were impressed: Hampton George, Lowell's older brother. He hadn't seen Lowell since the Factory days, and he was working for Hilton hotels in Honolulu as a food and beverages director when he got a call from Lowell saying he'd be in town. "I had no idea how many albums they'd done—I knew nothing about them," he admitted. And how did his kid brother do? "They blew me away," said Hampton. "I hadn't imagined he was so good."

With Clayton, Gradney, and Barrere in the fold, a new Little Feat had come together. It was time to make an album. Time to take that third swing.

Chapter 7

FINGER-PICKIN' GOOD

By adding Kenny Gradney on bass and Sam Clayton on percussion, George was taking Little Feat further South than ever before. The first two albums had reflected his and his bandmates' affection for the blues, R&B, country, and other American roots music.

But now, with two players with Louisiana hot sauce streaming through their veins and adding propulsive percussion as well as with a solid new guitarist whose presence allowed George to explore new turf with his own bottleneck, in 1973 Little Feat was not only renewed; it was a new ensemble.

As a quartet, Little Feat were a truckin' country-rock band, despite frequent emphases on rock and blues. Songs like "Willin'" and "Truck Stop Girl" put them in the ranks of pioneers of what would be called in the radio business "Americana" music. Now it had gone marching into Louisiana territory, with its second-line rhythms and syncopations, all the while maintaining a strong roots-rock base and a wide range of sounds, including soulful numbers like "Roll Um Easy" and "On Your Way Down," a bluesy number by New Orleans's Allen Toussaint. "We were influenced at that point by Dr. John and

Professor Longhair," said Payne, "and then also to a degree by Van Dyke Parks through the veil of Randy Newman."

After inviting Templeman back as producer and being turned down ("Ted didn't have the time," George said. "He was busy making hit albums with the Doobie Brothers.") George appointed himself producer of the next album.

Templeman was not surprised. During sessions for *Sailin' Shoes*, he said, George's ability to come up with ideas and solutions impressed him, prompting him to remember George's interest in the mixing process. "I think he always wanted to be a producer more than an artist," Templeman said. George agreed: "My head is directed toward production anyway. I really like it, and the group thought my chops were up enough to give it a try. Making records is equally as much of an instrument as anything you can sit down and play. You can record your guitar and play it back and then augment it and modify it any way you want. It's just like playing it."

Beyond the new band members, George called in additional vocalists, chief among them Bonnie Bramlett, Bonnie Raitt, and Tret Fure. They would add greatly to the choruses of the title track, "Dixie Chicken," as well as other enduring Feat songs like "Roll Um Easy" and "Fat Man in the Bathtub." The band—and friends—gathered at Clover Studios in Hollywood.

As producer, George gave himself more leeway as a vocalist than he felt he had received from Titelman and Templeman. "*Dixie Chicken*," he told one writer in 1976, "was the first album I was really allowed to sing on, and to experiment, with microphones, et cetera. It's real tough, because there's always the budget hanging over your head, and that was an expensive album, but you have to live with these things for the rest of your life and it doesn't go away. You try to do your best."

In the studio George also gave the rest of Little Feat a lot of room. Kenny Gradney, the bassist, said that with Delaney and Bonnie, the music was structured. With Little Feat, "I just played, and Lowell goes, 'I love this.' He goes, 'Play it like you feel it.' And I did."

Gradney also appreciated the band's policy on songwriting royalties. Although George wrote or cowrote seven of the ten songs on

Dixie Chicken, he told the new band members: "'We split the publishing. Everybody gets a piece, whether you write it or not.' And that's what really got me into Little Feat," Gradney said. Incredible. "So I have publishing on everything, from *Dixie Chicken* on."

Sam Clayton said his congas and other instruments fit in immediately: "Richie didn't want it, but Lowell said, 'No, man, I need him [Sam] to hold you down.' He knew I played straighter and more on the rhythm and stuff like that. That's why I was hired. He'd say that to Richie or anyone." "Richie's such a loose cannon," Kenny says with pride. "They were ready for it. . . . They were having trouble finding someone who could play with him because he's out there, but it was just what I was looking for."

Hayward, of course, disagreed. He thought he was doing fine by his brother-in-law, George, and by the band. He also felt that the Feats' southern drift was only beneficial to his evolution as a drummer. He told Robyn Flans of *Modern Drummer* that songs like "Fat Man in the Bathtub" "were important stepping stones in my growth because I got to learn different ways to play 4/4 time, different ways to enjoy a backbeat. 'Fat Man' was one of my first experiments in second line. It began with that straight Bo Diddley thing you hear in the intro, and through the course of the tune, it changes feels about six times. They're all at the same tempo, but they feel completely different."

With Clayton and Gradney on board, Hayward said, "it got a lot better really fast. . . . There was much more input, more people to play off of. Groove-wise, there was a lot of psychic arm wrestling going on for the next bunch of years. We were all coming from different places, and to make it work there were a lot of compromises made, voluntarily and involuntarily."

In the *Dixie Chicken* sessions, Barrere recalled, George never asserted a leadership role, but because he wrote and sang most of the songs, the band assumed he was the leader. But, Barrere said, "Anybody who had a song could bring it in, and we would play it, and if everybody dug it . . . His only rule was Rule Number One: There were no rules. And any kind of music was fair game. He was the one who really encouraged me to broaden my perspective musically, which helped immensely." Barrere credits George with expanding his musical horizons, giving the rock guitarist country and pop records as well as encouragement: "You can write songs with more than three chords." Barrere cowrote "Walkin' All Night" with Payne, and the jaunty tune fit right into *Dixie Chicken*. He also cocomposed the instrumental "Lafayette Railroad."

George himself wrote "Fat Man in the Bathtub," "Two Trains," "Juliette," and "Roll Um Easy." As for the title song, that dated back a year, when he and Martin Kibbee met, fueled up with espressos, and tried to come up with songs for *Sailin' Shoes*. "Dixie Chicken," Kibbee says, was inspired by a sign for a chicken restaurant that he saw as he left an all-night songwriting session with George in Laurel Canyon. "It said, 'Dixie Chicken.' He'd been playing the damn thing all night, you know, '*Duh-duh-duh*,' which was going through my brain. By the time I got home, I had written this song."

That left two songs from outside the Little Feat circle. One was "On Your Way Down" by Allen Toussaint, a musician and producer best known at the time as the writer of the sixties hit "Mother-in-Law." The other was "Fool Yourself," a gently cautionary song by multi-instrumentalist and writer Fred Tackett. Then, in 1973, he had no way of knowing that, fifteen years later, he would become a member of Little Feat.

Actually, if it weren't for the fact that his credits as a session player stretch longer than most red carpets, Fred Tackett could have joined Little Feat far earlier than he did. Tackett, a native of Hot Springs, Arkansas, was playing guitar with various groups in and around Oklahoma City when he got wind that he might soon be drafted into the military. "I just said, 'Screw it, I'm gonna tune in and drop out.'" He jumped into a car with one of his bands—comprised of four Filipino musicians—and wound up in Hawaii, where the group got a gig in a bar. Among the clientele one night: Jimmy Webb. Tackett recalled, "He found me playing 'Ode to Billy Joe' and said, 'Come out to Hollywood, Man.'"

Composers aren't the most recognizable faces in the business, and Tackett wasn't sure who his admirer was. "I thought he was a drug dealer—this dude all dressed in white," he said. "It turns out he was

Jimmy Webb. He brought me to Hollywood and got me started play-ing with Glen Campbell, and through Glen's producers I found other country guys." And, through Webb, he and Lowell became friends and, at one point, neighbors.

Over the years they would hang out at each other's home or at Jimmy Webb's and jam or trade songs. One of Tackett's was "Fool Yourself," which Bonnie Raitt would later record. "And Lowell hears it and said, 'I'm gonna record that one,'" Tackett recalled.

Now, with the new Little Feat together, George made good on his promise, putting "Fool Yourself" on *Dixie Chicken*. "He did it, and I came in and played acoustic guitar on it." Thus, Tackett became part of what he would call the "Feats Auxiliary," a corps of musicians al-ways willing and able to hit a Feat session and help out.

At Clover Studios the help also included Danny Hutton, one of Three Dog Night's lead vocalists. He was a pal of George's and had dropped in to visit one evening when George was at work by himself. George got him to sing harmony on "Roll Um Easy," despite Hutton's protest that he'd just come off the road so his vocal chords were shot. "He said, 'C'mon, man, let's try a harmony.' I did it once, and it sounded terrible. He said, 'That was great. You sound awful—it's wonderful.' And that was it—one take. I sound like a rough old man on that track. He really knew what he wanted."

The Auxiliary would come also to include Linda Ronstadt and Emmylou Harris, joining Bonnie Raitt. Raitt was a fellow Warner Bros. artist who, like Little Feat, had yet to find her way to the charts. Like George, she played slide guitar and loved the blues. They had met only recently, when George, on one of his side excursions, produced singer-songwriter Tret Fure's first album (on Uni, the label the Factory had been on). It was George's first outside production work since his stint with the GTOs. Raitt met Fure through Fanny, the band fronted by June and Jean Millington, and Fure was Jean's girlfriend. Early in their friendship June had played "Sailin' Shoes" for Bonnie, and she became an instant fan of Little Feat. "This was like my dream," she said, "to see somebody do to blues what Lowell was doing. Between him and Bill, the vocabulary was sophisticated, with the Latin feel on 'Texas Rose Café,' and I had to meet him." She wound up singing on

Fure's album and meeting George. "The connection was immediate," she said, noting that there was both musical and physical chemistry: "He was really a fox. I mean, he was one of the most attractive men I've ever seen. I mean, I fell hard for him." She did not know that he was, in his own way, a committed man. In 1972 he was still legally married to Patte, but they had separated, and he was living with Elizabeth. Said Bonnie: "He neglected to mention that he had a family."

The unsuspecting Raitt tried to combine the personal with the professional. She joined in on vocals for *Dixie Chicken* and told a VP at Warner Bros. that she'd like George to produce her next album. George, she was told, would be tied up touring to promote the Feat's album. Raitt had an idea: she'd join the tour, even though she'd just completed an East Coast trip for her second album, *Give It Up*, and George could produce her album afterward. Raitt was a popular concert attraction and had no concerns about hitting the same areas again. "And I went back out, with Little Feat opening for me. We played Max's Kansas City, and I introduced them to Philly and DC and Baltimore—all those places that ended up being their most rabid following."

The band tried to do their part. In selected cities they agreed to promote *Dixie Chicken* by visiting radio stations—in costumes. Barrere remembers a stop in Atlanta. "Lowell's wearing a chicken suit, and the rest of us are in busboys' costumes, going to radio stations, handing out Kentucky Fried Chicken that had the Little Feat cover of *Dixie Chicken* on it. It says, 'Finger Pickin' Good.'" George didn't want to wear the chicken head, so Barrere wound up putting it over his busboy's uniform. Clayton and the others wore paper caps, and Hayward chose a top hat and long scarf over his white jacket. He liked playing Mr. Rock and Roll.

"So," Barrere continues, "here we are, acting the fool, and [Lowell] comes to find out that there's no product in the stores. He got really pissed. He went and yelled and screamed at those people. He was talking about calling the whole thing off at that point."

Warner Bros. execs apologized; they didn't have control over retailers in every town. "It wasn't marketed the way it needed to be marketed," said Carl Scott, who helped book concert appearances.

"The point of these tours was to go out and put this band in front of people. It's not unlike today, but on a much smaller scale: colleges, small clubs; the circuit. And that's what I did."

As for not finding records in the local shops, Lenny Waronker, who signed Little Feat and would go on to become president of Warner Bros., explained that retail outlets decided what to order—and they usually went with bigger artists who were more likely to sell. "If you were selling," he explained, "it was rare that you'd go looking at a store to see if they were carrying your record. . . . When things aren't going as well, then you'd start to take a look at those things. So often they were right; sometimes they weren't right because something was back-ordered."

George understood. He was learning the business, saying, "The blame for our past lack of success is equal one way or another. We never presented ourselves in front of an audience at the right opportunity. We'd make a record, the thing would come out, and then three months later we'd go on the road. And then the sales of the album would never equate because the initial push would be lost. There was no chart position, so the buyers out in the boondogs wouldn't buy. The record company's a business. It's like if you have a product and it's not doing well, there's not much you can do about it unless you do a million-dollar push. And everybody was afraid that we were going to break up."

Which, in fact, George kept, hidden in his chicken suit, as an option.

In the meantime, back in Los Angeles, he went into a recording studio with Bonnie Raitt to work on her album *Takin' My Time*, but he would not complete the job. In one interview after the album's release Bonnie said she and George "got too close to be able to have any objectivity." Choosing her words carefully, out of deference to Liz George, she told me: "It got a little bit complicated emotionally." Soon after learning that he was married, she began going out with Barrere, "and that did not make Lowell happy." And in the studio there was more tension: "He wanted to play slide on a lot of the record, and I thought maybe as much as I loved the way he played slide,

I felt that he should have let me play. So that was kind of where we went astray."

Raitt would complete her album with John Hall, of the band Orleans, producing. She wound up with pretty much all of Little Feat—and her own auxiliary—chipping in, including Barrere, Clayton, Payne, Van Dyke Parks, and Lowell George, who played guitar and slide guitar. The album was a critical success and made the *Billboard* Top 100.

But still, George and company would continue to wait to crack the charts. Like their first two efforts, *Dixie Chicken* would underperform. Barrere says it sold about thirty thousand units—more than double *Sailin' Shoes'* initial sales, but still a modest number. This—despite George producing what would stand as Little Feat's finest overall effort, despite their tour and willingness to serve fried chicken to disc jockeys, and despite another round of positive reviews.

In *Rolling Stone* Bud Scoppa all but made a call for readers to come to the band's rescue: "We don't really need any more audacious, ingenious bands like Little Feat," he wrote. "We just have to support the ones that exist." Scoppa noted that although the Feats had moved away from echoing the Band and the Stones, comparisons, especially to the Stones, still might be apt: "There's even a rumor, possibly dreamed up by some lonely Little Feat fanatic, that as soon as Mick Jagger got to Los Angeles . . . to put together *Exile on Main Street*, he requested a set of Little Feat LPs for which he expressed a particular fondness. There are, in fact, several tracks on *Exile* . . . that have that dense, careening, nearly out-of-control feeling that distinguishes much of Little Feat's music."

On *Dixie Chicken*, the group seems to have returned the favor, using a number of elements also found on the last Stones LP. Rock critic Steve Stolder continued the comparison: "In many ways, *Dixie Chicken* stands as a kind of kissing cousin to the Rolling Stones' *Exile on Main Street*, which hit the streets one year earlier. While not as expansive as the Stones' magnum opus, its highlights are every bit as spectacular."

So George had proven himself as a producer but, in failing to get his band out of the red, left himself open to sniping about how he comported himself in the studio. Sure, he handled an expanded band well, gave each musician enough latitude to perform at their best, and supplied them with some of his strongest songs. He made the most of his engineering crew and studio equipment. Nonetheless, there'd be talk about the time he chased a couple of band members around Clover studio and unleashed the contents of a fire extinguisher at them, in the process putting the control board out of commission for a day. And there was, inevitably, talk about drugs.

As George's longtime friend and cowriter Martin Kibbee has noted, Frank Zappa influenced George. Although he found the Mother too autocratic and demanding for his taste, he liked being in charge. He admired Zappa's work ethic and workaholic ways, of toiling for hours in the studio; composing, performing, or editing music; or perfecting a mix. He loved tinkering with the latest technology.

But there was a crucial difference. As Kibbee put it: "Frank was so dedicated, so hardworking, such a no-bullshit guy, and that model of how the group ought to be run was what Lowell aspired to. But he was not that guy. It would be like having Bill Clinton run the military. Frank was more of a Colin Powell sort of guy."

So what was Lowell George like? Rick Harper, who was by his side as his road manager throughout his music career, from the Factory through Feat and beyond, said, "When you look up the word 'hedonism' in the dictionary, there should really be a picture of Lowell there." Some who got close to George believe that, in some cases, drugs were exactly what they were: drugs, meant to relieve pain, whether mental or physical. "He was caught up in that period of the culture," said one friend. But sometimes he got high just to get high. Hutton maintained a "party house" in Laurel Canyon and said that George was a frequent visitor, "ingesting huge amounts of cocaine, yet somehow getting fatter and fatter."

In some cases George's behavior cost friends real money. Kibbee contends that he wrote most of "Teenage Nervous Breakdown" but had his name left off the credits in *Sailin' Shoes*. And one day, while they were at work on the song "Dixie Chicken," Kibbee complained about it, only to hear George grumble that "Teenage" was "a terrible song."

"One day," Kibbee recalled, "he shows up with a paper bag with $10,000 cash in it . . . and he says, 'Hey, this group covered our song. Some Irish group . . . I got ten grand here.' So I said, 'Okay, give me five.' And he said, "I know this great Puerto Rican coke dealer. And we can spend all of this.' And . . . he bought this huge quantity of cocaine, he got so strung out, he gave it to Liz for safekeeping. It was the last I ever . . . Anyway, that group was Nazareth . . . "

Fortunately, "Dixie Chicken" became one of the more popular items in the modest George-Kibbee catalog. (Besides "Teenage" and "Dixie Chicken," they had "Easy to Slip" and "Rock and Roll Doctor.") "Dixie" would be covered not only by John Sebastian but also by Clarence "Gatemouth" Brown, the blues, country, and jazz artist from Louisiana and Texas; Livingston Taylor, talented brother of James; the Big Wu, a rootsy jam band from Minnesota; and five or six others. The most surprising of all the interpreters was Jack Jones. Yes, that Jack Jones: "Wives and Lovers," "Dear Heart," and the theme from the television series *The Love Boat*.

Jones actually did a respectable rendition and earned praise from George on a radio interview. "In an odd way," said Payne, "it legitimized what we were doing." Jones was true to the song, and, especially for a vocalist in the "crooner" category, he sang without careening into Bill Murray-as-lounge-lizard turf. He may not have rocked, but he rolled with the southern tempo and horns with which producer Rick Jarrard embellished the song. Jarrard was a solid, contemporary producer, having worked with Nilsson, José Feliciano, and Jefferson Airplane. Jones's "Dixie Chicken" appeared on his 1977 album, *With One More Look at You*, which also included John Lennon's "Jealous Kind."

Warner Bros. picked "Dixie Chicken" as Little Feat's third single, following "Strawberry Flats" and "Easy to Slip." "We were hoping that something like 'Dixie Chicken' would be a commercial success," said Barrere. "I mean, there were songs that were 'single-esque,' like 'Two Trains.' But the thing about Little Feat's music that I love is that it's timeless. But that's also the problem with it, because we never would jump on to what was *au courant*. We never fit in with the 'hot' scene of the day, so I guess it was a marketing person's nightmare." The record, Payne added, "has the chords, the verse, and a little bridge, but it's played in a New Orleans style, which doesn't hit the zone that would make it a hit record."

George, who often argued that commercial success was overrated, did, nonetheless, try for hits, beginning with "Easy to Slip" and "Sailin' Shoes." Sometimes, he would announce to the band that he was going to single-handedly compose a hit song, appease Warner Bros., and rake in some money.

So where, I asked Payne, did that leave him and the rest of the band?

He paused for a few seconds. "It left me on the level of: 'Can he pull it off?'"

Chapter 8

FEATS DON'T FAIL

IT WAS AS THOUGH LOWELL GEORGE, UPSET AT WARNER BROS. FOR screwups with marketing and promoting his band's records, took it out on his own brother-in-law. Soon after it became apparent that *Dixie Chicken* would not do much better than its predecessors, George got his bandmates to agree to dismiss Richie Hayward.

Family had nothing to do with the move. (Besides, by early 1974 George's marriage to Patte, sister of Richie's wife, Pam, was over, even if they hadn't done the paperwork.) It was all about Hayward's work—and attitude.

"Richie and Lowell were like brothers," said Kenny Gradney. "They would argue. Lowell would want him to play one thing, and he would play what he wanted, and Richie could never play the same thing twice. He'd play something great, but he could never remember what the hell he did. He's an artist—he paints—and has this whole different concept. That used to drive Lowell nuts."

In an article about Hayward, written in 2010 after the drummer's death, Payne said that when he was asked "to pull it back a bit and just play a regular groove . . . his attitude was defiant. Lowell said, 'Let's get someone else.' We all went with the flow."

"I didn't think it was what should have happened," Payne continued, "but on the other hand, none of us stepped up to back Richie up either."

The band brought in Freddie White, brother of Maurice and Verdeen White of Earth, Wind & Fire. Freddie, who had worked with Donny Hathaway, played a number of concerts and began jamming with Little Feat. In the process he had also helped develop a jazzy Payne composition, "Day at the Dog Races," that would materialize on a future Feats album.

With White on board, the band found a new rehearsal space on West Cahuenga, out toward Burbank. Sam Clayton credits the development of George's composition "Spanish Moon" to the space, the new kid on drums, a beat, and a growing openness to jamming, to seeing what might happen. "I just started doing this beat," he remembered, "and Lowell came in and said, 'Just hold that—and do *this*.' And he showed Kenny a bass line, and he said, 'I've got this song.' And he started doing this thing, and that's how we got it." Those, he said, were fun times.

But White was with the band for only a couple of months when George called things to a halt. As he told Andy Childs of *ZigZag*: "We broke up for about two days. I think I called Bill on the phone and called him a son-of-a-bitch and said 'fuck you' and hung up." Payne confirms the chat. "We just told each other to get screwed," he said.

Payne recalled numerous such blowups. "I just was frustrated with the lack of communication we had," he said. "We're trying to write songs together. He wants to do his own thing—that's fine, that's understandable. It had more to do with direction: are we having rehearsals? Is he being helpful or putting inordinate hurdles in the way of getting any progress done?" George didn't like rehearsing, Payne said, and often missed sessions. The lapses in communication and direction could be explained pretty simply, said Payne: "He was high." But of course, George wasn't the only one. "It was the age we were," said Payne. "It was the amount of drugs we were taking."

A couple of days later they spoke again. As George recalled, "I called him back and said, 'Hey, man, I'm sorry.'" Actually, George recalled, "I'm exaggerating the state of affairs. What really did happen was that it was a great hobby, but we weren't making any money. We really weren't surviving. So I suggested to everybody that we try and find employment while we either figure out a new hustle or get all the people involved with the management and the record company together under a banner-head, that being Little Feat."

There apparently was more to George's upset than the band's earnings. In late 1973 he had spoken about the possibility of his buddy Van Dyke Parks coproducing the next album with him. They had begun with "Spanish Moon," and there were problems right away.

As George remembered it: "I asked Van Dyke if he wanted to do it, and we got into an enormous argument with Warner Bros. because Van Dyke is famous for his huge budgets. He was going to do more, but we reached a point where we got stuck, and the band broke up."

During that time the guys had no trouble getting session gigs. Payne went out on tour with the Doobies—and even considered joining them—while reggae star Johnny Nash hired Barrere, Gradney, and Clayton for an album. George got an invite from Robert Palmer, the British rock and soul vocalist, to join him in New Orleans, where he had the Meters backing him on his next album, *Sneakin' Sally Through the Alley*. It was a chance for George, whose band's last album was so steeped in New Orleans, to go there and work in a recording studio. One bonus was the crack band, the Meters; another was Palmer's inclusion on the album of a robust, thoroughly contemporary version of George's "Sailin' Shoes." The mutual admiration society would continue, as George appeared on a Meters album, *Rejuvenation*, produced by Allen Toussaint, and all of Little Feat would later serve as Palmer's session band for his 1975 album, *Pressure Drop*.

While in New Orleans with Palmer and the Meters, George heard from the band's comanager, Bob Cavallo. "We have a studio ready for you to work in at an incredible rate," he told him. Best of all, it was far away from Hollywood. "And I dropped everything and said, 'Yikes, that's it!'," George said.

Steve Boone, who'd been the bassist in the Lovin' Spoonful, had acquired a studio in the Hunt Valley suburb north of Baltimore, Maryland, which he would name Blue Seas Studios. Thanks to Cavallo,

Little Feat were his first clients. "We got this studio for five thousand a month, locked out," said Barrere. "So, for fifteen thousand we had a zillion hours."

As a bonus the band could obtain the services of George Massenburg, the engineer who built the studio's console, who already knew Lowell George from previous projects and would go on to engineer Little Feat's subsequent albums, including George's solo project.

The new Feats album would be named after one of the songs, "Feets Don't Fail Me Now" (by George, Kibbee, and Barrere), with "Feets" changed to "Feats" for the LP title. "You could say it was a literal title," said Barrere, "because Lowell said, 'Okay, we're gonna sink or swim on this one.'" Little Feat was back together, and they invited Richie Hayward back.

Although George had expressed an interest in getting Freddie White back too—"I've always loved listening to two drummers," he said—he settled for Hayward and his percussive brothers, Gradney and Clayton.

And Hayward was happy to return. He understood that there had been—and would be—challenges. "There were personality clashes in Little Feat that made it very uncomfortable. But they also contributed to the tension you hear on the records," he said. "I kinda liked both Lowell's and Billy's directions, so I acted as the pressure relief in the band. I let a lot of stuff come down on me in order to preserve the group. Otherwise it would just have blown up."

Liz George thought the time in Maryland was a welcome break from Hollywood for the band. "Little Feat had been really in turmoil," said Liz. "Just getting away was great, because it was really touch and go at that point. Hollywood was getting to be not a very good influence, and so it was wonderful they all went to 'the country.' Everybody had a good time."

But "touch and go" may well have also referred to her and George's relationship, though she wouldn't say more about that. "I really do try to guard our private life," Liz told me, "because that's really all I can guard."

And in spring of 1974 Liz was pregnant. "I was about to give birth to Inara," she remembered, "six weeks to delivery. We piled the kids into a little car and drove across the country." The kids were Jed, her son from her marriage to Tom Levy, and Luke, George's son with Patte. They were both about five years old.

"We found a little house in Cockeysville, and we set up a home there. I rented furniture, and I found a new doctor to deliver the baby." They named her Inara after a friend, "an extraordinarily talented, beautiful woman, classical pianist, debauched, and I just loved the name and she will be everything Big Inara should have been but wasn't because of her debauchery." Inara George was born on the Fourth of July, 1974. (Massenburg remembers going to the house in nearby Cockeysville to babysit Luke and Jed while Liz and Lowell were out having their baby.) Inara would get her middle name later, when the album was finished and Little Feat, together again, were back on the road. "He called and said, 'I've got it—I've got her middle name!'" Liz said. "It's 'Maryland.'"

Baltimore evoked positive memories for several other Feats. It was during the session at Blue Seas that Payne met his future wife, Fran Tate, who was a recording engineer and a singer. She joined in, along with Feats pals Emmylou Harris and Bonnie Raitt, on backing vocals. And Barrere met Debbie Donovan, a native of nearby Towson, and they would go on to marry—briefly. In Los Angeles, he said, "it was a bit overwhelming to be thrown into the Little Feat world, so the marriage broke up after two years. But we had lived together for almost a year before we got hitched, and those were the happiest days—living in a small apartment in Laurel Canyon, next door to Sam."

Elizabeth and Lowell George, however, would not be married until 1976. They were still working out a few bumps. Before they took off to Maryland, the band had gathered at the Sound Factory, a sister to Sunset Sound, for Van Dyke Parks's production of "Spanish Moon." The sessions concluded with overdubs by the Tower of Power Horns, the soul ensemble from Oakland.

Emilio Castillo, saxophonist and cofounder of the band, knew Little Feat only as the name of a fellow act on Warner Bros. Records.

Castillo met Parks, who struck him as "one of the weirdest cats in the whole world. A really trippy dude, he talks in this weird language." Greg Adams, the horn section's arranger, agreed, stating, "He was an eccentric guy. He was just short of, say, an 'oddball.' Brilliant, a deep thinker, and always twirling his moustache."

Castillo asked Parks about what he wanted for "Spanish Moon." "He goes, 'Well, when you approach this song, I want you to think that you're standing outside an old funky red barn, and you're throwing cow pies at it.'" Castillo laughed. "I said, 'Okay, why don't you just play the track.'" Castillo cracked up at the memory. "He hit this track, and to this day I wished they had released it like that because Lowell George was singing 'Spanish Moon,' but he didn't sing it the way the final recording was. The original work vocal—he was down low, man. He was really *snakey*. It was so soulful, and Greg Adams wrote the coldest [horn] arrangement I've ever heard in my life. It maxed down the boulevard. I just thought it was *so* great. We left there, and I was like 'Man, Little Feat—Wow!' Slow, funky soulful tune; seductive lyric—it was just wonderful."

Recalling his one-track stint with Little Feat, Parks told writer Daisann McLane of *Crawdaddy* (April 1979) that George was distracted, stating, "Lowell was hanging out with Linda Ronstadt at the time." He continued: "Lowell and Linda were VERY close. And Lowell just disappeared from the studio. Left me holding the bag, as it were. When he finally showed up, I ended up chasing him out of the studio with a single-edged razor blade."

Ronstadt, having met George months before, had tried to learn "Willin'" from him, unsuccessfully. "He changed the rhythm arrangement of it, and I couldn't sing it very well." Actually, she could, and George, who enjoyed spotting and encouraging talent, told her so. "I couldn't believe he thought I was a good singer," she said, "because I didn't think I was a good singer, and I still don't . . . but he was a great singer. He wasn't a good singer—he was a truly great singer. And he just had technical ability, proficiency that was just beyond the pale."

She also found George physically attractive. "He was so delicious, and he was so different from the pretty-boy types, that I found him extremely pleasing to look at—those huge brown eyes. He wasn't what you would call a conventional male cupcake."

They became friends, and she helped him make an important

musical connection, introducing him to Massenburg, who would become his engineer, studio mentor, and buddy. "He [Massenburg] liked George so much," she said of Lowell, "that he brought him back to L.A., and he built a recording studio there—the Complex."

Linda was recording songs for *Heart Like a Wheel* at Track Recorders in Silver Springs, Maryland, with her manager Peter Asher producing and with Massenburg engineering. Massenburg recalled, "Here's this guy in white overalls, has one of those floppy hats on, had a thick beard." He was there to play on "Keep Me from Blowing Away." "We got along really well," said Massenburg, "and he's a fascinating storyteller, is very smart, and he liked the way I worked and asked if I would consider working with him."

By now, apparently, George had adopted white overalls as his outfit of choice, both on and off stage. As his pal Danny Hutton had remarked, George somehow managed to gain weight while "ingesting huge amounts of cocaine."

"I'm sure it had to do with his weight," said Payne. Both Payne and Fred Tackett figured the overalls afforded more comfort than shirts and slacks, but Barrere had a more practical explanation: "He did it because any laundry service in any hotel can knock that thing out in no time."

One day in March, Lowell and Linda appeared on WHFS, the progressive rock FM station in Bethesda, Maryland, serving the DC metro area—a hotbed of Little Feat support, according to the DJ, Cerphe. Several friends accompanied the pair, including members of the bluegrass ensemble the Seldom Scene as well as Paul Craft, composer of "Keep Me from Blowing Away." Encouraged by Cerphe, George proceeded to perform "Willin'," with Ronstadt in perfect harmony. George then declared, "I've never had so much fun on the radio." He also sang a song he wrote with Ivan Ulz, friend of his soon-to-be former wife, Patte. It was called "Heartache."

Heartache would become part of Lowell and Linda's story. It's a funny tale she's about to tell, she says, but adds that the incident must have caused Elizabeth George a good deal of pain. "And being a mother now, I can understand. She was pregnant with Inara when

I first met her, and Lowell would not mention certain things, like he was married. . . . Basically, first he told me he wasn't married. Then I found out he was married. Then he told me he broke up with her."

One day George visited Linda at her home and stayed over. The next morning her doorbell rang. It was Liz. "She turned up at my house early. I thought it was over with. Turned out it wasn't over with—she was pregnant. Nor had it ever been suggested to *her* that it was over with.

"And I said, 'Well, come in.' I felt some solidarity with her at that point—you just do. . . . So she came into my room, and he woke up and said, 'Hi, Liz, where's the coffee?' He didn't know where he was. And I realized that he'd been lying to me and lying to her, so the two of us are standing there like, 'Hmmmm! What's your story here, boy?' Anyway, that was the end of that."

Looking back, Ronstadt believes George had something akin to bipolar or manic-depressive disorder. "I don't know, I'm not a doctor," she said, "But I just know what I saw." In the recording studio George would change a song "in some little tiny way, and we would learn it that way and record it, and then he'd say, 'No, I'm changing it to this . . . ' and we worked on this song all night long. There was another song too, but I can't remember what it was . . . but I remember somebody had to come over and just lock Lowell out of that studio because he'd been in there night and day for like several days . . . without sleeping or anything. That's another symptom of bipolar disorder . . . and he was undiagnosed and untreated."

If George had a mental condition, he fooled a lot of people, especially in the Blue Seas Studios, where he once again took the reins as producer and once again mixed excellent new songs, like Payne's "Oh Atlanta" and his own "Rock and Roll Doctor" (and a couple of old ones—a medley of "Cold Cold Cold" and "Tripe Face Boogie"), with stellar performances from the band and his growing penchant for experimentation with technology and sounds. The new "Cold Cold Cold" kicked off with a bit of George's technical tomfoolery. He used what became known as the "Donka-matic," which Hayward described as "the first electronic drum machine I ever heard of." Engineer Massenburg said the box, about ten inches square and a couple of inches deep, and painted red, was a rhythm generator. It was, said Parks, "the metronome of Lowell's ear."

A knob allowed one to select from various tempos or grooves, said Hayward, adding, "'Groove' is a loose term for this." For "Cold Cold Cold," Hayward remembers George handing him a cassette tape that he had edited with an old-fashioned razor blade, "with a guitar part and a Donka-matic part on it. The beat turns over like two or three times because of Lowell's edits." Hayward then played his drums to it.

Barrere remembers a similar setup for "Rock and Roll Doctor." "Lowell would do a lot of demos on cassettes," he said, "and then he would cut up pieces of tape, patch them together, and then play them for us. So that was how we got those quirky half-beat measures and turnarounds going on things like 'Rock and Roll.' Lowell would give the tapes to Billy and say, 'Normalize this as much as you can and teach it to the band.'"

As anyone of a certain age who tried repairing a broken cassette knows, splicing a tape was near impossible. Massenburg doesn't think George did that, especially since cassette tapes were bidirectional—recording both ways—and, as he recalls, Lowell "had big fingers." Most likely, George edited regular quarter-inch tape and then copied the results to a cassette to give to his bandmates.

Nonetheless, the razor wizardry and Donka-matic grooves added to Little Feat's myriad syncopations, but as always, the album came down to performances and songs. George had a hand in composing five of the seven original numbers, but Barrere and Payne each got a solo credit, Barrere for "Skin It Back," a jam-friendly song on which he sang lead, while Payne came up with one of Little Feat's all-time favorite songs—and he did it in response to a not-exactly friendly challenge.

As Payne explained, "What people sometimes discount is that Little Feat was a band. . . . We affected each other; we pushed each other, and it was that type of camaraderie that produced the music. Lowell would say, 'You can't write a commercial song . . .' And I'd say, 'Yeah, I can.' My idea of a hit record then was basically something with a chorus coming in at around forty-five seconds. The result was 'Oh

Atlanta.' It was not a hit record, but it was one of those songs that's stood the test of time."

The song was inspired by a girl Payne met in Atlanta and by his memory of being in an airport in Cincinnati, watching airplanes taking off. The wistful tune, in which the singer wishes he could be on his way to Georgia, was picked to be the single off *Feats Don't Fail Me Now*. And although it didn't chart, it's a favorite of Feats fans. And perhaps more important to Payne, it earned some respect from George. In an almost brutally candid interview with Bill Flanagan of *Musician* magazine in mid-1979, George recalled, "One time I said, 'Bill, these songs you're writing.' I was real blunt with him one time. And right after that he came up with 'Oh, Atlanta,' which to me is a very successful song." (In her 1981 album, *Evangeline*, Emmylou Harris, briefly a member of the Feats Auxiliary, did a hard-charging version of the song.)

Feats Don't Fail Me Now fared well with most critics; some declared it to be the band's best effort yet. But others came close to giving the album a failing grade. *Rolling Stone*, which had been supportive from the start, expressed disappointment that the "perfect tension" of "material, performance and production" had slackened. The critic, Ben Gershon, guessed that George was "not quite as dominant as he once was" and that he also adjusted his songwriting to be "less reflective of his own slant than of the new, corporate Little Feat." Gershon took note of "Rock and Roll Doctor," saying the song was "too choppy to be uplifting." Still, that song, along with "Feats Don't Fail Me Now," "Down the Road," and Barrere's song, "Skin It Back," "qualifies as fine dance music," wrote Gershon.

As it turns out, that was just fine by Little Feat. As George said in 1976, "*Feats Don't Fail Me Now* was a party record—have a beer or two and dance . . . that's the frame of mind we were in for that record."

To the surprise of probably everyone, the album, which was released in August 1974, was a hit. Not a number-one hit, like Chicago, the Beach Boys, CSN&Y, or the Stones, but a pretty satisfying number thirty-six, after initial sales of about 150,000 copies—more than their first three albums combined. Over the years its sales would climb past 500,000 units, good enough for a coveted gold record.

Little Feat had themselves to thank. They could also thank their managers, who went to Warner Bros. executives and pled for support. And they could thank their residence at the Blue Seas Studios. While they were in Maryland they became local favorites. "We started playing DC concerts," said Payne, "and it just caught on, and people said, 'This is a cool band,' and so everybody was showing up." Barrere added, "We played the colleges, and we would go up and down the Atlantic Seaboard, and I think it was just the fact that we were more present, live. . . . People embraced us as if we were a local band just from the three months we'd spent there recording—it was amazing."

One concert, at Lisner Auditorium in Washington, at George Washington University, remains a reminder that, for all his wanderlust, Lowell George was a family guy. Luke George, who was four, going on five, remembers being in Baltimore for the summer and attending the show on June 20. He told me that at one point "Jed and I kinda got bored and jumped up from our chairs, and we ran up on the stage. I think it was during 'Fat Man in the Bathtub,' and the light guy shined the lights on us, and Jed and I started dancing around, and the crowd just stood up and went crazy. And it was just a perfect example of what a family-oriented band Little Feat was."

While Liz George, who said she was "extremely pregnant," remained in her chair, Luke remembers seeing his father onstage: "Lowell just lit up. The smile he had. I can still see it—that sparkle in his eye, seeing his kids dancing around to his music, and the crowd appreciating it, and Richie not missing a beat, Sam Clayton just smiling, and Paul grooving in the moment. It was like this euphoria . . . a huge euphoria for everyone."

It was, all in all, a very good year. By its end the estimated sales figures for *Feats Don't Fail . . .* were close to two hundred thousand. Little Feat did a triumphant three-night run at the Troubadour followed by several concerts at Bill Graham's Winterland Arena in San Francisco. Back in Los Angeles, sitting with a reporter from *Rolling Stone*, George allowed himself to gloat in his typically self-deprecating way. "Now we're a third rate *known* band," he said. "Maybe even second rate. And I think now's the right time to go to Europe."

LATE IN 1974 Warner Bros. began plotting out a promotional tour for a half dozen of its acts, ranging from unknowns to the Doobie Brothers, who'd had five visits to the Top 40. The Warner Bros. Music Show would be a two-headed invasion of Europe, with a "Red Tour" and a "Blue Tour," each comprising three acts, all of them backed up by Warners executives, publicists, and dozens of road managers and other support staff—all together, more than one hundred people.

Besides the Doobie Brothers and Little Feat, the bands were Tower of Power; Graham Central Station starring Larry Graham, formerly of Sly and the Family Stone; Montrose, a Bay Area rock band fronted by Ronnie Montrose; and Bonaroo, recalled by Emilio Castillo of Tower of Power as "protégés of the Doobie Brothers."

The three-week tour, traveled mostly by train, was mapped out by Warners' Artists Relations team, composed of Carl Scott, who'd managed and booked the label's acts into clubs and college dates, and Georgia Bergman, better known, then, as Jo Bergman, who'd worked for the Beatles, the Stones, and other artists in the UK, primarily in publicity. She anchored Warner Bros.' New York office, but for this tour she worked with Scott in a trailer in the parking lot at the company's Burbank headquarters. The company was growing rapidly, she said, adding, "There was no space. We were next to the mailroom trailer."

Joe Smith, president of the record company, led the executive team. Between concerts they would meet with Warner Bros. licensees and labels the company owned in Europe. Smith also acted as scoutmaster. At one train station, as the troupe was headed to Germany, he gathered the bands and warned them to dispose of anything they might be carrying that might be deemed illegal. "I want to tell you about the prisons in Germany," he said. "You get good food, and you will be in them." Smith recalls one of the Doobie Brothers telling him later that in the next hour "almost a million dollars' worth of drugs were flushed down the toilets in the train station."

The tour began in Manchester and London, moved into Germany, with stops in Frankfurt and Munich, and, after a Warner Bros. bash in Hamburg, rolled through Dusseldorf, Amsterdam, and Brussels, winding up with two evenings at the Olympia in Paris, with Little Feat opening for Montrose and Tower of Power on a Monday night and with the Doobie Brothers headlining the final show over Graham Central Station and Bonaroo.

Sometimes Tower of Power, whose horn section had just appeared on *Feats Don't Fail Me Now*, would team with the band—in more ways than one. Said Castillo: "We got really tight with Little Feat, friend-wise and, I must say, very much drug-wise. We wound up sitting in with [Little Feat] a lot. When we sat in, the whole level of the performance would just skyrocket. . . . We worked up a little Dixieland thing for 'Dixie Chicken.' Every time we played, the audience would go wild."

It was a Sunday, January 19, the fifth date of the tour, when the audience went surprisingly wild. It was the tour's third day in London, at the Rainbow Theater, an old movie house in north London, and it'd be Little Feat's first performance there. The Doobie Brothers had headlined the two previous concerts over the other bands. Sunday there'd be two shows, with the Doobies headlining both again. Little Feat would open the afternoon concert; Graham Central Station, the evening set.

Two prominent rock journalists were eyewitnesses at the Rainbow. Andy Childs was the editor of the rock magazine *Zigzag*. He and other staffers were Feat fans. They traveled to Manchester to catch the band in the opening concert and waited anxiously for the Sunday show. There, he reported, "it was refreshingly apparent to note that the overwhelming majority of people had primarily come to see Little Feat, and I can't imagine that anyone left the Rainbow that evening without the feeling that they'd seen one of the best bands in the world . . . they were just magic. No way could I even begin to think of watching another band after that performance, and I genuinely felt sorry for the Doobies, who clearly found it impossible to follow them, and ended up playing as meekly and politely as they could."

That is, when they could begin playing. The audience got several encores from Little Feat, causing George to address them. "We weren't quite expecting this," he said, to more cheers. "You people are crazy!" he declared. "It's Sunday afternoon. Why aren't you home in bed?" After Little Feat finally left the stage the audience continued to cheer, all the way into the Doobies' first number. Then a good number of the crowd, satisfied and sated, left. Childs was one of them.

Barney Hoskyns, who was a teenager at the time and would go on to become a prominent pop writer and editor, put it this way in *MOJO*: "Little Feat took the stage that Sunday afternoon and proceeded to wipe the floor with the Doobies, who'd enjoyed fleeting hipness a year before but were henceforth doomed to be remembered as just another American Band with Facial Hair."

Joe Smith put it more gently. "The Doobies had the name power," he said, "but Little Feat were the underground act that everybody loved. Little Feat was constantly being interviewed in all the different countries we went to. The esoteric people loved them. When we went to France, it wasn't the Doobies or anybody else—everybody wanted to see Little Feat. They had one of these followings of people who were hip to whatever is new, and looking for great new things." Rock fans in the early seventies were getting their fill of pop music, of glam-rock, of art rock. Little Feat was a band of mystery, never appearing on their own album covers, a band of musical adventurers.

But a record company always keeps one eye on the bottom line. Smith asked, rhetorically, "If you walked through the streets of this country and say 'Do you know the Doobie Brothers or Little Feat?' Little Feat would lose all the time. It was hard getting airplay for them—they weren't a singles band. They went out on tour, but their tours were not Madison Square Garden."

Warners loved and nurtured acts like Little Feat. But they needed bands like the Doobie Brothers. Still, Smith couldn't deny the band's achievement overseas. "It was a Little Feat show from the beginning," he said.

Paul Barrere, along with the rest of his band, didn't witness what happened with the Doobies, having gone backstage. But he would later see a headline in one of the British rock papers that cruelly but conciscly captured the moment, to the effect that the Doobie Brothers had become the Smothered Brothers: "'Trampled by Little Feat' . . . which made it very hard for the rest of the tour."

Jo Bergman doesn't recall any tension on the rest of the tour. "My sense is . . . we were all in this together. Nobody wanted to feel that they were getting more attention than anybody else. But clearly they realized that something had happened."

Bob Regehr, her boss and the head of Artists Relations, held nothing back. Observing the commotion over Little Feat, Bergman said, "Regehr got really excited. We had to leave for Frankfurt for the next show. So we get to the Holiday Inn in Frankfurt, it's the middle of the night, and he's just nuts. He has all of us in his room, and he's saying, 'Okay, we got a star here . . . we have to let everybody know about it. . . . We gotta set this up. We gotta set that up.' And we're all going, 'We gotta go to sleep!'"

The members of Little Feat cooperated with an expanded media schedule in Germany, but they took no joy in any discomfort the Doobies may have experienced. But to hear Tom Johnston, founder, guitarist, and vocalist with the band, there were no ill feelings—to the contrary, even if he's speaking almost forty years after the fact.

With the passage of time he doesn't remember that afternoon in North London. "After a while it all became a blur," he said. "But there were certain bands that stood out . . . one of them was Little Feat . . . and if the crowd was really going for them, then rightfully so . . . they definitely deserved it.

"They put on a great show," he said. "You had Richie just killing it on drums. Nobody could play second line quite like that guy, and he was also the king of Boogie Rock. . . . You had Kenny as funky as hell on the bass. You had Lowell's very distinctive vocal style and guitar style, his lyrics . . . nobody else was doing that. And then you had Billy, who's like Professor Longhair in whiteface. . . . And Sam Clayton playing the percussion as well. . . . Little Feat to me, were completely underrated, undervalued by the press. They didn't get the credit they deserved."

During Little Feat's first hiatus, after Roy Estrada's departure, the Doobies employed Payne for some sessions, playing on their 1973 hits, "Jesus Is Just Alright," "Rockin' Down the Highway," and others. Also, said Johnston, "He was instrumental in helping me come up with lyrics, even though he didn't mean to, for 'China Grove.' If he hadn't played that piano lick, I wouldn't have come up with those lyrics. I've always given him credit for that."

A week after the Warner Bros. Music Show tour had hit Frankfurt the bands were in Amsterdam. That's where Little Feat met the Rolling Stones. As Payne remembers it, it was at the Jaap Eden Hall, just outside Amsterdam, where Little Feat topped the bill over Tower of Power and Montrose. (The three other bands had played there the night before.)

In his interview with Bill Flanagan in 1979, shortly before his death, George was asked about the visit. "Yeah," he said. "I supposedly said, 'No,' and I did, too. They just showed up. If one of them had come up individually and said, 'Hey, can we do something?' 'Can we play with you guys?' . . . I would have said, 'Yes.' But they had some roadie come up: 'Do you think the *guys* could come up and play a little *ditty* with you?' I said, 'What are we gonna do? "Mona" all night?' To me, the decadence of them not being one-to-one with me was rude. . . . I just decided that the last thing I wanted to do was have the Rolling Stones sit up there and play out of tune."

Despite Mr. Cranky Overalls' rejection of the jam, at least one member of Little Feat was pleased to meet the band. Bill Payne remembers, "They were on both sides of the stage. I talked to Keith Richards down in the dressing room. I'm gushing, like, 'Oh, my God, it's Keith Richards.' He put his arm around me. Then he goes, 'Aw man, we're all part of the same cloth.' In other words: 'Welcome to the club.' And I tell that story on my solo shows where I'm introducing local artists, because in his own biography Keith is talking about being backstage, part of a concert he's involved in when he's just starting out as a musician."

From Richard's book, *Life*: "We went everywhere . . . big gigs, small gigs. There was that amazing feeling of, wow, I'm actually in a dressing room with Little Richard. One part of you is the fan, 'Oh, my God,' and the other part of you is 'You're here with the man, and now you better be the man.'"

"That's probably what he was sharing with me in Amsterdam," said Payne. "That inclusiveness—'You're one of the guys now'—and I never forgot it. What a gift. So I've been doing it to people and letting them join me on stage."

On the surface all was well in Featsville. But within the band there was trepidation. Leadership was unstable, to say the least. There had been more divisions, near-breakups, and actual breakups than were ever made public. Where was Little Feat headed next?

One clue, perhaps more, could be gleaned from the album cover. Once again Neon Park conceived and executed it. The artist did not intend them to be literal. He might hear the music for *Sailin' Shoes*, *Dixie Chicken*, or *Feats Don't Fail Me Now*, but he would never be expected to feature shoes, chickens or, say, an R. Crumb takeoff of big shoes parading up a street, hoping to avoid failure.

And yet to Bill Payne's eye, Park nailed it. "He painted a pretty bleak picture of the band's state. We had just gotten back together to give it one more try. I don't mean to make it allegorical, but you couldn't tell if the car on the cover was going uphill or downhill, there was all that thunder and lightning in the background, and Marilyn Monroe and George Washington [passenger and driver] represented our concept of the business then. Riches and bitches. Of course, you can see everything worked out."

Chapter 9

NOT QUITE
"THE LAST RECORD ALBUM"

THINKING BACK TO THE MAKING OF *FEATS DON'T FAIL ME NOW*, BILL Payne smiled. "The mood at that point was one of hope," he said.

Asked to reflect on the follow-up, entitled *The Last Record Album*, Payne was sober: "This was the beginning of the rift . . . the atmosphere was 180 degrees the opposite of what we experienced on *Feats Don't Fail Me Now*."

Immediately after each Little Feat album was completed, Lowell George would compose a list of thank yous. Those acknowledgments would grow to become liner notes, always written in run-on sentences sans punctuation and capitalization, the product of a run-on mind. For *The Last Record Album*, George, well aware that the band had picked a doomsday title, even if it was a play on the title of the movie *The Last Picture Show*, offered a few words of reassurance: "the real name of this record is the first record album so let no paranoia ensue." He mentioned a few people he'd forgotten to thank in the previous album's notes, and as he ran out of space, he closed with "there were more but i'll once again have to remember them on the next record album."

There would, indeed, be more albums. But this one did, as Payne indicated, signal the beginning of the end—at least of Little Feat as we had known it. Through the personnel changes and hiatuses and breakups, it was Lowell George's band. Now, as the band steamed through a post-Europe tour of the East Coast, from Boston to New York and on to Washington, where Feats faithful gathered over three nights at the Lisner Auditorium, and then south to Oh Atlanta, changes were in the air.

Little Feat fans and historians have portrayed the shifts in power as some sort of a rock 'n' roll *coup d'état* engineered by Bill Payne and Paul Barrere.

The real reasons are more complex—and simpler too. For one thing, George had a hand in those shifts. As he said, "I wish for everyone in the band to step forward. For a long time I was getting a lot of attention, but, for example, Bill Payne is a magnificent musician and also deserves a lot of attention. Basically the idea . . . is that we should all do our best and have a good time. If it doesn't happen, that's the breaks, and if it does—great."

In the liners he would compose for the not *The Last Record Album*, he announced, "I'm Lowell George the so-called producer slide guitar player who sings but let that end right there cause all I did was sit in the control room and watch the rest of the folk in the group bring forth an identity that represents the so-called musical statement about the whole being the sum total of the parts."

Talking about his authority as a producer, he told one writer: "It's left up to me until somebody says, 'That stinks.' It's more or less a matter of getting in there and trying to get the feel for the song, and putting it down the best we can, and sometimes it takes years."

In and around Little Feat, Payne and George were still in their mutual fuck-you society. George was never quoted complaining about Payne during this period, but Payne was frustrated with his own songwriting and the fact that he was no longer able to count on George as a collaborator. "I just felt somewhat dismissed with my own material, in some cases," he said. "It felt so chaotic. I'd also been doing a shitload of sessions over the years with the Doobie Brothers, Bonnie, Jackson, and a lot of others, and I knew that not every session you walked into would be half as insane as ours were. Why does it have to be so adversarial? And you know, I was contributing to that because of my personality, not to lay it all on Lowell, which I was doing at the time. The truth is, it was part of what we were."

Feeling spurned by George, Payne began partnering with Barrere. Even though they hadn't cowritten a song since "Walkin' All Night" on *Dixie Chicken*, they now produced three songs together: "Romance Dance," which would lead off the album, "One Love Stand," and "All That You Dream." They teamed on the music, and Barrere wrote the words. "He really hit his high watermark there," said Payne about "Dream." It was a high mark not only for the album but also for the entire Little Feat discography, with its gorgeous blend of melancholy and melody.

> *I've been down, but not like this before*
> *Can't be 'round this kind of show no more . . .*

Barrere explained the birth of the tune: "I was living up in Laurel Canyon next to Sam Clayton, and across the way lived this great blind organist named Gordon De Witty. One day we were jamming, and I came up with the chord progression to 'All That You Dream.'

"Lowell absolutely loved the song and wanted to sing it. But his time was becoming more split. He had a daughter and didn't like going on the road, so he relinquished a lot of things to us. It was a strange time, plus we were doing things to our streams of consciousness which were not helping."

George knew he was falling behind his bandmates, but he never mentioned drugs as a reason. He told *New Musical Express*: "Life gets too taken up with airports and getting to the gig on time that there's no time left for writing. Nowadays I'm really screwed to come up with a page of lyrics, which is no fun."

The proof of his decline in songwriting was in the credits. Of the eight tracks on *The Last Record Album*, he wrote or cowrote only three: "Down Below the Borderline," "Mercenary Territory," and "Long Distance Love." And the latter was actually planned for the previous album, *Feats Don't Fail Me Now*. Payne and/or Barrere had a hand in the other five. The most radio-friendly song from the album was "All That You Dream," although both Payne's "Somebody's Leavin'" and George's "Long Distance Love" earned high marks. Also, another song by Barrere, "High Roller," apparently was cut at the last minute after the lyrics had been printed on the back cover. Written over them is the message: "Maybe next time."

Martin Kibbee, George's early songwriting partner, had dropped out of sight. He admitted that drugs played a part in his absence, stating, "There were times when I was doing some other stuff, and I was ill, and I wouldn't show up, and we just didn't get together." The songwriting team didn't slow down, he said. "It was only that Lowell wasn't spending as much time writing."

Sam Clayton agreed. "It wasn't like they had more say," he said about the songwriting shift to Barrere and Payne. "It was just like Lowell sort of withdrew. He wouldn't have new material. He had material and stuff, but he was saying, 'Let these guys go and do this.' And he just let them do more stuff."

Payne gave George due credit for his songs, including "Long Distance Love," which would be the first single from the album. It was a "terrific ballad," said Payne. However, he got mixed signals from George, who encouraged input but, as Payne noted, could be dismissive of it. "We battled with each other almost every day," he said. "I was so pissed and frustrated. And Lowell was getting really high all the time, so his ability to focus on things was completely scattered."

There's no denying the impact of drug use on the musicians—not all of them, but enough that, as George said, a song could take years.

Barrere fessed up about his own nasty habits. "Lowell and I and Richie were the main culprits," he said. "We used to call ourselves 'McHale's Navy.' We would surrender at a dime bag. But it was mostly cocaine and marijuana and alcohol."

Payne may not have been part of that sitcom crew from World War II, but he did regularly get stoned, he said, until he was about twenty-four, in 1973. He decided then that, unlike his band mates, "I'm not able to function. I thought, 'Okay, so you're not cut from that particular cloth, so do what you need to do to stay alive, 'cause if you don't, you're not going to be around to worry about it.'"

Sam Clayton says that, out of concern for off-stage performances, he never got into drugs. As he explained, "There was one time, when they had you up there and wanting to try coke and all that. I'd never done that . . . it made me sneeze, and I'd been trying to be with this girl, and then you can't do anything. You're impotent, man. That, right there, was it. '*Ohhh*, that's what it does? No, thank you.' That's very embarrassing. So I just never did it."

George, by all accounts, always did it. His main man in the control room, engineer George Massenburg, moved from the Baltimore area to Los Angeles, partly at Lowell's encouragement. He would build his own recording studio and, as Linda Ronstadt recalled, became good pals with George. "Well," said Massenburg, "we did a lot of drugs together, for sure." As for music and recording: "We did a lot of experimenting together. . . . He liked it because I would leave him in the studio, a couple of nights he just wanted to be alone . . . and I would set him up with a mike in front of the console, and I would teach him everything I knew . . . how I did things, and why I did things. . . . So I would set Lowell up with a microphone and a tab of acid, or whatever, and he'd put together the wildest things you ever heard in your life."

They wouldn't be useful for Little Feat, but once in a while George's all-night flights might lead to something. "But," Massenburg said, "it's hard to say that a song came out of it."

As for how his marathons and their impact on the recording process, the creative process, and the budget affected the rest of the band, Massenburg was candid: "It was pretty tough, because especially when he had had a lot of blow, he would go off on a cocaine tangent that could last for days. So he would prefer to do work on his own and make tapes and bring it in and show the guys what he wanted and get them to experiment with him." You can almost hear the ensuing "fuck yous."

Considering his addiction to both work and recording equipment and studios, Lowell George did attempt to find time for his family and for a favorite pastime dating back to his childhood: fishing. As Elizabeth remembers, "Once he caught a fish here in Malibu, sand surfing, and cooked it, a red Snapper, Chinese style. He loved Chinese food, was a great Chinese cook, and so sometimes we would get to-gether and cook a family-style meal. One of the things we did, 'cause we had kids all over the city—except for Inara, who was here with us—we tried to get them together every weekend. One of us would do the pickups, in Hollywood, Studio City, Sunland, and back to Topan-ga . . . and the other would do the returns. We went out on the Aquar-ius Fishing Boat off the Malibu pier, and it was something everybody could remember with great joy.

"But he was a driven man, I would consider even calling him a workaholic, he would get so impassioned with whatever he was do-ing that, like, hours and hours and hours would pass by . . . so that was sometimes very difficult in terms of having a balanced life."

Back in the recording studios the band had a forced shutdown when, one afternoon early in July, Hayward had a motorcycle spill. He did not offer details to media, but others did. *Circular*, the newsletter of Warner Bros.' publicity department, noted: "A Laurel Canyon mongrel caught itself in the spokes of Richie Hayward's mo-torcycle. The machine was moving at the time, causing the Little Feat drummer to sustain serious facial injuries after being vaulted over the handlebars."

Rick Harper, the road manager, recalled, "Richie just went face-first off the bike and slid for about thirty-five, forty-five yards." Low-ell added, "He looked pretty bad there for a while." George went to see Hayward at Riverside Hospital in North Hollywood, later relat-ing that "I went along and suggested they should sew his big toe onto his forehead so he could wiggle them when he played, which was the first joke that anybody had told him at the hospital, and I think it cheered him up a bit—though the plastic surgeon did not laugh. That happened in the middle of recording the album, which broke things up. There was very sporadic activity in and around that album, and at one point I just finally said 'Stop!'"

But not for long. Thanks to the fact that the band dark-humoredly reproduced pages from the hospital bills on the back of the album cover, it's clear that Hayward, admitted on July 7, was discharged on the afternoon of July 12. Soon he was playing again. And a couple of months later he was rehearsing with the band at Alley Studios. "I had to heal quick," he told the *Circular* newsletter. "It seemed like the only thing to do."

For all the tumult within the band, in 1975 Little Feat had increasing incentives to work—and to make things work. Album sales had reached respectable figures, and Warner Bros. was showing a willingness to reward the band, but with certain conditions.

In negotiations for a new contract with Little Feat, Warner Bros. asked that George include a solo album in the deal. The label, it was said, wanted a buffer in case the band broke up. In return for agreeing to a solo deal, George and the band's management received a $1 million advance. Barrere believes that, as part of the deal, George received promises of increased promotional and marketing help from the label "so we could, as he would often say, 'break through the bullshit barrier.'"

In the midseventies major record labels did things in a major way, with lavish parties to promote new albums and tour support akin to the Warner Bros. Music Show that rolled through Europe. To celebrate its re-signing of Little Feat, the company had a ceremony at The Forum in Inglewood, just outside Los Angeles, where the band was performing in December. As Barrere remembers, "All the bigwigs showed up, and they gave us these Everlast robes, and on the back it said, THE BIG DEAL, and everyone was happy about it." The band had signed initially for $15,000. Now they'd get a check for $1 million.

That was a lot of money to pay out to a band that had yet to sell that many records and that in four albums had yet to produce a hit single. But Warner Bros. was a different kind of record company, with an attitude toward artists that was considered unique in the industry. While it went after, developed, and nurtured major stars, including James Taylor, Joni Mitchell, Jimi Hendrix, and the Kinks, it also had Captain Beefheart, Zappa, Randy Newman, Bonnie Raitt, Ry Cooder, and, yes, Little Feat—"Feathers in their cap," as Hayward once put it.

"That was our reputation," said Joe Smith. "We would go after the Ry Cooders and the Van Dykes on the basis that having them would attract other artists. 'This is a freer company—they're doing this and that.'"

And there was talk that if Warners wasn't interested in the band's services, Capitol and Columbia Records were. Regardless of the reason, however, George's agreement to a solo deal was credited with giving his band members their first big payday. "Everybody took a hundred Gs," said Barrere. "Management and business managers got their pieces, and it was kinda swallowed up really fast. We all went out and bought houses and what have you."

But George would take his time holding up his end of the deal, as his solo project stalled, time and again, until 1979. But the new contract paid off for Warner Bros. long before then. *The Last Record Album*, released in fall of 1975, sold an estimated three hundred thousand units, easily shading the estimated two hundred thousand figure for *Feats Don't Fail Me Now*. Just like its predecessor, it reached number thirty-six on the *Billboard* album chart and, for the first time, also made the charts in the United Kingdom. Alas, neither of the two singles from the album, "Long Distance Love" and "All That You Dream," would dent the charts.

Not surprisingly, music critics were all over the place. In Little Feat's home away from home, England, Myles Palmer raved in *Time Out* magazine about "Little Feat, as you've never heard them before." He wrote, "This time, the groups' favorite group has made more of a group album, sharing the writing credits. *Feats Don't Fail Me Now* was body music. This is late night head music—much looser, more laid back, six men jamming with supreme stoned rapport."

Dysfunction? What dysfunction?

Palmer, who caught Little Feat's transcendent moment at the Rainbow Theater in London the previous year, continued, "I have heard nothing since that phenomenal Rainbow gig to alter my frequently expressed opinion that they are the finest group in the world today. . . . I look forward early to their next five albums."

Uh-oh.

Another British publication, the *New Musical Express*, would put the album into its 1975 Best Albums list, ranking it number four, behind only Bob Dylan's *Blood on the Tracks* and two albums by Bob Marley and the Wailers, possibly for *Natty Dread* (released in 1974) and *Live!*, issued in December of 1975.

As for *Rolling Stone*, critic Jean-Charles Costa seemed to like the album enough; he just didn't want to say so. Several of his remarks sounded critical, but weren't, like: "Little Feat are on the verge of being too proficient for their own good," or "Payne is a gifted and versatile player, but adding George Duke/Herbie Hancock keyboard styles to a band that is already so well-defined . . . is a risky undertaking at best." Then Costa wrote, "Any more tendencies toward being cute and 'ingrown' will cause them to risk becoming as much a self-parody as their home turf, Hollywood," which no doubt puzzled many readers.

But he gave an unqualified rave to Barrere's "All That You Dream": "Highlighted by Payne's brilliant electric piano and John Hall's phase-funk Stratocaster picking, this one is a classic hit single possibility." And he wrote, "Overall, Little Feat still have a much higher batting average than just about any other American band."

Another way of saying, "one of the finest groups in the world today."

Another critic, Stephen Thomas Erlewine of *Allmusic*, called the production flat and uninspired, but he did name three outstanding songs, "All That You Dream," "Long Distance Love," and "Mercenary Territory," which he called "sublime." Elizabeth George said that she was the inspiration for that song: "I was really bugged at him and wrote him a very strong letter . . . it inspired the song." Sure enough, the words could be addressed either to a lover—or to Little Feat:

> *Is it the style*
> *Is it the lies*
> *Is it the days into nights*
> *Or the "I'm sorrys" into fights . . .*

On the album and CD the song is credited to George and Hayward ("for the drum fills," said Liz). But on the 2000 compilation, *Hotcakes and Outtakes*, Liz, who oversees Naked Snake Music, gets a cocredit. And the last word.

Looking and listening back, Barrere sounds like one of *Last Record Album*'s tougher critics. "To me," he said, "the record always seemed so compressed, clean, very pristine—stifled."

He did have praise for Neon Park's cover art, however. It's a surreal landscape of a Hollywood street, with desert land where the street and sidewalks normally would be. A jackalope sits in the foreground, flanked by various cacti and trees. Landmarks like Frederick's of Hollywood, the costume shop that specializes in campy, sexy under- (and over-) garments, and the Pussycat Theater are clearly in view, and in the distance sits a mountain, created by a Jell-O mold, bearing the HOLLYWOOD sign and wearing a cap of whipped cream.

"We wanted to set up vague parallels to *The Last Picture Show*," said Payne, referring to the poster depicting a small Texas town, with, in place of Jell-O Mountain, Cybill Shepherd and Jeff Bridges looming over the buildings. "Anyway," said Payne, "Paul says Hollywood is nothing but a fruit dessert with Cool Whip."

Speaking of cool whips, Frederick's of Hollywood was the site, a few months after the album was released, of one fabulous Feat event. Although there already was a star—Charlie Chaplin's—on the Hollywood Walk of Fame in front of the store, there was Little Feat, ready to receive its own star on Hollywood Boulevard. Standing just in front of Frederick's window display of glittery negligees, padded bras, and see-through panties, fans, Warner Bros. staffers, and a few curious passersby surrounded Little Feat.

The band lapped it up. They ventured inside Frederick's, and when the store manager's teenaged son approached George with praise, he got a glossy Little Feat photo, which George signed, "With full support."

Bonnie Raitt accompanied the band on their big day, and when a DJ asked for a comment, she said, "Little Feat are the greatest rock 'n' roll band in the world."

The band celebrated with a four-night run at the Roxy on Sunset. Raitt, along with Jackson Browne and other friends, attended, and each night a very fortunate audience member received a $25 gift certificate—from Frederick's.

As it turns out, Little Feat never got an official star on the Walk of Fame. It was all a publicity stunt to hype *The Last Record Album*.

"It was all about promo," said Payne. "Welcome to Hollywood!"

Chapter 10

"WHAT IS THIS? WEATHER REPORT?"

It was a see-saw; it was a roller-coaster ride. It was the state of Little Feat in the spring and summer of 1977.

Time Loves a Hero, released in April, had been the band's first release in a year and a half, and some of the rock media were beginning to ask questions about this band—a band who seemed always to be on the verge of a breakup, despite increasing sales and a renewed deal with Warner Bros.

In the June issue of *Circus* magazine Payne had his meet-and-greet-the-press face on. Responding to rumors about a yet another breakup, he told writer Peter Crescenti: "The group has done anything but broken up. We haven't felt this good about it in a long time."

Barrere, sitting in on the interview, added a touch more reality: "We're not breaking up. There's no way. It would cost us too much . . . due to our contract."

Besides, said Payne, "Outside of *Feats Don't Fail Me Now*, which we cut in Hunt Valley, Maryland, this was the smoothest record we ever made. It was relatively hassle-free in the studio."

Barrere saw success as being "all very possible, since everybody,

attitude-wise, has gotten so much better. . . . Things are actually looking more positive than they've ever looked before."

Little Feat also put on a show of unity with an appearance on
The Midnight Special, a music show on NBC that usually presented
an array of pop, rock, and R&B acts performing before a studio audience. On a late Friday night in June Little Feat and Emmylou Harris
cohosted the show (George shared Feat's portion of the MCing duties with Barrere), presenting a dazzling array of roots music talent,
including Neil Young, Jesse Winchester, Bonnie Raitt, and the jazz-
rock ensemble Weather Report. Little Feat, with the telegenic Harris and Raitt on backup vocals, performed "Dixie Chicken," "Old
Folks Boogie" (with Barrere taking the lead), "Rocket in My Pocket,"
and "Rock and Roll Doctor." America got to see Little Feat, both
its strengths—its solid performances—and its weakness: not a lot of
charisma, as George sang and played with little energy and without
attempting to connect with the audience. But that appeared to be the
Little Feat way: let the music do the talking. It spoke well enough,
though, and they introduced two songs from the new album. Mission
accomplished.

And as Barrere said, it was a big step up from another television
show he'd recently done. He recalled: "Richie, Sam, and I got to be the
'secret square' on *Hollywood Squares*." He remembers little about their
adventures in game-show land except that the Feats shared one square
and that center square star Paul Lynde "got fed up with us and left."

Just days after the *Midnight Special* appearance, *Rolling Stone*
published an article with the headline, "Lowell's Retreat from Little
Feat." John Swenson, the writer, noted that Feat fans were beginning
to split into factions, one supporting George's inventive songwriting
and playing of eclectic roots rock, the other approving of Payne and
Barrere's move into jazz fusion and funk. He also called *Time Loves
a Hero* the band's breakthrough album and noted that it was the one
record on which George had the least to do.

Although George did not talk with Swenson, others associated
with the band made it clear that if George, who had begun work on
his solo album, were to leave, Little Feat would go on. "We'd have

to find another golden throat," said Barrere, "but we could do it. But he's not gonna leave the band. No way that's gonna happen."

In fact, the next month, August, George led the band onto two stages on which the old Little Feat had triumphed: at the Rainbow Theater in London, then at Lisner Auditorium in Washington, where they played and fought their way through enough performances to come up with one of their best, which became one of their best-selling albums, *Waiting for Columbus*.

But here in spring and summer, the roller-coaster ride continued. In public—at least to media—all was well . . . and please buy our record. In private there were serious concerns about how *Time Loves a Hero* really went in the studios and how long the battles with Lowell George could continue to go on.

Warner Bros. Records, having made a heavy investment in Little Feat's future and well aware of the rifts within the band, maneuvered to move George out of the producer's seat. As George Massenburg, engineer and George's pal recalls, "Lenny [Waronker] and Mo [Ostin] kinda lost faith in Lowell after *The Last Record Album*, which was eight tracks, and he spent a God-awful fortune on it, and so they made a deal with Lowell where he could have a solo record if he'd let Ted Templeman produce *Time Loves a Hero*."

Templeman, who by now had enjoyed great success with the Doobie Brothers, Van Morrison, and other Warner Bros. artists, was delighted to return. It had been five years since he worked with the original band on *Sailin' Shoes*. Now he found an entirely new dynamic. For one thing, George often was missing. "I don't know where the fuck he was," Templeman said, "but he wasn't around for a lot of that."

Besides an increasing distance from his fellow Feats and his beginning to turn some of his attention to his solo project, George was ailing. He had contracted the infectious disease of the liver, Hepatitis C. He'd been diagnosed with the infection, often related to chronic drug usage, when *The Last Record Album* was being produced. "I worried about him, just like everyone else did," said Rick Harper. "He was always putting off seeing doctors until it was almost too late."

Martin Kibbee, who admitted to his own drug problems, thought his old friend was functional. "I wasn't aware of him having hepatitis," he said. "He always had sinus problems. He was steaming, had a hacking cough. He was a shit-kicker. He was overweight, but he was one of the strongest men I knew." In fact, he said, "Lowell was carrying on grandly and having a great time, unaware of how sick he was becoming."

But the impact on his musical output and his position in the band—no matter that he continued to front it, as usual, in concert and on television appearances—was clear. Despite Payne's portrait of the sessions as smooth and hassle-free, Barrere admitted that the previous October they got off to a sluggish start: "All that we managed to accomplish at that point was a recut of 'All That You Dream,' a few demos for the singer Valerie Carter, and one tune that was Billy's, called 'Front Page News,' which did not make the record." (George played on Carter's album, which Massenburg produced and would include a song by George, Payne, and Carter: "Back to Blue Some More.")

Barrere, talking to the press in 1977, proudly recalled a workmanlike schedule, with the band in the studio from noon to six in the evening. "We went in with the idea of getting things done," he said. "Having rehearsed the tunes just enough not to spoil them, the energy really came across superbly."

Many years later, looking back on that time, Barrere and Payne understand that George contributed little to that energy. Whereas Barrere wrote or cowrote six of the nine songs, including the title track, which would be the single, George had two songs, including the rowdy "Rocket in My Pocket" and a cowriting credit, with Barrere, on the bluesy "Keepin' Up with the Joneses." He did do three excellent lead vocals on "Rocket," Barrere's "Hi Roller," and "New Delhi Freight Train," composed by Terry Allen, a friend of George's.

Bassist Kenny Gradney remembers George encouraging his bandmates to chip in: "Lowell said, 'I don't want to be the only guy writing all these tunes. You guys get out there and write.' On *Time Loves a Hero*, he just went, 'Do an album.' Warner Bros. was banging him to do a solo record. They were on him, and he wanted everybody to create."

That's when the power shifted. Payne recalls George telling him and Barrere: "I need you guys to take over, at least start to steer." With his health problems, Payne said, "he was in the same spot that Jerry Garcia was in, where Jerry was with the [Grateful Dead], and then he disappeared for a week or two. And then came back. 'Oh, he's back—great.' We were going through the same shit they were."

Although rock journalist Barney Hoskyns thought that George "had effectively ceded leadership of the band to Paul Barrere," Barrere didn't see it that way. There was always that see-saw effect on the band. "He wanted us to do more," said Barrere, "but he wanted the control."

With Ted Templeman in the producer's seat, George and Payne began to wrestle over creative input. "I think Billy wanted a bigger piece of production, more input, more responsibility," said Barrere, "and Lowell was still kind of holding on to it all, even though he had told us that 'you guys need to step up and participate more.' And then when we did, it was a shock to him."

Even more of a shock, apparently, was the jazzy number the rest of the band had come up with, called "Day at the Dog Races." "Lowell hated it for some reason," said Payne. He thought it was just too fusion-like, so he'd go offstage while we'd play it." His attitude surprised the band, especially given George's own background, playing flute and, as Kibbee recalls, listening to such artists as Herbie Mann and Rahsaan Roland Kirk. "He thought we were just kind of copying Weather Report in a certain fashion," said Barrere. "I didn't see it that way at all. I just saw it as another step musically, to have fun."

"Day at the Dog Races" came out of rehearsals, which George generally shunned. Barrere says many of the practices turned into jam sessions. "Sam and Kenny and Richie were having their connection on the rhythm side, and Billy and I were having a connection melodically that was just phenomenal. . . . We had a ball doing that kind of stuff. I don't know if that's what flipped Lowell out, but he was not totally sold on that kind of thing. He knew we weren't going to get any airplay with that."

Payne had recorded a number of the jams and mapped out the song, which kicks off with him on a synthesizer, making Flamenco sounds for a few bars before the jazz took over. He did have some concerns about the still-new technology, even though it had made appearances on *Sailin' Shoes* and *Dixie Chicken*. "When I was first introduced to the synthesizer," he said, "I thought, *Will I begin to sound like these disco people?* No. I look at it in terms of a piano. I've got a pretty good orchestral ear. I tried to make it work on that level."

"I was taking my cues from Joe Zawinul of Weather Report," Payne said. "Look, every step of the way we've bastardized everything we've done. Very little of what Little Feat does is original, but what makes it Little Feat is this voice we have behind it. We've never been afraid to take certain elements and mix them up."

But George didn't care for the newest elements. When he heard the tapes he was upset, according to Templeman: "He said, 'What is this? Fuckin' Weather Report?'" Templeman relayed that to Bud Scoppa, writer of the extensive band history included with the CD anthology, *Hotcakes and Outtakes*, issued in 2000. But speaking to me recently, he said there was no friction over the song. "He was so easygoing," Templeman said. "He didn't say, 'What are you trying to do? Be Weather Report?' I liked it . . . nobody ever raised their voice."

Speaking to Bill Flanagan in June 1979, just eleven days before his death, George sounded pretty reasonable as he laid out his case against the song. For starters, he had taken notice of Weather Report when that crack band appeared, with Little Feat, Emmylou Harris, and others on *Midnight Special*. Even in rehearsal Jaco Pastorius and company knocked him out. Payne's playing, George thought, didn't compare. "Instrumentals in that form, of chord progressions and textures, are done well by a few people. Herbie Hancock, Weather Report are the best at it. But if you shoot at something and you know it ain't gonna make it . . . why bother? . . . And it didn't fit. It made me crazy. It was completely the antithesis of everything else Little Feat played. And it approached boredom to the extent that I had to leave. I had to get offstage and go elsewhere."

But not always. "Occasionally it made it, though," said George. "I would say that later on, one out of six was real hot and came across. But the other five, you had to sit through."

Unfortunately, by now George was outnumbered. Producer Templeman, although aware that Lenny Waronker, who'd signed the band, was with George in opposing the Feats' direction, sided with Payne and company. "I'm a jazz player and I love jazz. I would just let them go, especially on things like 'Day at the Dog Races'—they were kickin' ass. Billy came up with that incredible intro. I think he was playing an Oberheim—he was ahead of his time with that shit. Billy had hit his creative stride, and Paul too. I was just sittin' back and letting Billy roll."

On stage, when the song came up and George retired backstage, Payne, for one, shrugged it off. "I just figured, when in doubt, lay out," he said. "If you don't like it, don't play it. By that time I'd pretty much had enough of him and his tango of two steps up, one step back, two steps back, one step up dance." Further, it was unfortunate, Payne said, that the distancing took place even as the band was beginning to play larger concerts. Barrere accepted some responsibility for the deteriorating communications between himself and George, who still was the closest in touch with management and the record company. "Looking back on it, probably we should have stayed in better contact," he admitted. "Discussed whatever it was that was causing problems and so forth." The so-forths, he said, included George's health issues. "But we didn't . . . we just, I think Billy and Lowell maybe talked a lot, the rest of us just waited until we got the phone call. 'Come rehearse, we're going on the road.'" Barrere, for one, was happy to leave business details to Payne and George. "I wasn't really a very deep thinker back then," he said. "I wanted to play, have fun, drink, smoke, snort, play."

Even on his own song, "Rocket in My Pocket," George's lowered energy level almost cost him dearly. Templeman found himself pushing the putative Big Feat. "When we did 'Rocket in My Pocket,' he was singing, and I kept telling him, 'Lowell, you're not getting any soul into this.' He got so pissed off that he wouldn't sing. And he was big, but he actually jumped and got off the ground in the middle of singin' it."

One day, later in the recording process, it was time for the slide guitar solo on George's one big song on the album. As Templeman remembers it: "I couldn't get Lowell out of bed." Templeman wasn't sure whether his star had "a hangover, the Peruvian flu, or was just lazy.

"He showed up for all the other dates," he said. But this was an important one. "I called Bonnie Raitt, and she came down and just kicked it. I called Lowell and I said, 'Listen to this. What do you think?' He actually got out of bed and came barreling down, in his pajamas. He came right in there and played it. Technically, they were neck and neck, although he was better at the time. She idolized Lowell."

Raitt loved and respected George so much that, as she recalls, she resisted Templeman's invitation, stating, "I didn't really want to do it, and they just said they were really on some kind of time limit, and would you go do this? There was probably a subtext to this, about why he wasn't able to show up . . . he had been being late quite a bit, and the rest of the band was kinda pissed off about it, so I think they wanted to use this as a lever to get him to show up. I wasn't thrilled about it, and I think at the time I said I knew what was going on and he should rise to the occasion."

Although Raitt's emergency guitar didn't make the final cut, the Tower of Power horns and Fred Tackett represented the Feats Auxiliary, with Tackett playing mandocello, an eight-string instrument, and guitar on the title track. The Doobie Brothers, having enjoyed Payne's services both on the road and in the studio, lent three brothers—or Doobies—to the album. Jeff "Skunk" Baxter played dobro, Patrick Simmons played acoustic guitar on "New Delhi," and he and Michael McDonald added vocals on "Red Streamliner," giving it a smooth vocal sheen.

Templeman, who by now had scored numerous hit records with other artists, was pleased with the end result. Little Feat, including Lowell George, had shown up and, through all their travails, delivered. As Templeman told Scoppa: "I've produced all kinds of people and had hits with them, but I've gotta say, in terms of learning from an artist or just enjoying the talent, Little Feat is definitely up there for me. We had a mutual respect. We got along well. Those guys were truly one of the great musical groups of all time."

Even so, they had to face the critics with their finished products. J. P. Gelinas of *Perfect Sound Forever* wrote that *Time Loves a Hero* "was considered by the press and public alike to be a major disappointment."

But that's too broad a brush. The fact is that the album was another success by Little Feat's still-modest standards. Like the two albums before, it reached the charts, getting to number thirty-four and staying on *Billboard*'s weekly compilation of the 200 Top LPs and Tapes for four weeks, one better than *Time Loves a Hero*. It would go on to achieve sales of five hundred thousand units, giving the band its second gold record.

Rolling Stone, which had been disappointed in the previous album, this time around was more cognizant of the band's evolution. Peter Herbst neatly placed Little Feat's albums into two categories: the three that George dominated, and the three that he had not. The odd syncopations, the idiosyncratic, cartoonish lyrics, even much of George's vocal and guitar stylings were diminished.

But Herbst found much to like about the direction in which Payne and Barrere were taking the band, writing, "Little Feat combines rock and funk better, and certainly more naturally, than other, similarly-inclined groups; and . . . the new material not only takes advantage of a strong, flexible rhythm section but also provides better melodies than did the previous two albums."

As for the big dog in the room, Herbst said that "Day at the Dog Races" "partly succeeds" in showing what the band had gleaned from Weather Report, the Mahavishnu Orchestra, and Jeff Beck. Herbst preferred Payne's "Red Streamliner," which he approvingly likened to Steely Dan.

Critic Don Snowden, writing for *Rock Around the World* in mid-1977, described the album as "stylistically scattered," whereas he found *The Last Record Album* unified. The band, he said, failed to develop "a cohesive group sound out of the diverse elements that make up their music." That written, he thought the album "excellent," with two highlights demonstrating Feat's range of musical sources: "Day at the Dog Races" showed off Feat's musicianship "in a progressive context," and "Old Folks Boogie" killed with its knockout drumming and the line, "You know that you're over the hill / when your mind makes a promise that your body can't fill."

(Barrere confesses, now, that he took that line from his father, who'd been an usher in a vaudeville theater in New York and would walk around the house repeating jokes he'd heard at work, such as "You ain't old when your hair turns gray, you ain't old when it falls away." He gave his father—Gabriel Paul Barrere—due credit.)

In his review Snowden made it a point to give Little Feat overdue credit. He spoke for numerous fans of the band when he noted the unfairness of it all, that even though Little Feat earned raves from fellow musicians (including Led Zeppelin and the Marshall Tucker Band) as well as critics, they were "something of prophets without honor in their own land," even as the likes of Jackson Browne, Linda Ronstadt, and the Eagles had been anointed to represent Los Angeles. Snowden argued that the musical voices of Los Angeles were not the Eagles, soaring high—sometimes very high—above the streets and canyons, but rather Little Feat, who chronicled truckers and low-lifers, narrated life in the land of stars and Jell-O mountains topped with Cool-Whip.

The press, by and large, maintained its affection for the band. But this could well have been a different story. While work was going on for *Time Loves a Hero*, George gave an interview in which he responded to rumors that he had a particularly inflammatory idea for a title for that album. As he told Paul Kendall of *ZigZag* magazine in its August 1976 issue: "I'd love to call it 'Nigger Rich,' but I'm afraid I'd get some hate mail." He said his idea had to do with the cover art, being done, as always, by Neon Park. "It's one of the first concept covers that I've laid on Neon, and it has to do with, not necessarily black folks, but the gigantic middle class, who think they are 'doing well,' but at the same time they are destroying our surroundings: *More roads! More pylons! Put another piece of asphalt through! Let's have a ski resort here!* That kind of attitude. Recreation is a wonderful thing, but in the States, it becomes de-creation, and also very expensive. It's a lot of crap, and that was the purpose of the idea 'Nigger Rich.'"

George envisioned, to Park, "some old folks in a camping van, and the old man's watching a football game on the TV . . . and his wife is sitting on a camping stool reading the *National Enquirer* with a picture of Cher on the cover, and they're in orbit over the moon, which is covered with beer cans." "As in 'Beer Cans on the Moon?'" asked Kendall. "Right, the Ed Sanders idea," said George, thinking of the founder of the anarchic rock band, the Fugs. "A juxtaposition of time frames, elements, and things we've all seen, which is kind of what the covers have been to date."

Fortunately, George's vision never came to light. In *Time Loves a Hero*, the only song with a middle-class theme was his and Barrere's "Keeping Up with the Joneses," which began,

> *Keepin' up with the Joneses is killin' me*
> *Go on and hang that man who says*
> *The best things in life are for free*

The song contained nothing ecological; there were no beer cans on any moon.

But many critics noted George's low profile in the new album. For instance, Don Snowden ventured, "Lowell George, probably due to working on his solo album, seems curiously out of place here." Others ventured that Payne, Barrere, and perhaps others had hijacked creative control from George and kept him from getting more of his own songs onto the album. "We got blamed for all this crap," Payne said, "for blocking Lowell out of the writing arena. And that wasn't true. The guy just wasn't coming up with songs."

Initially, Payne thought George might secretly be stockpiling material for his solo project. He was suspicious about the solo venture, afraid that it might take away from Little Feat. "But I gotta say, keeping an eye on what Lowell was doing, as best I could with regard to his solo project, I said, 'Put two and two together. It took this guy five years to make a solo record, which has very little original material on it. In what way were we blocking this guy?' Obviously, he blocked himself."

What a far remove from the Payne of the feel-good interviews earlier in the year. The band of musical renegades who had attracted critics like Don Snowden was disappearing. Still, Snowden, who'd seen the Feats on stage many times, remained a believer. Although the band had broken into the charts with respectable sales, the critic thought it could go farther. What they needed "to put them over the top," he wrote, "is a double album of one of their live performances with an appropriate push from Warner Bros."

Snowden may have had some inside dope on the band's plans for concerts in August, shows that would, indeed, be recorded and lead them close to, if not quite over, the top.

Chapter 11

WAITING FOR COLUMBUS

DESPITE ALL THE CONTRETEMPS FROM THE SESSIONS FOR *TIME LOVES a Hero*, it was Little Feat's modest version of a three-peat: their third consecutive time in the Top 40 of the *Billboard* album charts. But insiders knew that the end had begun.

Loathe to return to the recording studios anytime soon, George had suggested, early in 1977, that the band record several of their concerts that summer and produce a live album. The guys, equally disinclined to get back into the tedium and tensions of studio work, readily agreed. Whatever George's reasoning—Payne guessed that the idea "might have been his way of reinstating himself"—the band welcomed George's show of assertiveness, despite the irony of his situation. As he receded in productivity and authority, Little Feat were doing increasingly well. (In the United Kingdom *Time Loves a Hero* scored rave reviews and made the Top Ten.)

They knew they were a strong stage act. Looking back many years later, Hayward would name *Waiting for Columbus* his favorite Feat album "because it shows what we did with the stuff from the studio records."

They invariably took that "stuff" to new places, if not always new heights. With Little Feat, as with all bands that thrived on changing things up, with challenging themselves and their audiences, nothing was guaranteed. There were always good nights and bad nights. What they did not know was that on certain nights they could bring all the tension, the conflicts, even the potential for violence onto the stage.

For this live recording they decided to embellish some of their songs with the Tower of Power horns. There would also be a few special guests. In London it'd be Mick Taylor, including Michael Mc-Donald and Patrick Simmons of the Doobie Brothers. Talk about good sports.

Little Feat wisely scheduled recordings in August in two strong fan bases of theirs: London and Washington, DC. After a warm-up of sorts in Manchester, they opened at the Rainbow Theater, the site of their shocking success two years before as part of the Warner Bros. Music Show. They returned in triumph, and after a solid opening night, they partied. Hard.

Some of them did, anyway.

In 2009 Emilio Castillo, saxophonist with Tower of Power, tried to remember for the music site Jambands. Little Feat, he began, "were really celebrated over there by the Brits and the Europeans, so there were a lot of famous people hanging around, and there was a lot of dope and stuff."

Uh-oh.

He continued, "This one night, they wound up calling it 'Black Wednesday' because on Tuesday night, after the show, all the guys stayed up partying. Mic Gillette [trumpet, trombone] was partying all night with Paul Barrere, Richie Hayward, and Lowell George. . . . They stayed up all night . . . and came to the concert on Wednesday for the sound check. A lot of the guys who were straighter were really upset."

Wild guesses: Bill Payne; Sam Clayton; Kenny Gradney.

Castillo went on: "I remember right before we went on there was a big fight between Richie Hayward and Lowell. They were cussing each other out, and Richie turned around to walk away in a huff, and Lowell punched him . . . right in the back. And I mean *hard*. Our road manager Doug Zahn grabbed Richie because Richie turned around and he was going to kill Lowell. And that's how we walked on stage. Paul was completely obliterated. He couldn't talk. He was barely standing. Richie and Lowell were completely ready to kill each other, and the other guys were angry as hell, and that's how we walked on stage."

Little Feat fans know that the band, by tradition, huddles before a concert and sings a bit of the old spiritual "Join the Band" as they head up to the stage. In fact, that ritual was captured and is the opening moment of *Waiting for Columbus*.

Regardless, Castillo continued his recollection of George ordering the road manager on stage to turn Barrere's amplifier off. "And Paul kept turning around and fiddling with it," Castillo wrote, "and every time he turned it on and started playing, the roadie would reach around and turn it off. That's how the night went. It was atrocious."

And yet, Castillo concluded, anger propelled Hayward and George to stellar performances. "They played with a vengeance. And we played really well. Mic Gillette—even though he had been partying all night—played *astoundingly*. He took everything up a notch . . . and they wound up using that for the record." Castillo laughed and added, "They re-recorded all the other stuff. We were stunned when we heard that. We couldn't believe it. Then, when you think back, a lot of times when you're over emotional like that, you play your heart out, and I think that's what happened."

Or not. The meticulous credits in the booklet for the expanded CD of *Waiting for Columbus*, released in 2002, indicate that nothing from "Black Wednesday" made it onto the album except for a bite of "Dixie Chicken" and Mick Taylor's appearance for "A Apolitical Blues," on which the Rolling Stones guitarist played sizzling counterpoint to George, then engaged him in a friendly duel.

Bill Payne, who was also there and, unlike the horn players, was there the entire concert, said Castillo's story was "pretty close." But for starters, it was him, not George, who had Barrere's amp turned down. He was compelled to act from the first song, he said. "It was 'Walkin' All Night' [which Barrere had written with Payne]. And when Paul started playing, it was way off rhythmically, and I said, 'What is he doing?' And I motioned to the guitar tech, Paul Bruno, and I yelled at him, 'Turn his amp off. Turn his fuckin' amp off, NOW!' He did, so a good portion of the evening Paul was looking at his amp, playing, shaking his head. . . . Okay, now I got him, he can't do any further damage . . . Lowell had a greater capacity for handling the downers or whatever it was that put these guys in trouble in the first place. Hayward was not a part of that, nor was Sam Clayton or Kenny Gradney, and we looked at each other, and I said, 'We gotta hold the ship together or this thing's going off the front of the stage.'

"What did happen is, following the show, everybody just went bananas again. . . . We're walking up the steps at the back of the stage to go up to the dressing room. Richie said something to Lowell, I heard a couple of quick little *pop-pops*, I saw a little rabbit punch to Richie from the back, and we're all upstairs yelling and arguing with each other, and I said, 'We gotta go back out and do the encore, these people are not gonna stop!'

"So we marched back downstairs. It was 'Teenage Nervous Breakdown,' and Richie had a quiver of sticks, so if he broke one he could reach in and grab another one. Lowell was up front, and 'Teenage Nervous Breakdown' is like a double-time, almost triple-time tempo—very fast song. Richie is reaching in, grabbing these sticks, and throwing them at Lowell's head while Lowell's on the mike. Lowell is a black belt, or a brown belt, so he's dodging these sticks, and the audience is picking them up for souvenirs. It was comedic in a sense, but not really. . . . It was a high-wire act that night, so that's the way that evening went."

George Massenburg, the engineer, called the evening "fucking tragic. . . . Richie was bleary, and Kenny, Sam, and Bill were trying to keep it together. And Liz was there to try to keep Lowell straight. . . . She would try and keep Lowell away from drugs, so she wouldn't give him any money. Monday before the show nobody can find Lowell, and he has grabbed armloads of T-shirts off the table and is selling them to people for cash so he can score some coke.

"Black Wednesday," Massenburg said, "sort of went on all night . . . and Paul keeps looking at his left hand, then he looks at his right hand, and he doesn't know why his guitar's not working, and the band is furious with each other all night long. . . . Lowell turns

Hampton George
(left) with Lowell
and their mother,
Florence, at home,
1949. *Courtesy of
Hampton George
Collection*

The George boys are flanked by their mother and stepfather, Andy,
on a cruise to Asia, 1963. *Courtesy of Hampton George Collection*

The Factory on *Gomer Pyle, U.S.M.C.*, 1967. From left to right: Martin Kibbee, Lowell George, Warren Klein. Richie Hayward is in the background. *Courtesy of Lynn Hearne Collection*

The Factory play a festival, The Fantasy Fair, at a raceway in Northridge, California, sharing the stage with the Doors, Canned Heat, the Sunshine Company, and others, July 1967. *Photo by Jill Klein*

Early Little Feat rehearse on a Warner Bros. soundstage, 1970.
Photo by Linda Wolf

Little Feat in an early publicity shot for Warner Bros. Records,
1970. From left to right: Richie Hayward, Bill Payne, Roy Estrada,
and Lowell George. *Courtesy of Lynn Hearne Collection*

On tour to promote *Dixie Chicken*, 1973. Clockwise from Afro:
Kenny Gradney, Richie Hayward, unknown colonel, Paul Barrere,
Sam Clayton, Bill Payne, Lowell George, unknown civilian. *Courtesy of Lynn Hearne Collection*

Little Feat in a 1975 Warner Bros. photo. *Courtesy of Lynn Hearne Collection*

Little Feat sit with DJ Cerphe Colwell (second from left) at Track Studios in Silver Springs, Maryland, in 1977. *Photo by Dave Nuttycombe*

Craig Fuller joins the reunited Little Feat in 1987, on guitar and vocals. *Courtesy of Lynn Hearne Collection*

Shaun Murphy had a long run as a Feat vocalist. Here, she hoists one on New Year's Eve 1998, in Richmond, Virginia. *Photo by David R. Baus*

Richie Hayward, drummer and rock star, in Vancouver, British Columbia. *Photo by Polly Payne*

Acknowledging Feat fans at Stamford, Connecticut, in 2007. *Photo by Hank Randall*

At the 2012 Jamaica fan fest, Bill Payne escorts Diane Pelis to a renewal of her vows with husband Jerry. *Photo by Polly Payne*

"Shag" with Bill
Payne, 1998.
*Courtesy of Lynne
Hearne Collection*

Little Feat today. Front to back: Gabe Ford, Sam Clayton, Bill
Payne, Paul Barrere, Fred Tackett, and Kenny Gradney. *Photo by
Ashley Stagg, courtesy of Little Feat*

around and glares at Richie, 'cause Richie had speeded up and slowed down, then Richie retaliates firing a drumstick at Lowell, and that was onstage . . . as they walked off stage Lowell did a karate thing."

And what did Barrere the Blitzed have to say about all this? Amazingly enough, he has some recollection. Barrere says that the night before "Black Wednesday" he hosted a little party in his hotel room, including some horn players, and that George and Hayward dropped in. Refreshments included "the nefarious white powder," lots of alcohol, and, in his case, some pills. "I think it was Tuinols," he said. Downers. He remembers room service ringing with more drinks, him moving to the door and keeling over. While he was out, he says, "Lowell gave me a hot foot." The injury to his not-so-little foot lasted awhile.

More immediately, the next day, onstage, "It was abysmal on my part. I was definitely gone." He doesn't know what he did during the set. But, he said, "A lesson learned, and never repeated."

"Black Wednesday" was one of the most eventful gigs in the band's history. In the audience music critics were divided. Pete Erskine of the British music weekly *New Music Express* called the four-night Rainbow run "anti-climactic," showing the band "as tired, bored, ill-looking and uptight, with Lowell resorting to strange behavior and the almost cynically obvious ploy of climaxing each set by throwing his maracas into the audience. By then it had all simply become a stage act—and Lowell and Richie Hayward, at least, were far too intelligent and humane to actually believe in the hoax."

J. P. Gelinas, on the online music 'zine, *Perfect Sound Forever*, wrote in 2008 that he thought the album restored the band's credibility and did "an excellent job of capturing the onstage improvisational interplay that characterized many of Little Feat's best concerts. George, in particular, brings a renewed sense of energy to his singing and playing."

That George did, from openings that included his singing and dancing with an Afro-haired, tambourine-banging dervish (portrayed by "Doc" Kupka of Tower of Power) to his seamless duet with Mick Taylor to his emotional, stops-out readings of his songs. Similarly, Payne, the keyboard wizard, had his spotlight moments, as did Barrere, who took occasional lead vocals, as well as the percussion department of Gradney, Clayton, and Hayward. Both in London and in Washington, DC, at the Lisner Auditorium, the Tower of Power horns added a party atmosphere as well as solid backing for "Mercenary Territory" and many other songs.

But the concerts were one thing; the resulting album, another.

After the two mostly triumphant runs it was time to gather all the tapes and hunker down in a recording studio, with Lowell George as producer, overseeing the editing. There would be a lot to do.

At Westlake Studios in downtown Los Angeles George, along with Massenburg and Warren Dewey, the recording engineer for the shows in Washington, convened to select the best performances and fix the rest. "We did a lot of overdubbing on *Waiting for Columbus*," said Bill Payne. "Some vocals were redone, a few guitars, maybe a bass or two. No drums were redone, no keyboards." Payne recalled some minor surgery on "Dixie Chicken" "to put something in that was not recorded on that night."

The CD information backs him up. "Dixie Chicken" was a blend of the "Black Wednesday" performance with the horn break from the next night. "Tripe Face Boogie" got similar treatment for the piano solo. In the studio George and company also decided to put the sound-check version of "Mercenary Territory" onto the album.

The most significant overdubbing involved George's lead vocals. He replaced pretty much all of them with freshly recorded versions. As engineer Dewey told Bud Scoppa: "Lowell sang almost every song over, usually in one take, and then we would decide whether the original or the overdub, or a combination, was better." George also reviewed all his guitar solos. As Dewey noted, "Lowell liked a guitar recording technique that put super-hot levels on the tape, and we hadn't done that on the original recordings." Also, he said, "For one tune, Richie Hayward set up his drum set to fix some tiny error."

Payne himself was pleasantly shocked with the results. "The way that album opens up with the applause, and you hear the band singing—it just raised the hair on my arms," he said. "As I sat there and listened to it, I felt that we really had something. Whatever was done through Hollywood magic, it has a feeling of being right in your face. For a change, I thought, *Man, Lowell did a great job on this record. He nailed it.*"

Waiting for Columbus, issued in 1978, earned mixed reviews but became the band's best-seller to date, reaching the top twenty in *Billboard* and, over time, has outlasted the most critical of critics. A recent poll of *Rolling Stone* readers for "the ten best live albums of all time" resulted in a number seven spot for *Waiting*, behind the Who, the Allmans, Peter Frampton, the Stones (*Ya-Yas*), KISS, and Deep Purple, and ahead of Nirvana, the Band (*Last Waltz*), Bob Seger, and everybody else, including Dylan, Springsteen, the Dead, Phish, Jimi, Aretha, Ray Charles, Monterey Pop, and Woodstock—even James Brown and his Famous Flames at the Apollo. *Rolling Stone* noted, "Little Feat never became true household names like many of their peers, but anyone who spends time with this album will be quickly converted."

George, while wrapping up *Waiting for Columbus*, doing on-and-off work on his solo project and beginning work on the next Little Feat album, took on various gigs with other artists. In some cases he was a session player; in others he worked as a producer, overseeing recording sessions. And in several instances one or more of Little Feat joined him. From the time of the band's debut album its members were sought out—or simply welcomed—as session musicians.

By 1977 George had compiled some thirty such credits. These are only roughly chronological, as release dates of albums don't indicate when they actually were produced. Please hold your applause until all have been mentioned, and these aren't necessarily all of them. Some have already been noted, whereas others don't quite measure up to being notable, but they include:

1972: Carly Simon, whose album *No Secrets* featured George and Payne playing on one track.
1973: Most of the band worked with:
- Chico Hamilton, a drummer who ranged from big band to bebop,
- John Cale, cofounder (with Lou Reed) of Velvet Underground (George, Payne, and Hayward sat in), and

- Bonnie Bramlett, whose *Sweet Bonnie Bramlett* LP featured Little Feat, albeit uncredited, on half of the album.

1974: Credits for George included:

- Mike Auldridge's *Blues & Bluegrass*,
- the satiric comedy troupe the Credibility Gap's *A Great Gift Idea*,
- Rolling Stone Bill Wyman's *Monkey Grip*,
- R&B legend Etta James's *Come a Little Closer*,
- Maria Muldaur's *Waitress in a Donut Shop*,
- the Meters' *Rejuvenation* (produced by Allen Toussaint, with whom George worked on Robert Palmer's *Sneakin' Sally Through the Alley* in '73),
- Howdy Moon, a band including Valerie Carter, and
- John Sebastian's *Tarzana Kid*, on which, besides playing on "Face of Appalachia," the lovely song they wrote together, George played on Sebastian's version of his "Dixie Chicken."

1975: George got an "executive producer" credit for singer-songwriter Tom Jans's album *The Eyes of an Only Child*; fellow Feats Bill Payne and Sam Clayton, along with Feats Auxiliary faithful Fred Tackett were also on board. On his own, George backed UK soul artist Linda Lewis on her album *Not a Little Girl Anymore* and played guitar on Linda Ronstadt's *Prisoner in Disguise* on his own song "Roll Um Easy."

1976: In addition to producing most of an album by Akiko Yano, entitled *Japanese Girl*, George's sideman credits included:

- his pal Jackson Browne's *The Pretender*,
- J. D. Souther's *Black Rose*,
- Carly Simon's *Another Passenger*, and
- the Canadian folk duo Kate and Anna McGarrigle's eponymous album.

And in 1976 and 1977, while weathering health and band crises, he managed to work with his friend Jimmy Webb on his album *El Mirage*. He played in a session for banjo player Herb Pedersen's *Sandman*. He contributed some slide guitar and got to meet Dolly Parton when he, she, and Ronstadt sang together on "If I Lose."

Finally he and some thirty fellow musicians, including Feats' Payne, Barrere, and Clayton as well as Pederson, Ronstadt, Browne, Maurice and Fred White, Jans, and Sebastian, lent support to Valerie Carter, an obviously popular backup singer who'd moved up front. For her debut album, *Just a Stone's Throw Away*, George coproduced two tracks, provided "Face of Appalachia," and joined in writing "Cowboy Angel" with her along with "Back to Blue Some More," with her and Bill Payne.

No matter his role in any situation with a musician, George was protective of that musician's work and demanded control. One evening in 1976 he was in a studio with Carter and George Massenburg when Linda Ronstadt dropped in, accompanied by Mick Jagger. Ronstadt no longer remembers why Mick was with her, but she remembered George's hostility toward the Rolling Stone: "Massenburg was producing, and Mick came in and tried to run the session. And Massenburg is plenty strong but kind of a quiet guy, and Mick thought he could just take over and run the session. And I was trying to sing with Valerie . . . and then Lowell kept saying, 'Okay, lose the teabag'"—meaning the Brit. "Mick was interfering," said Ronstadt. Besides possessing an impressive range and a crystal-clear voice, Carter was, as Ronstadt put it, "ridiculously pretty. And Mick Jagger was really noticing, you know. I think he just wanted to take her under his arm and ride off in the sunset with her. And Lowell's hissing, 'Lose the teabag!'" That night, at least, Jagger rolled home, alone.

George, who was widely praised for encouraging new talent, was also credited with boosting the career of Rickie Lee Jones, a twenty-three-year-old neo-Beat singer and songwriter from Chicago. George is often credited with discovering Jones.

George remembers their first encounter as clear as any day outside of Los Angeles. He was in Topanga Canyon., not far from his home. "There was a little joint called the Post Office that had a Fender amplifier with the microphones plugged into it," he recalled. "Rickie got up and sang that song, and I went, 'Holy Moley, that's a great song.' So I cut it a couple of months later. She got a manager, and he took her to Warners. The folks there had heard that I had done one of her songs, so they listened to her." She got a deal, made a record, and, as George concluded, "Here we are. She's gone platinum."

Holy moley, indeed.

But that's not how it happened—at least not according to Jones and another principal player. Yes, she said, there was a post office on a patch of Topanga Canyon, with an ice cream parlor and a small nightclub nearby. "I wasn't playing there," she explained. "I just met him there. I was playing pinball, and I feel he watched me play pinball a little bit, and we struck up a conversation. I think that was the first time, but I think I met him when my friend Ivan Ulz called him up and sang 'Easy Money' on the phone . . . but we just met briefly that night."

Ulz was the singer-songwriter who, visiting Patte Price in 1969, met George and told him about hearing "Willin'" performed the night before at the Troubadour. George wound up helping out on Ulz's album *Ivan the Ice Cream Man.*

Ulz and George also wrote a song together that would wind up on George's solo album. "We wrote it fast," Ulz said. "I had a fight one morning with my girlfriend and left the house and went over to see Lowell. And that same morning Patte was storming out of the house. She and he had had a big fight. So we sat down and wrote 'Heartache' in about an hour." Before he recorded the gorgeous lamentation, George would give it to Valerie Carter for her debut album.

Ulz's own career didn't take off at that time, and in 1977 he was working at a pharmacy, Disco Drugs in Santa Monica, when he helped a friend to launch hers. He had met Rickie Lee Jones as a neighbor in Venice. "We had a romance for a while," he recalled, "and I was astounded by her talent, what a great singer she was." He was even more impressed when she sang him a song she'd written, called "Easy Money."

"I couldn't figure out how a twenty-one-, twenty-two-year-old girl could have the smarts to write such a song. It showed such great awareness. I loved it, and I sang it all the time." One day while at Disco Drugs, Ulz called George, told him about Rickie and the song, and sang it to him. "And I gave him her number and it went on from there."

Jones picked up the story, stating, "Lowell came right over, with a Sony tape recorder—reel to reel—and he recorded 'Easy Money.' I think I sang him a couple other tunes. I saw him a week later, and he came back with an instrumental version of the song." He told her he wanted to put the song on his solo album. He pressed "play" and pointed out a passage. "This is gonna be the solo on the record," he said. Rickie was delighted. "And then we started hanging out."

Jones recalled going on drives with George: "He started coming over, and we would meet people that lived in Beachwood Canyon," in the Hollywood Hills. "He seemed to still have a crush on Linda Ronstadt. We went by this one house, and he said, 'That's where Linda and I used to live.'" Of course, George was married, but he added Jones to his list of lovers.

"Well," said Jones, "all I can tell you about that is, gosh, I guess I should've checked. . . . He was obviously not the most faithful of people. I feel it was kind of understood but not discussed. I know that he probably went to bed with . . . " She paused and restarted. "He truly loved women. He really liked women, and they liked him."

With George on her side, Jones would land a recording contract with Warner Bros. Russ Titelman and Lenny Waronker would produce her first album, a smash hit that included "Easy Money" as well as "Chuck E.'s in Love."

By the time Jones made her debut, Little Feat were enjoying the success of *Waiting for Columbus*. The album was released in February of 1978. But just two months before, George had a motorcycle spill while he was still working on the final mixes.

Four months later he recounted the incident—and its consequences—to T. E. Mattox of the Armed Forces Radio and Television Service in Tokyo, where the Feats were playing at the Nagano Sun Plaza. "I had a small accident on a Yamaha . . . on a motorcycle, in the dirt and crazy. Trying to have a good time and overdid it." He was doing wheelies and got thrown off the bike, rupturing several disks in his vertebrae. He suffered a loss of sensation in his left hand. At the time of the accident he was wrapping up postproduction on *Waiting for Columbus*. "I was supposed to have some physical therapy and said, 'What the heck' and didn't do it, of course, because I'm stupid. It got out of hand. I had a couple of discs removed from my neck. Put on twenty pounds lying in a hospital."

George was on the operating table for six hours. As he recalled, "That particular operation, you have to sit up for it. They put you out and strap you in. It takes more time. In my case the guy realized that I was a musician and made a real concerted effort to revive the nerves that had stopped in my hand. Cause I couldn't play the guitar anymore. And I have to say, only when I get tense does it bother me at all. And it's mostly just minor pain in my back. I went back to work two weeks later."

George was back to his juggling act. With Little Feat, that meant tours in the spring and fall along with the start of another studio album. For himself, it meant continued work on his solo project and any side gigs that interested him.

And the Grateful Dead interested him.

The Dead, five years Little Feat's senior, were the musical symbol of the San Francisco music scene of the sixties. Jefferson Airplane had become a starship; Big Brother, Quicksilver, Creedence, Country Joe, and all the rest were long gone, but the Dead kept that freak flag flying.

But in the midseventies that flag often drooped. Even though the Dead were still beloved, had built a following of "Dead Heads" around the country, and could seemingly do no wrong, even when they did. In the midseventies, when they signed with a new record label, they were perceived to be making some musical missteps.

Even more seriously, they seemed to be falling apart, physically as well as musically. In 1978, as Dennis McNally, the band's publicist and, later, biographer, would say, "the band was at a low point in its playing" in a year that included an auto accident that laid drummer Mickey Hart up for the summer, an accidental gunshot wound in Bob Weir's shoulder, and, perhaps most frightening of all, Jerry Garcia's discovery of heroin the year before. Garcia was also exhausted from two projects, *The Grateful Dead Movie*, which he had a heavy hand in editing, and a solo project, *Cats Under the Stars*, that failed.

The band, after issuing several recordings under their own label, signed with industry powerhouse Clive Davis and his Arista Records. Their first effort, *Terrapin Station*, had come up short. That album, which was produced by Keith Olsen of Fleetwood Mac fame, had featured strings and horns, some of it to the Dead's surprise. For its twelfth album in their twelve years together, the Dead decided to get back to basics. As their longtime associate and occasional manager Rock Scully wrote, "None of this cool professional attitude in fully automated studios. This time we're going to use someone certifiably funky—Lowell George of Little Feat—to produce."

When the band came up with that idea, they assigned guitarist Bob Weir to make the contact. "I was the guy," he recalled. "I had manners . . . so I got to do virtually all the diplomacy for the band. So I got the gig to interview potential producers. I called him, and he wanted to fly up and see our studio and facilities, which made sense."

One fall evening in San Francisco Weir drove to the airport to pick George up. "We went to Chinatown. There'd just been a Chinese gangland shooting, and we went to the Golden Dragon." That was the restaurant where, in September 1977 an attempted hit on a youth gang very early one morning led to what the press described as "the Golden Dragon Massacre." Five people, all innocent diners, were killed. But that didn't bother the two musicians. "We were putting our fingers in the bullet holes," said Weir, "stuff like that. We wanted to absorb the ambience of the situation."

Whether it was the setting, the food, or their musical bonds, Weir remembers them having "a pretty glorious time. We became real good friends. Others in the band won't have as fond a recollection as I do, but to me he was a genius. He was a California boy with a California sensibility about music." By that, Weir, who came from a wealthy family in the Peninsula, just south of San Francisco, meant that, in the fifties and sixties "there are a number of intelligent Californians who grew up in a culture where most all music was available on the radio, and there's a certain culture in California of kids who found it on their own. It was disparate, spread out everywhere, where kids were playing the buttons on the radio and listening to everything. Jerry Garcia was one of those kids, I was one of those kids, and Lowell was one of those kids. And we spoke the same language."

According to Scully, Garcia and other band members had another reason to like George: "Lowell reminds the Dead of Pigpen and their roots, and Jerry loves him for that." "Pigpen," of course, was Ron McKernan, their original keyboardist, an R&B-, blues-, and jazz-loving player and singer, one of those California boys Weir was talking about, who died in 1973 from liver disease—that is, excessive drinking.

Lowell did not hurt his case when he inspected the Dead's rehearsal and storage facility, Club Front, a funky garage on Front Street in an industrial sector of San Rafael and declared, "I like the old Dead. Let's get that sound. How did you used to play 'Good Lovin'?' How would Pigpen have done it? Guys, let's boogie."

George was hired and set about getting that sound. He told the band: "We're not going into the studio, period. This is where you rehearse, right? We'll do it right here. We'll get some baffling, put up some curtains, and deaden it down a little bit, hang some stuff from the ceiling, and we'll get it right here." As George would explain on a radio show in West Hartford, Connecticut, in 1979: "There was no control room . . . the recording equipment, everything was right in the same room as the musicians."

Going old school, George asked the band to lay down the basic tracks live, without isolating the drummer in a booth or having Garcia adding his guitar parts later.

The Dead were right about getting a peer, a musician, to oversee the sessions. "Lowell was like a member of the band more," said drummer Bill Kreutzmann. "If we were working on a song and he didn't feel it was going right, he'd just grab a guitar and come in the studio and show us how he felt it. That was one of the ways he'd communicate, and it worked great. I had a tremendous amount of respect for him. Basically, though, I think the Grateful Dead produces itself best."

George himself said as much. On the radio in Hartford, Ed O'Conell, the DJ, asked how he handled Garcia, and George responded, "I'll tell you the truth . . . Jerry Garcia is entirely capable of producing the band, but he'd rather not have the headache, and to tell you the truth, I would not want the headache again myself." He swore that he had "a great time" working with the Dead, who he called "extremely good musicians" and "so far out they're really funny."

As it turned out, as good a match as George and the Dead appeared to be, they may have been too similar in areas, which might work against producing the best possible songs, performances, and albums. Both George and the band liked recreational drugs, and with those in hand, they often lacked discipline. George, Weir concedes, wound up being as much "a traffic cop" as a producer, and things dragged on so long that George never finished his work. On the Dead's side, there was a major event: a trip to Egypt for several concerts at the Great Pyramids. For George it was another Feats tour. Garcia would end up supervising the final mixes, and the album would be released in November, to tepid reviews.

Weir, who says that he and the rest of the band later became huge fans of *Waiting for Columbus*, swore that he was pleased with the results. "That was a lot of fun for me," he said. "Some of the guys didn't fare so well with Lowell at the helm, but me, I liked it just fine."

Percussionist Mickey Hart did admit to having a problem with George. "Lowell George was mad," he said. "We wrote a great song one night. . . . It was called 'My Drum Is a Woman.' We wrote this song about all my instruments and what I thought about them, how I address them. Lowell played good guitar, but he was no producer, certainly not for the Grateful Dead. He did too much coke. There's no way for him to have any kind of judgment."

McNally, the Dead's publicity director and historian, told a more colorful variation of that story. "Once," he wrote, George "spent the night at Front Street with Mickey Hart, snorting coke and writing a never-recorded song called 'The Drum Is My Woman' instead of doing the overdubs they were supposed to be working on. At dawn, as they were leaving, Lowell turned to Hart and said, 'You know the conga drum sound on *Diga*? I hated it. It sucked.'" *Diga* was a solo project of Hart's, an album he had worked hard on and had sunken without a trace when the Dead's label issued it in 1975. McNally continued, "Always gracious in the face of criticism, Hart tackled him and began to choke him, at which point Lowell began to hyperventilate and have heart palpitations."

With that, George's short, strange trip with the Dead was over.

Chapter 12

WARPED BY THE RAIN...

HIS THEME SONG, SUCH AS IT WAS, SEEMED TO HAVE COME AROUND to haunt him. In George's last months bandmates and other friends observed that he had been warped by various rains; driven by snow (and other drugs); and drunk, if not dirty.

And he was still more than willin'.

In spring of 1979 he was full of plans and, even if he was overweight, at 250 pounds, full of fight. He would continue to make music—on his terms. And he was still juggling myriad projects. Having finally finished his solo album, he was mixing the tracks Little Feat had come up with for what would be titled *Down on the Farm*. At the same time he was preparing for an East Coast tour to promote his solo album. He was calling it *Thanks, I'll Eat It Here*, and it was adapted from the slightly more enthusiastic *Thank You! I'll Eat It Here!* that had been intended for what became *Sailin' Shoes*.

But at least he was home. With the success of *Waiting for Columbus*, Little Feat were kings of the road for a good part of 1978. And their mode of transportation, including limousines, did not escape notice. Barney Hoskyns wrote that "they now epitomized everything punk rockers detested" and that George was "travelling on a separate bus from the others."

But no, Little Feat weren't copying the Eagles or Fleetwood Mac. Gene Vano, who was a road manager for the Feats, did drive George, apart from the rest of the band, in a large, sleek motor home from General Motors called the Eleganza. But this was for George's health and his nonstop work schedule; the vehicle contained tape recorders and other recording equipment. "He was recording and writing music as I was driving him around the country, because his ears were such that he could not fly."

But while he worked, Little Feat were falling apart. What exactly happened and who made it happen is unclear, despite—or because of—statements from George saying he'd been fired, by Kibbee saying George had fired the band, and by Bill Payne saying he had quit.

The principal actors in the fallout were George and Payne, and the story most likely began at the end of the *Waiting for Columbus* tour, in the chill of Buffalo, New York, where the band had played on November 6, 1978. "Everything was going off the rails at that point," said Payne, who recalls having several conversations with George. "We had one more record to do for Warner Bros, *Down on the Farm*, and I asked him, I wanted to coproduce, and he told me flat out, 'No.' And I went, 'Well, if that's the answer, then screw it, I don't really want to do this.' . . . I was pissed off."

Then, whether it was anger or just another pickup gig while Little Feat were off the road, Payne and Barrere went on the road with Nicolette Larson, a singer on Warner Bros. who had a close relationship with Ted Templeman. Fran Tate, who married Payne, was also in the troupe. In an interview with the *New Musical Express* of London, George noted, with chagrin, that her band "started picking up rave reviews. . . . The next thing I know about it is that Bill comes around to tell me that, as from now, it's official that Little Feat have broken up." This, George said, was around March or April, while he was in a studio doing mix-downs on *Down on the Farm*. He told the *NME* reporter, Pete Erskine: "I must admit I got pretty tired of everybody . . . seeing me as some kind of ogre. . . . For years now they've seen me as an ogre." He said he'd heard that Bill and Paul had been "bad-rapping me to people in the record company for what they have called my 'ex-cessive behavior.'"

Payne admits that he called George out on some of his behavior, but not because he saw him as any kind of an ogre: "I said, 'Man, you were . . . this is the guy I met when I came down when I was a kid. You were up on a pedestal to me . . . but what you've been doing since, you're just this tortured individual. You're killing your-self, you're pissing everybody off, within the band and without the band. . . . Nobody can read you, we think we're taking five steps up to do something that will move us forward, you want to go back the other way. You can't sing, you're unhealthy, you're this, that. . . . Look, I want to get out of this band, I've had it. You don't need me torturing you and vice versa. If you want to keep going with the band later, great. My suggestion to you is to do something you love to do. . . . I know you love to write music, you love to record it.'" He advised George to "take a breather. Do some things to take the weight of the band off of him, and produce some things."

But when Payne added that, in the meantime, he and Barrere "were looking at other people to play with," George didn't take it well. He began telling interviewers that he'd been "fired" from his own band. Payne didn't understand why George would say that. Per-haps, he said, "Metaphorically, he felt we did that."

George continued to work on *Down on the Farm*—by himself. Later he would tell interviewers that Payne had betrayed him by quit-ting. One such instance was his appearance on WHCN, the station in West Hartford, Connecticut, one of the stops on his solo tour. He told Ed O'Connell that he would complete the new Feats album when he got back to Los Angeles, adding, "It was about two-thirds done when Bill Payne came in and went, 'I quit.' Which was really a big help, which really did a lot to my ego."

Hadn't Payne said he'd quit before? O'Connell asked. George re-plied, "He said, 'If things don't get better after this record's done, I'm going to quit.' And he went back on his word and quit right in the midst of it. And I have to say, that really got to me."

Soon George would be telling the press that Little Feat was still part of his future. "I might want to revive the band," he told John

Rockwell of the *New York Times*, "but I don't know if the original members would want to be part of it."

That was fine with Payne. After all, he had given notice. But it was still emotional for him late one evening in June when Lowell George came to visit at his home in Woodland Hills, in the Valley, just before he went off on his solo tour. "He drove out on his bike," Payne said, "and he drove up on my lawn, and I went out to talk to him. He had his mouth open. His eyes were as dark as saucers. He started to say something, but he couldn't talk. He had tears in his eyes, and he drove off. That's the last time I ever saw him."

Little Feat, as they had known it, was over.

George turned his attention next to promoting *Thanks, I'll Eat It Here*, which had been released in March—around the time when his hostilities with Payne and Barrere were peaking—and had received decidedly mixed reviews from critics and plenty of questions from reporters: Why did the album take so long? George had said he'd begun work in September 1976, shortly after the "Big Deal" with Warner Bros. Had he kept songs from Little Feat to use on his own album? If so, where were they? Why only five songwriting credits out of ten tracks, with the only sole credit being "Two Trains," which he'd done before on *Dixie Chicken*? Why covers of soul tunes like "I Can't Stand the Rain" and Allen Toussaint's "What Do You Want the Girl to Do" instead of more originals? And where's his slide guitar?

Back in 1977 he told the late Timothy White, writing for *Crawdaddy*, that he'd had problems booking studio time for the project, and he had a musical agenda already set, saying, "The basic emphasis of the solo album will be on the kinds of tunes I try to get through on as an individual within the band. 'Long Distance Love' [a ballad from *The Last Record Album*] was close to the type of thing I'll be doing, because it was not really group-oriented. The record will contain original material, with one or two all-out rockers by other people. I really like Jackson Browne's 'Doctor My Eyes,' for instance."

By the time the album was out, Browne's song was also out. George told Erskine of *NME* that he'd long wanted to record "I Can't Stand the Rain" and "What Do You Want the Girl to Do." When Erskine asked why there was so little of his bottleneck on the album, he responded with a question: "Yes, but what did you think of the singing?"

In fact, George's singing sounded slick and soulful on several ballads. When he and Little Feat were in Tokyo in March 1978, he sat for an interview on the Far East Network with T. E. Mattox. There he named Marvin Gaye and Stevie Wonder as two of his favorite musicians. "I'd crawl on my hands and knees to beat on his shoes with a pair of sticks," he said about Wonder. He said he'd met Gaye once at a session, and Gaye dropped his work to talk with George for some fifteen minutes. "What he's writing about in his songs is honesty. I try real hard to do the same thing."

"The Japanese have an expression, '*Gom-bah-ru*,'" said George. "Don't quit—do your best."

But his best, this time out, would not be all that good. The album reached only number seventy-one on the *Billboard* album charts.

No matter. George had done his best under difficult circumstances, given his health problems, back surgery, and sore Feats. In a way, *Thanks, I'll Eat It Here* was a respite from all that and was, in some ways, a family affair.

In his typically rambling and incomplete liners, in which he admitted to forgetting some of the contributors, he made certain to say, "This is all for Liz." He noted that "20 Million Things" had a cocredit for his eight-year-old stepson, Jed, who had received a tape recorder as a Christmas present. Jed and a friend began singing into it, and one day, when they were playing a tape, George heard giggling, along with the line, "I've got twenty million things to do, but I'm only thinking of you." As for his daughter, Inara, at three and a half, George said, she "started singing silly songs in a limousine with Little Feat. Maybe she's motivated by artistic jealousy. Anyway, maybe she'll have something on the next album."

Longtime Little Feat fan and rock journalist Barney Hoskyns, while calling the record "a typical L.A. album of the time . . . all very Boz Scaggs-ish," pointed to "20 Million Things" as the best song on the album, "as good as 'Willin'' or 'Long Distance Love' or any of Lowell's other great ballads."

In *Rolling Stone*, reviewer Alan Platt panned the album as a "strangely faceless collection of tunes." With all the help George had—he thanked forty-two musicians, including himself, in his liner notes—the result, Platt wrote, "sounds like the product of a committee." The closest things to Little Feat—a new version of "Two Trains" and "Honest Man," which he wrote with Fred Tackett—struck the critic as "leaden." The two standout tracks were novelties, a mariachi send-up, "Cheek to Cheek," which Platt dismissed as a "throwaway," and "Himmler's Ring," a Jimmy Webb composition that Platt liked, calling it "One of those perverse quickies that satirize a syrupy style with a sick lyric."

George, who acted as producer of his own album, hardly intended to create any throwaways. As Linda Ronstadt recalled, when she and Wendy Waldman had shown up at one of his sessions, "Cheek to Cheek" was the song he was working on. "We were in there with him for a whole day and a night," she said, "and he kept changing the parts. They were incredibly complicated parts, and then he would change them just a little bit . . . what I didn't realize but I think Lowell had bipolar disorder. But he would change it in some little tiny way, and we would learn it that way and record it, and then he'd say, 'No, I'm changing it to this . . . ' and then we'd record it another way, and we worked on this song all night long. I remember somebody at some point called . . . there was Mo and Lenny over there, Lenny and . . . Teddy Templeman . . . I think he was involved in that record, he was trying to produce it . . . somebody called Teddy and he had to come over and just lock Lowell out of that studio, because he'd been in there night and day for like several days . . . without sleeping or anything." Again, said Dr. Ronstadt, "that's another symptom of bipolar disorder."

Appearing on WHCN in West Hartford, George spoke about "Cheek to Cheek." After the DJ played the song, George expounded on his serious excursion into Mexican mariachi music. He credited Van Dyke Parks for turning him on to the Mexican singer, composer, and actor Miguel Aceves Mejía—and made a tongue-in-cheek accusation that Browne had ripped him off for his own south-of-the-border song, "Linda Paloma."

(George enjoyed being on the radio. He affected an exaggerated announcer's voice, à la George Carlin or Ted Baxter, as he read a weather forecast or a commercial. At one point, he sang along with the jingle for Michelob beer.)

Rolling Stone was on George's side, and even a bruising review like Platt's concluded with compliments on George's singing and voice. "It's still the perfect rock instrument—lyrical, expressive and assured," the critic wrote. "But it's almost wasted here" on this "featureless" album. "The obvious conclusion is Little Feat is Lowell George's truest identity. Some bands were just meant to be together."

When that review appeared in June of 1979, George must have felt pretty certain that they were meant to be apart. By then, he had a new band. He had called on Fred Tackett in May, and within a month an eight-piece band, including singer Maxine Dixon, who'd appeared on the album, was set to go. "We got a band of New Orleans dudes that I played with in a club on weekends," said Tackett. "Lowell came down and basically hired everybody." Besides Tackett, the lineup included Peter Wasner and Eddie Zip on keyboards, Armando Compean on bass, Don Heffington on drums, and Lee Thornberg (from Tower of Power) and Jerry Jumonville on horns.

George told reporters that his contract with Warner Bros. called for him to perform a minimum of twenty-one shows "to get the right degree of promotional support" for his album, but on the tour that was mapped out for him, he would not come close to meeting that requirement. It began with a show and a radio interview in Chicago on June 15, followed by mixed radio and club appearances going to the end of the month. He and the band played in Providence and West Hartford, Connecticut, before heading to New York for two evenings at the Bottom Line. After a stop in Philadelphia for a radio show, George would perform in Browns Mills, New Jersey, before heading to Washington, DC, and the comfy confines of the Lisner Auditorium. According to Gene Vano, the band would wrap up the tour with stops in Richmond, Virginia, and Atlanta, Georgia. They would have done only nine or ten shows.

(Vano was no fan of Warner Bros. around the time of George's solo tour. Warner Brothers, he said, had a stingy promotional budget, recalling, "They gave me five thousand little yellow buttons that said, 'Thanks, I'll eat it here.' And that's all they gave us.")

Lowell arrived into Washington, DC, on a high. They loved Little Feat—and him—there. He'd just scored a nice review in the *New York Times*, despite the fact that he had a cold—"a wicked cold," Vano said. But he made the shows at the Bottom Line and, on June 28, did a strong show at the Lisner, mixing Little Feat favorites with songs from his solo album. Feat fare included "Fat Man," "Rocket in My Pocket," "A Apolitical Blues," "Dixie Chicken," "Roll Um Easy," "Spanish Moon," "Willin'," and "Two Trains." New songs included "I Can't Stand the Rain," "Easy Money," "What Do You Want the Girl to Do," and "20 Million Things."

It comes from confusion
All the things I've left undone
—"TWENTY MILLION THINGS," L. GEORGE AND J. LEVY

THE NEXT DAY, June 29, around the time that most people were getting up or arriving at work, Lowell George hit the sack in the suite he was sharing with Elizabeth and Inara at the Twin Bridges hotel in Arlington, Virginia, across the Potomac from Washington, DC.

At age thirty-four, he would have only a few more hours of life. As with everything about George, reports vary regarding his last hours, his death, and the cause of death.

The official word was that he had died of heart failure. The *New York Times* called it a heart attack. Quoting someone from George's management firm, the *Times* said he had been up until eight in the morning "doing interviews," went to bed, "and woke up two hours later complaining of shortness of breath and chest pains." Elizabeth called for help, "but by the time medical aid arrived a half-hour later, Mr. George was dead."

Elizabeth says that her husband was not in good shape during the tour: "He was very overweight, and he was very sick—like a bronchitis chest infection . . . taking over-the-counter medication to try to keep himself able to perform." Traveling to Washington, she said, "he was curled up in the back of the bus, barely conscious."

The show had to go on, and it did—triumphantly. But she was in fear. "I was always concerned about his health, to the point that it got to be like, 'Can we do this anymore? If you don't care, how can I care?' I mean, I didn't give up, but . . . let me put it this way: the day before he died we had a conversation, and he said, 'I know I need help, and when I get home I will get help.' Because I said that was required. And home he never got."

Because he was Lowell George, a rock artist with a hedonistic reputation, the official cause of death came to be challenged—drugs had to be involved. Bill Flanagan of *Musician* magazine, who interviewed him only days before his death and described their conversation as "rambling and sometimes revelatory," noted, "He was overweight, overtired, and had a bad cold for which he was taking antihistamines. He was also inhaling lots of cocaine."

I asked Elizabeth about such talk. "I'm not going to comment on that," she said.

Perhaps the only person who was with George most of that night, from after the Lisner show to his return to his hotel room, was Gene Vano, his faithful road manager and driver. George's first post-concert activity was to go backstage for interviews with two reporters, Joanne Ostrow, a *Washington Post* reporter who was freelancing for a small magazine called *Washington Rock Concert*, and the late David McQuay, a writer from the *Baltimore News American*. Ostrow remembered George sounding upbeat, mentioning his review in the *New York Times* of his Bottom Line appearance, in which critic Robert Palmer wrote, "He is singing strongly and confidently and playing dramatic slide guitar, and he is getting performances of his music that are tighter and more idiomatic than those Little Feat usually delivered." Palmer (not the British singer but rather the *Times*' chief pop critic) was, in childhood in Arkansas, a buddy of Fred Tackett. He had singled out Tackett and saxophonist Jumonville and concluded about George: "He has a personality and style all his own, so that instead of attempting to recreate traditional idioms, he reinvents them. We need more of this, and we need more of Mr. George, and soon."

Ostrow recalls George telling her that he was having more fun playing with his band than with Little Feat. He talked a bit about song lyrics, and he addressed his health issues. "I'm having to be really careful of my health," he said, with Elizabeth's warnings perhaps echoing in his head. "I still drink straight alcohol, but not a quart at a sitting, and I won't try to stay awake for five nights in a row."

But one night? Maybe so. Vano, who'd driven George through three tours as they shared the motor home, knew George could handle it. "His overall health was great," he said. "He was the strongest human being that I knew. Even at 250 pounds—and he was about five-eight—he could jump in the air and do kicks [which George enjoyed doing, onstage with his fellow Feats], so I never worried about him long term." I asked Vano, who was a young man at the time (he now operates a travel agency in the Los Angeles area), to take me through the night as best as he could. We began with Lowell George, after completing his interviews backstage at the Lisner Auditorium.

Gene: He went to a party. In Washington, DC, Little Feat was king, and everybody wants to give you drugs. Some of that went down. He liked white wine, he liked his brandy. . . . I honestly don't remember the time frame—whether I was with him at the party—I know I certainly wasn't in the "secret room," which is what they called the places where the drugs were going down. I didn't worry about him because, like I said, he was the strongest human being I'd ever met. He was like an Iron Man . . .

Ben: When you say "party," I'm thinking about, like, the scene in *Almost Famous*, where fans have a house party and invite whoever they have just heard onstage . . .

Gene: That's what it was. But we played Washington, DC, a lot, so we had almost, like, family there. Some of our crew came from Washington and lived there . . . and their friends and girlfriends . . . so the party was a mix of those and fans.

Ben: You mentioned a secret room . . .

Gene: Well, the secret room was any place where the guys who did drugs would sneak off to go and do the drugs. There could be a secret room backstage . . .

Ben: And you've heard there was talk about how hard the drugs were that Lowell might have imbibed, but you guys did work, on the *King Biscuit Radio Show.*

Gene: Lowell could do drugs and drink and function.

Ben: Gene, what do you say to the talk that he might have taken hard drugs that night, like heroin?

Gene: Heroin? He did it. Why, is there a question that he didn't?

Ben: Well, there are a lot of people saying No, this is just a heart attack . . .

Gene: Well, okay . . . I didn't see him take anything. Like I said, most of the time he did drugs it was to stay awake and keep writing.

When he came back . . . I'm not sure if I brought him back to the hotel . . . his wife Elizabeth and his daughter were in the room with him. . . . The reason he was up and about, he went to parties but didn't party like other people do, to get silly and stupid. He did drugs so he wouldn't sleep. He liked to be able to keep doing things.

One of the things we were working on that night was the *King Biscuit Flower Hour,* which we were going to do in two days. We had a day off, then we were gonna drive to Richmond, Virginia, where the *King Biscuit Hour* was going to do the whole hour of Lowell's show. We were on the phone back to Los Angeles, 'cause George Massenberg was going to fly out as the engineer. California was three hours [behind] us, and it was midnight there, and we talked to George. I said to Lowell, 'I'm gonna go down to the coffee shop.' [It was open twenty-four hours.] And we went down and had something. I don't remember if it was breakfast—you know the rock 'n' roll lifestyle. And then I think he went up to his room.

So I sat in the restaurant and read the *Wall Street Journal*, and when I finally got tired I went up to my room. . . . A few minutes later Liz was knocking on my door and saying, 'Gene, you've got to help me. . . . Lowell is having problems breathing. And I can't turn him over. One of his arms is under him, and he's struggling to breathe, and I can't budge him.' I went in and rolled him over. His face was full of mucus, so she cleaned his face, and he seemed to be breathing easier, so back into my room I went. Twenty minutes later she comes over: 'Gene, he's not breathing,' so I try to give him CPR. I was compressing his chest, and the EMTs came in with the clappers. . . . They worked on him, and they weren't there two minutes, and they said, 'There's nothing we can do,' and they began packing.

Vano was in hysterics, trying to get the technicians to give George another try. Soon, at the Arlington Hospital, he was declared dead. Suddenly it was Vano's job to let people know what had happened and to coordinate transportation home for the musicians, crew members, and George's family.

On June 29 Inara George was five days shy of turning five. "I was there when he died," she said. "I do have a recollection of that day." She paused. "I remember . . . it was traumatic, the excitement, I know it sounds odd, there was something about it that was so different. I remember my mother, in shock, she couldn't wake him up, getting help. And I remember another member of the band, he was the drummer . . . Don." Years later, when Inara had become a musician, she found herself in need of a drummer. "And somebody gave me his name, and he called me back, and he told me the story of how he had taken care of me that day." It was Don Heffington. "I remembered him vaguely, in the dark recesses of my brain, and he told me the story and it made sense to me—I think I even had a little girl crush on him . . . he sort of watched over me while they were dealing with everything."

Luke, George's son by Patte, was nine years old and had hoped to be on tour with his dad, but his mother told him he'd been invited to go to the San Juan Islands, just off Washington state, where a family friend, the record producer Gary Usher, had a new home. Luke was friends with one of Gary and Susan Usher's kids. "I remember us all watching a movie that night," Luke recalled. "And when I went and crawled into bed, I had a dream, and it was Lowell came to me, and we're in a dark room, and we're holding hands, and he looked at me and he said, 'Luke, I love you, and I will always be with you and around you, and part of your life, but you won't be able to physically hold me anymore.'

"And in the morning I woke up early, and I packed my stuff and put it in my suitcase, and my friend's mom walked in and she was crying, and she said, 'Luke, we've got to take you to the airport.' And I said, 'I know.' And she said, 'What do you mean?' and I said, 'My dad passed.'"

Susan Usher had heard the news on the radio but had said nothing. In Los Angeles Patte got the word from her sister Pam and, with help from Lowell's mother, arranged for Luke's immediate return. "And they put me on a little Cessna, and on a big flight," said Luke. "I landed, and it was surreal—it was like a dream sequence. I remember getting into my mom's car, and she turned and said, 'Luke, your dad has passed.' I remember screaming and crying, then it went black."

Hampton George had not seen his little brother since catching Little Feat when they played in Honolulu. "It was a shock," he said, and worse. "There was an airline strike in Hawaii. I couldn't get back to the Mainland." He had to miss the small, family-only gathering, which included Florence (their mother), Liz, and the children. During the ceremony Lowell George's ashes were scattered from a fishing boat, a final salute to a favorite pastime of his, into the Pacific Ocean. "I think about him," says Hampton, "especially when I'm doing something I know he would enjoy or that we'd done together."

Among Little Feat, his most estranged bandmate was silent at first. One of Bill Payne's first acts was to inquire with the band's accounting firm about George's life insurance and whether the policy adequately covered his family. Hearing that it did not, he next telephoned Linda Ronstadt and began planning a concert. It would feature many of George's musical friends paying tribute to him and raising money for Liz and the children.

When Daisann McLane, who was writing the obituary for *Rolling Stone*, called, Payne said nothing about their disagreements or the band's dissolution. He said he thought George had begun writing more songs, and he spoke about his impact on the Los Angeles music scene. "He surrounded himself with mystery, and that drew people to him," Payne said. "It's amazing how many people that guy touched." He named Emmylou Harris and Rickie Lee Jones as two among many. He concluded with something he'd told George in their last conversation: "Without the pressures of Little Feat, Lowell would have become a very good producer."

Paul Barrere describes himself as being "emotionally devastated" by the news. "Death is a funny thing," he said. "When it happens to you there's that first moment of shock, and then for me there's a feeling of, 'Okay, you have to be kind of responsible through this whole thing . . . you can't just let down or let your emotions go. You have to take the steps that are necessary to get everything back to normal.' When Lowell passed I remember I didn't even cry til after we did the big show at the Forum with Jackson and all those people. And at the end of that show we were all backstage, and I just found a corner and sobbed like a baby for a while."

A few years younger than George, Barrere considered Lowell a mentor, from those first tryouts for Little Feat to the last albums. "I wouldn't say [he was] a life mentor, but musically he gave me so much to work with, broadened my horizons. And we had a lot of fun together on the road. I mean, Lowell and I, we partied a lot together."

Roy Estrada, the original Feats bassist, spoke from his Texas state prison. He was "devastated" when he got the word, he said. "He seemed like he was in good health, other than being so overweight. He must have been working hard, just like Frank. That's what got

Frank." But when I began asking about George and drugs, the line went dead. I would learn that it was not authorities at the prison who terminated our conversation but rather Estrada. Instead of saying something like "No comment" or "I don't know," he simply hung up, ending our interview after some twenty minutes.

Richie Hayward heard the bad news about his former brother-in-law while in traction in a hospital. He had suffered another motorcycle accident; this one took place just before George's solo tour began. Hayward, in fact, was riding home from visiting the new band during rehearsals at the Paramount Ranch in Agoura Hills, west of Los Angeles, where Little Feat had done some recording for *Down on the Farm*. According to Payne, Hayward was navigating a curving road when "some kids speeding by in a car yelled something at Richie, who turned to take a look and drove the bike into a huge rock." The drummer suffered a crushed femur and tibia—and an insult as well. As Hayward remembered, "While I was laying on the side of the road, a couple of guys pulled over and said, 'We don't think you're going to need this,' and they threw my motorcycle in the back of their pickup truck and took off. I think it was really my guardian angel with a sense of humor.

"Two weeks after the accident Lowell died. My first marriage was going down the tubes, and I felt robbed. I wasn't even able to play the memorial concert for Lowell." Hayward was out of commission for a year.

Kenny Gradney got a call from Vano. "He told me that Lowell had passed away. I went, 'Okay.' I hung up the phone and went back to bed. My wife goes, 'What was that?' I said Lowell died. And that was it." What more was there to say? Now, thinking back, Gradney reflects, "That broke my heart. I was down for about a year. He was on his way up, and he really didn't want to go. But he was apprehensive about fame, like anybody else who runs from it. But he was a great guy."

George, Gradney said, had a huge impact on him. "Musically, he changed the way I looked at rock 'n' roll, because we played it totally different . . . we didn't play it like any other rock 'n' roll bands."

Sam Clayton says he was out of the loop about the band's break-up, even though he considered himself close friends with George. "We roomed next to each other a lot," he said. "I used to go to his house. We'd hang out and talk about women, martial arts, Indian music—everything."

The night before he died, Clayton said, George phoned him. "He called me from the road. He said, 'Look, man,' and he was high—I knew he was high. 'Just hang out man, don't worry, you're in. When I get back, we're gonna get this thing restarted,' and, see, I didn't know they broke up like that. . . . I just thought we were on a little hiatus, just hangin' for awhile.

"And then they called me the next day. Man, I couldn't believe it. . . . I couldn't even respond. . . . No tears or nothin'—just shock. And I'm wondering, what's wrong with me, how can I . . . then after you think about it, later on, you think about it, and you're *gone*."

Fred Tackett offers an anecdote with a punch line that could elicit both laughter and sadness: "Right before he died we were driving down the highway on the New Jersey turnpike, and there was this pizza joint. I remember the entire band bought one cheese pizza and shared it, and Lowell bought one with everything on it, and sat in the back of the bus and ate the whole thing." This would have been after the two evenings in New York, when the band was heading to perform on WMMR, a progressive rock station in Philadelphia. "And after he died," said Tackett, "everybody was speculating about this or that, and I was just being facetious, but I said, 'I'll tell you what killed him: it was the pizza on the New Jersey Turnpike.'"

Bonnie Raitt maintained her friendship with George and the band through the years. She toured with them, expanding the audiences for both, and took turns as the closing, headlining act. "It looked like he wasn't really taking care of himself," she said, "'cause he was kind of expanding. I also knew that a lot of us were dipping into some stuff that came at a cost, and I was happy to hear that at some point he'd cleaned up his act and absolutely heartbroken to find out that he had slipped. Nobody can carry that much weight and booze and smoke and stay that high without there being some kinda health implications." She paused and added, with a laugh: "Unless you're Keith Richards, clearly."

Rolling Stone asked several musicians to offer remarks about George. Raitt praised both the man and his band. "Little Feat was one of the most innovative bands ever," she said. "I mean, once you get Feats-itis, you never get rid of it." As for George, the words that came to mind were "fire and ability," she said. "In the end, I guess, he paid for his true genius by having poor health. But I want to say— and this is not just being said in a moment of emotion—that he was the best singer, songwriter and guitar player I have ever hard, hands down, in my life. I don't expect to hear another like him."

Ted Templeman, who'd become close pals with George since meeting on Little Feat's second album, got a call from Liz George. "It was horrible. I honestly couldn't speak," he said of the phone call. Templeman had come to enjoy phone conversations with a few close friends, among them Lenny Waronker and George. "Every night I would talk to Lenny or Lowell, or both." With George, "a lot of it was politics, but he would talk music too. He'd talk about every-thing . . . he liked Led Zeppelin, he liked the Beatles, and I think he was always trying to find his way."

Linda Ronstadt spoke with George just days before he died. "He was someplace on the road, traveling with Inara and Liz," she re-called, "and he wanted to ask me about something—can't remember what it was—and that's the last time I talked to him. About two days later he was gone. We lost a lot of people in those days, but for me, that was the worst one, because no matter what, Lowell, we loved ya. We just loved him! He was so charming and smart, and he'd just get up and play the best song you ever heard, and sing it better than anybody you ever heard sing, and then just tell you some funny story and commit some incredible act of generosity."

George's charm could cut two ways, though. Martin Kibbee, his childhood buddy and erstwhile writing partner, was shocked by the news. "I thought he was virtually indestructible," he said. "If he had a problem, we all had a problem to some extent. Looking back on it now, I can see that it was more serious than we thought. And who knew? I think I was not alone in not perceiving it as a problem. And the guy had tremendous charm and, by then, was certainly dismissive of any criticism. I was probably more interested in participating than criticizing."

Rolling Stone magazine's coverage of George's death took up a full page and portions of three more, but he didn't get the cover photo. That spot had been planned, ironically, for one of the musicians he helped bring to the fore, Rickie Lee Jones. The singer-songwriter with the Beat sensibility was upset at the coincidence. "It just felt like doom," she said. "I mean, why does the obituary have to be on the . . . why does he have to die as I rise?"

In San Francisco the mourners for Lowell George included Lynn Hearne, the teenager who'd gotten George to sign his first autograph ever, thirteen years ago, after the Freak Out at the Shrine Hall in Los Angeles. She was at work in the office of Rip Off Press, the hip comic book publisher in San Francisco, when her boyfriend called with the news. "I went home, cried my eyes out, and later on, I went to KSAN." Little Feat had lots of supporters there, and several of the DJs knew the girl called "Shag." She knew that Tony Kilbert would be on the air, and so she showed up unannounced. "I knocked on the door, and he said, 'I knew you were coming. I knew I'd see you tonight.' He put on a long cut, threw his arm around me, and held me."

"What do you want to hear?" he asked.

She responded, "Some Howlin' Wolf—for Lowell."

Chapter 13

FROM THE FORUM TO THE FARM

ALL THOSE FRIENDS AND FANS OF LOWELL GEORGE'S GATHERED FOR his family on the night of August 4 at the Forum, the go-to site of major musical events in Los Angeles.

After Payne's initial call to Ronstadt, he and Barrere began hearing from other musicians offering to perform. The result would be a gathering of glittery LA rock stars and members of the Feats Auxiliary, including Jackson Browne, Emmylou Harris, Bonnie Raitt, Fred Tackett, Nicolette Larson, Fran Tate (now married to Payne), Michael McDonald and Patrick Simmons of the Doobie Brothers, and the Tower of Power horns.

To supplement Little Feat, which anchored one of six segments, and to back up the other featured acts, Ted Templeman joined in on percussion and Jerry Jumonville, from George's tour band, chipped in on saxophone. Feats insiders might have noticed that for Larson's opening set, her backup was the band Payne and Barrere had put together, the one that, as George had ruefully noted, was getting media attention. They included Rick Shlosser on drums (effectively subbing for Hayward), Bob Glaub on bass, Bobby LaKind on congas, and

Craig Fuller, the singer and guitarist from Pure Prairie League who would have a major role with a future Little Feat.

Later there was talk that the Eagles, Bob Dylan (who had met George), and other megastars were turned away because they were too late with their offers to play. Said Payne: "If they expressed interest, it never reached my ears. I think that would have been absolutely fine . . . but I kind of shut it off at one point, but certainly not to people like that." Payne delegated some of the booking duties to others, "and they might have pretty rightfully said, 'Hey look, it's all pretty well lined up.'"

Payne hosted rehearsals at his home in the Valley, and everybody showed up. "In fact," he noted, "Linda Ronstadt came out there with Governor Jerry Brown."

Performers were told that although the evening would be recorded and videotaped, there would be no attempt to market it. "This really wasn't done for money or grandstanding," Payne told *Rolling Stone* a few days after the concert. "The reason we were all here is because Lowell George had brought us together during his life. He wasn't as well-known as some of the people who were there that night, but he'd influenced each and every one of us."

On that summer night at the "Fabulous Forum," as it was called, some twenty thousand fans gathered for the tribute. Onstage the performers moved smoothly in and out of the spotlight, forming groups of lead and backup vocalists and any number of combinations of musicians.

True to the spirit of the man, his friends put on a happy face, which wasn't easy only five weeks after his death. But these were seasoned performers, much of the cream of the L.A. music scene, and they were not about to stage a downer. They entertained to the hilt. The petite Larson had on floppy white angels' wings behind her cascade of hair. She and Ronstadt flashed big smiles as they teamed up on Nicolette's "Rhumba Girl."

Also true to the spirit of Lowell George, mostly women composed the forefront. The sets, ranging from three to six songs, featured Linda, Bonnie, Emmylou, and Nicolette, with Little Feat and Browne fronting the other two. Additional vocalists included Fran Tate and

Rosemary Butler, from Browne's troupe. No matter their relative star status, they sang with and behind each other, happily harmonizing behind whoever was up front.

Jackson Browne, who'd become a close friend of George's, performed several songs and spoke before "Your Bright Baby Blues." He mentioned that he'd traveled with Ronstadt and George and that Lowell was the first to play guitar and sing with him on that song. He let the story dissipate and, with eyes glistening, began the song.

There were lighter notes. Raitt, introducing "Rock and Roll Doctor" with Little Feat behind her, told the audience, "People would call out for this one while Lowell was onstage, and Lowell would tell them, 'Rock and Roll Doctor'? You're *looking* at him, sucker!'"

The clear highlight, if only one could be named, was Ronstadt, in the finale segment, performing George's—and her—song, "Willin'." In fact, George, talking with writer Bill Flanagan just a week and a half before his death, had joked about Ronstadt's rendition of his song. "It's pretty good," he said, "except she gets a little bit 'WuhEEED, WuhHITES, AND WuhIIIINE!' Linda was a little bit too on." Well, Ronstadt told me, "He did it when *he* sang it." And she did a perfect reading, without the "Wuhs." The audience screamed at the first notes, as though the song was some kind of a hit, and Ronstadt, flanked by Emmylou, Nicolette, and Rosemary, carried it home, sometimes both singing and smiling through tears. It was the most emotional moment of the evening. As Payne told Daisann McLane of *Rolling Stone*, "That's when the tears started to come. My wife started to cry and looked at Linda, and she was crying, too."

Of thirty-four songs performed that evening, Lowell George had written only seven. His songs, Payne would say, were too complicated for the musicians to tackle many of them. And so the women did tunes fans associated them with, although Raitt did perform "Rock and Roll Doctor" and Larson sang "Trouble." Emmylou Harris stuck to her own songs, though she did ignite the audience when she sang "Love Hurts" for the first time in public since the death of Gram Parsons, a close friend of hers and another brilliant musician who went too soon.

Early in his set, Browne sang "For a Dancer" for a departed friend who indeed was always "dancing in and out of view" and "keeping things real by playing the clown." "Go on and make a joyful sound," Browne sang.

It was, as was almost always the case with one of his songs, the definitive performance. Until, perhaps, twenty years later, when it appeared on an album, *Western Wall: The Tucson Sessions,* performed by two of the women Lowell George had danced with: Emmylou Harris and Linda Ronstadt. "The world keeps turning around and around," they sang. "Go on and make a joyous sound."

Up on a riser, flanked by his keyboards, Bill Payne was focused on the music throughout the evening while keeping an eye out to ascertain that the personnel transitions were running smoothly. (Barrere, in a wide-brimmed straw hat, took care of emcee duties.) "It was sold out . . . it was a big, big deal. And I, at the very tail end of it when we were all in the dressing room, I just kinda broke down, we gave each other a hug. . . . It just was draining."

The concert grossed an estimated $230,000, and after expenses, proceeds went to Elizabeth and the George family. Said Liz: "It was a wonderful celebration of the man and his music, and it was very helpful to the family." But, she added, "It was a long time coming to grips, with mourning and moving on, for me."

SOON ENOUGH THE SURVIVORS went back to work. They had to. There was an album to be produced and delivered.

The band had begun work on it in April, around the same time that George had had his showdowns with Payne. But—and not for the first time—the band worked through the fussin' and fightin' and laid down enough music for George to begin mixing.

In the face of accusations that he was keeping songs from Little Feat, George contributed the most songs he'd had on an album since *Dixie Chicken* back in 1973. He wrote or cowrote five of the nine songs, including two with Payne ("Straight from the Heart" and "Front Page News"), one each with Tackett ("Be One Now") and Keith Godchaux ("Six Feet of Snow," from his stint with the Dead), and one on his own, "Kokomo," a sassy celebration of a young woman ("They call her Miss Demeanor").

Barrere, perceived to have taken the reins, along with Payne, of Little Feat an album or two ago, cowrote two songs, "Perfect Imperfection" with Tom Snow, and the title cut, "Down on the Farm," which he wrote with his son, Gabriel. Payne contributed "Wake Up Dreaming," which had his wife, Fran Tate, as cowriter. And Sam Clayton, the percussionist, earned a songwriting credit for the jam number "Feel the Groove." Although Gordon De Witty, the keyboard player and arranger who was part of the creation of "Spanish Moon," shares the credit, Clayton says that the song was not the product of a jam session. "It was done with Lowell, with us," he said. "He used to come over to my house all the time, so we just started writing this tune, and I said, 'Man, I've never done that,' and he said, 'Well, it's about time you did this and get your name on some music as writer.' I said okay. And that's how 'Feel the Groove' started."

By this time in the production process, George had been dreaming about building a mobile recording studio for himself. A couple of tape decks in a bus didn't quite cut it, and he liked the idea of recording music outside a conventional studio and running the controls and doing mix-downs in a truck. That's what he had set up at the Paramount Ranch, where Wally Heider, a prominent studio owner in Hollywood and San Francisco, provided a mobile recording truck. The plan was that the band would lay down instrumental tracks at the ranch, and the truck would then be transported to George's home in Topanga, allowing him to record the vocals there.

To Payne, this was a "mess," and his dismay was what led him to propose that he get to coproduce the album with George. "I would walk out into the main room," he remembered, "and there would be a microphone not even close to the amp. There wasn't a real 'room sound' there that I recall—nobody was paying attention. That just drove me completely over the edge. . . . I kept thinking, *What are we doing? We deserve better than this.*" When he was rejected, he made his mind up to quit. "*Down on the Farm* was the last straw—I hit the wall."

Others had lighter moments recording at George's home. Fred Tackett remembers working on the song they had written together, "Be One Now": "Lowell and I were trying to do an acoustic guitar part in the living room, next to a swimming pool, and this frog was makin' all this noise." That led to them making the frog part of another song—the title cut, in fact.

"At the very beginning of the album you hear Lowell coming out and talkin' to these frogs and stuff. You hear 'Ribbitt,' and then Lowell goes, 'Shaddap.' 'Ribbit' . . . 'Shaddup.'"

But George left all the frogs and everything else he'd recorded behind as he went off to his solo tour, never to return. It was up to Barrere and Payne, along with engineers, to complete the project. They found themselves with demos—but not finished versions—of George's vocals, with pieces of songs and early takes on his guitar parts. Some said that theirs was a rescue mission. In some cases they had to guess what George wanted songs to sound like in their completed forms. "I don't think we took that approach, that this was how he wanted it to sound like," Barrere said; instead, they came up with their own inventions. "For Instance, the slide that I did on 'Straight from the Heart,' Billy kind of coached me through it because he wanted a dual slide part, with a kind of harmony to it, which was fine. . . . I understand that [David] Lindley played some slide on it. But once again, it wasn't embarrassing."

George had left a scratch vocal—an early demo—on Barrere and Snow's song "Perfect Imperfection." While George would no doubt have recut it, Barrere and company decided it was "great. And then we brought in Bonnie to add some background vocals on that one. And it was sweet." In summary, he said, "I thought we made the best of a bad situation. There's some seriously funky grooves in that record too. And I wasn't even around when they did 'Front Page News.' But that whole track knocks my socks off."

Overall, Barrere told *Rolling Stone*, shortly before the album's release, he and fellow Feats made only a few changes here and there. "The band finished this album for Lowell," he said, "and because of that, it's probably gonna sound more like a group project than if Lowell were still alive." Payne acknowledged that *Down on the Farm* would not be the same album with George completing it. "It's not a perfect album, but the stuff he did is . . . great. There are cuts, too, that will bridge that personal feeling about Lowell George. And I'm quite anxious for people to hear that it's not a jazz-blues album at all. In fact, there are so many styles that this album is almost a revamp of *Sailin' Shoes*."

It was also another, perhaps final tribute to Lowell George. Several of his solo band members lent an instrument, including horn players Jumonville and Thornberg, along with Tackett and, on backing vocals, three friends who'd been at the Forum concert: Raitt, Fran Tate, and Rosemary Butler. Guitarists Robben Ford, "Sneaky Pete" Kleinow, and David Lindley, and drummer Earl Palmer also played.

The credit for the producer went to "Lowell George . . . with a little help from his friends," and the liner notes, signed "Little Feat," were all in capital letters, in contrast to George's writings, which went without capitalization and other grammatical niceties. This, the writer said, was the "real *Last Record Album*." The signoff read, "This is from us all to Lowell, straight from the heart. Good-bye, friend. Be free."

Neon Park was called, once again, for the album cover art. This time, he came up with a towel-headed female duck with ruby red lips, in a robe and nylon hosiery, lounging with a mint julep by a swimming pool, doing her nails while, across the way, a tiger rested with his own cocktail. In the tradition of Little Feat albums, there was talk that there had been another title considered for the album: *Duck Lips*.

Rolling Stone did not publish a review of the album. In the *New York Times* Robert Palmer, who wrote the positive notice of George's solo set at the Bottom Line, noted that "even in concert, Little Feat sometimes sounded schizophrenic. So it's a pleasant surprise to find that while *Down on the Farm* is a little schizophrenic, on the whole it's the kind of album Mr. George probably would have wanted it to be.

"It's very much an album of songs, with none of the longish solos and other experiments that often seemed out of place on Little Feat albums in the past."

Palmer liked most of the songs, calling "Kokomo" a "clever blues" and stating that "Be One Now," cowritten by Tackett, was "a lovely case of special pleading." He cared less for "Feel the Groove" and the "Steely Dan-like instrumental breaks and arrangement on 'Front Page News.' . . . For the most part, *Down on the Farm* does the band proud."

Released in November 1979, just in time for the holidays, *Down on the Farm* surpassed all previous Feats albums except *Waiting for Columbus*. It reached number eighteen on the *Billboard* album charts and stayed on those charts for seven weeks. But on the singles front Little Feat whiffed again. "Front Page News" failed to make any headlines, even though Warner Bros. released it twice. Little Feat, in its time with Lowell George, went oh-for-nine.

In the months before George's death Payne and Barrere had formed a new band, ostensibly to back Nicolette Larson. But not unlike the crew that played behind Linda Ronstadt only to go off and become the Eagles, Payne and Barrere were set to create an offshoot of Feats, with Craig Fuller on vocals, Bob Glaub on bass, and Rich Schlosser on drums. But after George died, the band collapsed. "That took the wind out of our sails," said Payne. Especially after he and others in the band were hired to go on tour with another singer—Linda Ronstadt.

Talking about the completion of *Down on the Farm*, Barrere commented, "Whatever doors were open to any more Little Feat albums are now closed." And Payne added, "Little Feat just does not exist without Lowell."

Those were words he would take back. But not for many years.

Chapter 14

LET IT ROLL, AGAIN

ONE OF LINDA RONSTADT'S FONDEST MEMORIES IS OF A GATHER-
ing in September 1973 at the musician and producer Al Kooper's
house in Atlanta after Little Feat had performed there. There, Lowell
George sang "China White," a paean to a painkiller or, as a *Rolling
Stone* critic would put it, a "tribute to heroin."

> *So cast away, cast away*
> *From this ball full of pain*
> *For it sinks beneath the waves*

"I thought it was staggeringly good," she said. "I still like it the
best of anything he's ever written. If you really want to analyze how
he structures the tuning and how he builds a melody on the tuning,
just listen to 'China White' with just him playing."

And then she wondered out loud: "Did he record it ever?" She
was pleased to learn that it had been included in an album called
Hoy-Hoy!

Around 1975, when he was in Baltimore with Little Feat, recording
at the Blue Seas Studio, George Massenburg, the engineer, remembers

Lowell George recording a Hank Williams song called "Lonesome Whistle." That, he said, may have been for George's solo album. If so, it would've been one of the first songs he considered. Regardless, it got lost and never made it into the solo project. According to Payne, "Liz found this version in a brown paper bag in the back of their garage." It too made it onto *Hoy-Hoy!*

"China White" and "Lonesome Whistle" were two of the rarities, obscurities, live cuts, and brand new songs that helped make up the nineteen-track, two-record set called *Hoy-Hoy!*, released in 1981.

Despite what he had said about Little Feat no longer existing without George, Bill Payne wasn't ready to let go. He went to Mo Ostin, head of Warner Bros., with an idea for a Feats anthology. The band had fulfilled its contractual obligations; it had gone from stiffs to solid gold. But, he said, it had not had a chance to bid farewell to its fans or to its founder and leader. Ostin gave him the go-ahead, and Payne got to work, with Barrere and Massenburg alongside.

Hoy-Hoy! didn't pretend to be a collection of greatest hits, as Little Feat didn't have any. It spanned old and rare ("Teenage Nervous Breakdown" in both a live and a studio version) and brand new (Payne's "Gringo" and Barrere's autobiographical "Over the Edge").

Payne and company put together an entertaining package, clearly aimed at existing fans. There were collages of Neon Park artwork, from Little Feat covers and from his days as a poster artist; reviews of Little Feat in foreign languages; and photos of the band, from younger, slimmer days to a shot of them doing high kicks on stage.

The liners included comments about every track—from band members, from Kibbee, from Massenburg, and from Elizabeth George. She traced "China White" back to the early seventies ("possibly even earlier"), saying it was one of those songs George "never felt could be rendered properly with the band" so he recorded it on his own. She ended with a not-so-subtle remark about one of her husband's nastier habits: "I think it was probably rather easy for him to write, if you know what I mean." (That last line was excised from the CD version of *Hoy-Hoy!*)

Rarities included "Framed," from the post-Factory, pre-Feats sessions of 1969, outtakes from the band's performances for *Waiting for Columbus*, Ronstadt's rendition of "All That You Dream" at the Forum tribute to George, and radio broadcast versions of "The Fan" (full title: "When the Shit Hits the Fan") and "Rock and Roll Doctor" from 1974. The latter was doctored in various studios afterward, with Allen Toussaint helping add horns at his studios in New Orleans.

Toussaint first met Little Feat when they toured together in 1975. Then best known as a composer and pianist, Toussaint was promoting his first album, *Southern Nights*. By then he'd had his song "On Your Way Down" included on *Dixie Chicken* in 1973, but he didn't know about that. Songwriters, he said, often are the last to know about other artists covering their material. Toussaint was aware of George in 1974, when they each had two songs on Robert Palmer's *Sneaking Sally Through the Alley*, but they met on the road. He recalled George as "a heartfelt man who was wide awake to emotions around him." Although he was seven years older than George, Toussaint became one of the many who George mentored, saying, "He gave me some encouraging words early on. When I went out to do that tour, that was new for me. I had spent all my time in the studio, never going out and being front-stage center."

Toussaint found it nerve wracking. "And Lowell saw that I was really torn about whether I was doing the right thing on the stage, and should I be there or not," he recalled. "And he told me such comforting words, and he told me, 'With so many wonderful things you've done, you shouldn't have to worry about it.' It was a really edgy time for me, and as simple as that was, it changed the next day . . . it worked."

Hoy-Hoy! received a lengthy review in *Rolling Stone*, written by the *New York Times*' Jon Pareles, who offered a brief band history as well as his assessments. He would have liked more demos and early Feats cuts as well as fewer repeats from previous albums, he wrote. In the end, though, he understood that "*Hoy-Hoy!* intends to be affectionate, not definitive, not a last gasp but, in the Little Feat tradition, a last laugh." (The title, says Payne, was inspired by Neon Park and could be interpreted either as an echo of a Howlin' Wolf line, "Hoy, hoy, I'm your boy," or "today-today!" in Spanish.)

The collection made the *Billboard* chart, Little Feat's sixth album to do so. But it only stayed two weeks and peaked at number thirty-nine, trailing the others. Payne, for one, has no regrets. It was, he says, "a gift to our fans. I'm still very proud of that record and booklet."

Hoy-Hoy! would be Payne's last connection with Little Feat for many years. He stopped writing songs, and he tried not to think about his old band. "It was too painful," he said. While with the Feats he had played numerous sessions and proven himself to be a creative and popular side man, both in studios and on the road. He spent most of the post-Feat years touring and recording with, among others, Ronstadt, Jackson Browne, Stevie Nicks, and Bob Seger, but primarily with James Taylor. In 1981 he declined a touring offer from the Rolling Stones because of a commitment to Taylor.

Actually, all the members of Little Feat were highly respected, sought-after musicians and had done outside work (of course, they needed to during the lean years). Now each could be as busy as he wanted. But, as Richie Hayward noted, "Some of us were fighting big demons at the time. That was the reason for all the dissension in the band."

As soon as the leg cast was removed after his second bike accident, Hayward was invited to tour with Joan Armatrading, with whom he had recorded an album, *Steppin' Out*. Six months on the road would have to serve as his physical therapy. Shortly after completing the tour he was in the doldrums. "At the point when I was at my lowest, I got the call from Robert Plant. I wasn't getting any work here, and he hired me. He hadn't heard the stories, I guess. I went over there with the determination to put my life back together."

Barrere had also been facing demons. "I fell into a very dark period of drug addiction and was not in a good place at all," he said. His wife, Debbie, had left to return to Baltimore, Lowell George had died, he had no band, and he fell out of contact with all his fellow former Feats. Then one night he got a visit from Payne, warning him to straighten out. "You're going to kill yourself," he said. "I was really touched, but did I straighten out? No."

On recovery he began playing "the chitlin' circuit," he said, with a band called the Blues Busters, headed by Bob "Catfish" Hodge, a native of Detroit and a popular blues bandleader in the DC area. Barrere also played in a side band called Chicken Legs.

Ironically, Barrere was the only Feats member who produced an album under his own name—two, actually. The first, *On My Own Two Feet*, came out in 1983 on a small label, Mirage, and although it didn't sell, it earned him a three-and-a-half-star review in *Rolling Stone*, whose reviewer, Steve Futterman, stated, "Paul Barrere has so perfectly captured the sound of his former band that one could easily mistake his first solo album for a Little Feat LP." The following year a second album, *Real Lies*, didn't do any better.

Sadly, he remembers very little of that time period. "I was barely conscious," he said.

Kenny Gradney hooked up with a band called the Romeos. He next joined Bobby and the Midnights, a band fronted by the Grateful Dead's Bob Weir. He also played with Mick Fleetwood's band, Zoo, with both Fleetwood and Billy Cobham on drums. "I was having a ball," he said.

Meanwhile, Sam Clayton, who'd been looking for a bigger-name band when he signed up with Little Feat, found one: Jimmy Buffett. Actually, he said, "I'd never heard of Jimmy Buffett." Fortunately, Buffett, who'd struck it rich with "Margaritaville" in 1977, knew all about Little Feat. "He loved our band. He loves the song 'Time Loves a Hero.'" Buffett held the Feats in such high regard that he wondered whether Clayton would even join his band. When his tour manager made the approach to Clayton, "I said, 'What are you talkin' about? It's about surviving!'" He had not worked steadily for two years since George's death. Now, he was off on an eight-year ride with Buffett—plenty of cheeseburgers in Paradise.

One day in 1986 Barrere answered his phone. It was the owner of the Alley, a rehearsal facility in North Hollywood that Little Feat had used along with Jackson Browne, Emmylou Harris, Bonnie Raitt, and dozens of others. He was informed that the studio had gone through a remodeling, and the main room had been given a Little Feat motif. The ceiling was given over to a recreation of a Neon Park invention: the somehow-sexy tomato from *Waiting for Columbus*, reclining on a hammock, between two palm trees. In one bathroom a wall mural depicted Lowell George, in a red beret and white overalls, with a guitar slung over his back, whistling as he strolled on a dirt road, near a horse that was about to make an escape over a broken fence.

A plaque on a wall carried a dedication of the room to George.

It was all about Little Feat.

Might the band members be interested or willing to show up and maybe do a jam session, "just to christen the room? Kind of give it that vibe?" Barrere agreed to make some calls. "Everybody was working," he learned, "but it worked out that everybody was in town."

Barrere would not have been surprised if some of the guys declined to show up. A year before, the band had been invited to a jam session at another rehearsal hall, S.I.R., which had numerous connections to Little Feat. Payne recalls everybody agreeing to play. But they walked into a mob scene. "There were so many musicians," Barrere remembered, "and everybody wanted to jam, and it didn't have the feeling of the five of us getting back together and just playing. It just turned into kind of a zoo."

"It was just not conducive to us really digging in," agreed Payne. Also, there was the issue of musical memory loss. "We couldn't remember anything. The material is complex enough to kind of throw us, and my suggestion was, we ought to do this again, but let's pull the crowd out of it and have just the band . . . and see what happens."

At the Alley it was all Feats, and they had a good time. Gradney remembers the evening: "I came in, and I couldn't remember any of the songs, but man, we were rockin'."

But a good jam did not a reunion make. Jimmy Buffett employed Clayton pretty much full time, and on the evening of the Alley jam Gradney got an offer from Warren Zevon's band. Actually, he didn't have one, but by the end of the phone call Gradney and Hayward were all but signed up, without an audition—hey, they'd been with Little Feat. Still, the reunion had gone so well that Payne and Barrere began talking. In 1986, said Barrere, "I'd been sober for about a year. . . . I'm starting to feel a little better about myself." Everybody, he noticed, appeared healthier and more mature than when the band broke up. "It was a no-brainer putting the band back together," he said. "I knew absolutely that I could do it."

Payne, along with Fred Tackett, had been touring with Bob Seger in 1986 and '87, but he was also interested in a full reunion. "We still sounded like Little Feat," he reasoned.

After Hayward, Gradney, and Clayton agreed to give Feats another chance, they began looking for additional members. Barrere would move to lead guitar, and they agreed that Fred Tackett would be natural as an additional guitarist and multi-instrumentalist. During the Seger tour, Tackett remembers, "Billy kept saying, 'I'm going to put Little Feat together, and I want you to play guitar with Paul.' I was like, 'Okay, sign me up.'"

Tackett was born to play music. He was surrounded by it at home in Hot Springs, Arkansas, a resort town famed for decades for its casinos and hangouts for gamblers and gangsters. "My parents," he recalls, "had stacks of Dixieland 78s, and I'd just sit there listening to Kid Ory and Bum Johnson. I used to take a calendar, roll it up, and pretend it was a clarinet while I was a little bitty kid. I'd stand there and pretend to play."

Musically, he was raised on hand-me-down trumpets. His father played, just for fun, and he and Fred's brother, Richard, who also played, taught him. "I had the lowest value trumpet. Every time they'd buy one, they'd all kind of move down."

No matter. Tackett was more interested in drums anyway, and he began playing—until Elvis came along. Fred, now twelve, had to have a guitar, and he had to see Presley when he came to Little Rock. His brother, who liked jazz more than rock 'n' roll, got tickets, and Fred tried talking him out of going himself. "Richard," he asked, "what are you doing going to see Elvis Presley? You don't like Elvis Presley. I love Elvis Presley. Why don't you let me go with your girlfriend?" Fred now knows that he was being . . . twelve. "I didn't understand what the whole agenda was."

Their mother consoled Fred, promising, "The next rock 'n' roll show that comes to town—I'll take you to see it." It was Little Richard.

King, queen—it was rock 'n' roll. "It was like, 'Oh, my God.' It was just the most insane thing I'd ever seen in my life."

By about age sixteen Fred was playing his guitar at night clubs in town and in nearby Little Rock. "Totally illegal," he says. "I was hanging out in the ghetto. Ninth Street in Little Rock was where all the black entertainment clubs were. There was the Tropicana—Gosh, Bobby 'Blue' Bland's band would spend weeks rehearsing there. Me and my friends, we'd sneak down there. They'd let us in the back door."

Once, he had a job at the Beverly Gardens. "This was like a greasy, dirty place—signs on the wall saying NO DIRTY DANC-ING. The cops would come out, and they'd shine a spotlight on me, I was standing there with these two guitar players, blues guys, and he would hold this light on me, and the club owner would go, 'Well, you know, he's a good guitar player, and he's not drinking . . .'

"I'd go, 'Oh, God . . . ' Always havin' to hide, playin' the guitar, kinda get down, don't let anybody see ya—all the way till I was twenty-one."

By that time Tackett had also learned to play trumpet and drums, and he continued his education in college, at North Texas State, be-ginning in 1963. He began working with a saxophone player, Joline Davis, in Dallas, in a quartet that worked every night as a show band. A solid gig at a new nightclub in Oklahoma City inspired Fred to transfer to the university there. "And that was my real education," he said.

For two years, six nights a week, Tackett played four sets of dance music, then some soft jazz. "Then we'd do a floor show in the middle of it, and the floor shows, they'd be like Two Jacks and a Jill, a come-dian, Don Cherry, a singer who had 'Band of Gold,' and we'd have belly dancers, magicians, and they would all have a book of music, like Judy Garland medleys, all this Las Vegas-y stuff, and we got so good at it, we'd sit in the coffee shop, and we'd see the act come in and instead of having a rehearsal, we'd say, 'Meet us half an hour before you come on,' and we'd pull out their music, and we'd sort of sing their part, and the act would stand there and they'd go, 'What in the fuck? . . .' And we were half drunk too and could read all those charts. It was amazing, and it was an incredible education. But that's all I ever wanted to do. I was totally, like, into Ricky Ricardo—I wanted to go to the club."

But that was before Tackett connected with Jimmy Webb in Honolulu, prompting him to move to California, where he got into session work and television variety shows (*Sonny and Cher*, *Donny and Marie*) and met Lowell George.

While performing on television throughout the seventies Tackett found time to head the Feats Auxiliary. Even when he was on other projects, he thought of George. In 1975 Tackett played on an album Webb was producing for Cher, which included rock and blues numbers like Neil Young's "Mr. Soul" and Eric Clapton's "Bell Bottom Blues." "We said, 'Let's do one of Lowell's songs, so Lowell can get some of the money,' and we got a version of Cher singing 'Rock and Roll Doctor.'" Sad to say, the album stiffed. "So all Lowell had was people coming up and saying, 'Wow, I heard Cher singing 'Rock and Roll Doctor,' and he didn't get anything out of it."

Now Tackett was willing to give up the lucrative world of session work to be a Little Feat. But who would be the lead vocalist?

In the later years of Little Feat Barrere and Payne had taken more of the lead vocals, but neither felt capable of filling Lowell George's earthpads.

Their first idea was Robert Palmer, a logical choice. Palmer had several connections with George and the band, having had George playing on one album and the entire band backing him on *Pressure Drop*. He'd covered a Feat song on each album: "Sailin' Shoes" and "Trouble." He didn't have George's blues growl, but he had proven himself with a wide range of music—rock, soul, blues, reggae. But in 1988 Palmer was on the road to massive success, with the number-one single "Addicted to Love," and he was not interested in joining a band.

The band next thought of Bonnie Raitt. By the mideighties she had become a consistent artist at Warner Bros., but like Little Feat, she had not broken through in any substantial way. In her fifteen years on the label she'd reached the upper floors of the *Billboard* album charts only three times, with *Sweet Forgiveness*, which reached number twenty-five and was her only gold record, in 1977, and, later, with *The Glow* and *Green Light*.

Like Little Feat, she was a darling of FM radio and had large pockets of fans in larger cities and college towns. Little Feat and Bonnie Raitt had recorded and toured together, and there was no question about their mutual affection. But the band had caught her at a vulnerable time. Warner Bros. had dropped her after the moderately successful *Green Light* album, so she was struggling for her music life.

"Yeah, I got dropped in '83," she said, just after she'd completed a new album called *Tongue and Groove*. That album was then shelved for two years, when Warner Bros. decided it wanted to release it. Raitt was in a battle with the label—she wanted to update the recordings—when the word was circulating that one of her favorite bands might be interested in her. The album, which she pointedly renamed *Nine Lives*, sank. She would regroup and sign with Capitol in 1988. By then its president was Joe Smith, who'd moved over from Warner Bros. Soon, with *Nick of Time*, she was a superstar.

When she heard the Little Feat chatter, her response was "I really wanted to do my own career." But, she added, "I don't think it was a real serious offer. I didn't actually talk to Paul and Billy and say 'No.'" But Raitt had made the right move.

Soon, so did Little Feat, when they found their new singer, Craig Fuller. Payne and Barrere already had been writing songs with him, he'd performed at the Lowell George benefit, and he'd been tapped for vocals and guitar in the band Barrere and Payne had put together behind Nicolette Larson in 1979. They also knew him as part of a singing duo that had served as their opening act on tour.

Fuller was best known as lead vocalist for Pure Prairie League, a seventies soft country-rock ensemble in the Poco vein. The band had one major hit, "Amie." As Fuller remembers it, he had attended practices for the 1979 band, put together during the Payne v. George disputes. When George returned from his solo tour he was seen as unlikely to welcome Payne or Barrere to be part of Little Feat—thus, the new band. But then George passed away. "It hadn't gotten very far," Fuller said about the new ensemble, "and it kind of knocked the wind out of everyone's sail."

Fuller actually went way back with Little Feat, to the beginnings of the band. In 1971 he had formed Pure Prairie League. "We were living in a giant, old-style hippie house in Cincinnati, and one of the guys was a promoter," he recalled. "He had a local venue called the Ludlow Garage, and he was on all the major labels' mailing lists, so we got a Little Feat record and wore it out. And when they came to town I went to see them play, and I was mightily impressed." That was one of the first concerts Feat ever did, and it was the show during which Richie Hayward, frustrated at the audience's lack of attention, pulled a sausage out of his pants.

So when Fuller says he was mightily impressed, he may have meant that Little Feat made a lasting impression on him. Their roads, as it turned out, would cross again, but not for a half dozen years. By 1978 Fuller had left Pure Prairie League and was working with the songwriter Eric Kaz.

A Brooklyn native who was once in the band the Blues Magoos ("You Ain't Seen Nothin' Yet"), Kaz wrote romantic ballads for, among others, Bonnie Raitt and Linda Ronstadt ("Love Has No Pride," "(I Am) Blowing Away," and "Cry Like a Rainstorm").

Fuller and Kaz formed a band, American Flyer, in 1975 and produced two albums before folding. They then began planning a duet album, to be produced by a friend of Ronstadt's, one Lowell George. But George was immersed in his solo album, so they found another producer, finished recording, and went on tour as the opening act for Little Feat.

It was mostly a college tour, Fuller remembered. "It was a good time, a memorable experience," he said. "Lowell, by that point, had gotten to a point where every other night he didn't feel like singing—his throat was sore, and he was really struggling. But everybody else had a good time." What ailed George? "I don't know," Fuller says. "It could have been that he just didn't take care of himself. I mean, he just didn't like to go to sleep."

After George's death Fuller returned to playing in various versions of Pure Prairie League. He continued to write with Kaz and, at one point, connected with Barrere for a songwriting session that produced "Hate to Lose Your Lovin'." Then, in 1987, he and Payne wrote a song. By the time Fuller was ready to send it out to publishers, Little Feat's surviving members had agreed to try a reunion.

Now, here was Fuller, calling Payne about music publishers. "And," Fuller remembered, "He said, 'By the way, we're going to try to put Little Feat back together.' I said, 'That's a great idea.' He says, 'We're having a hard time trying to get Robert Palmer to sing. We thought about getting Bonnie. We're not sure what to do.' And I said, 'I could do that.' And he said, 'Yeah, you probably could. Why don't you come out?'"

He met Payne and Barerre at Payne's house in Los Angeles. "We went up to the little music room above the garage," he said, "and I played them 'Hate to Lose Your Lovin',' and they said, 'Gee, that sounds like Little Feat.'" It should. After all, as Fuller remembered, when he and Barrere sat down to write it, "We may have even said, 'Let's do something Little Feat could do.'"

Then Fuller sang "Fat Man," and, Barrere says, "That was it." "So in fifteen minutes," Fuller said, "it was over. And the rest of the band heard the news."

Fuller, who describes himself as "kind of a straight arrow" when he toured with rock bands, was the flip side to Lowell George's partying ways. But they had one crucial thing in common: their voices. "It was eerie," says Barrere. "Especially on the old songs, like 'Cold Cold Cold' and things like that. It was very eerie."

"Lowell's voice and my voice were really similar in timbre," says Fuller, "and we all played the same music back probably when we were eighteen years old. We could've gotten together and done a set without a rehearsal because we all knew the same twenty, thirty songs." And, of course, he had a history, as a fan and an opening act as well as a musical peer.

"Most of those old songs—the things that stick out in my mind, 'Strawberry Flats' and 'Fat Man' and 'Two Trains'—things like that, they were right in my range. And remember, I wasn't trying to play a guitar too. I had a great guitar player on either side of me that filled all the guitar stuff, so all I had to do was sing."

But it was a little more complicated than that. George, after all, had an edge to him, a loopy sense of humor, that cartoon consciousness that he brought to both his life and his music. And Fuller knew he was not that guy. "I come from a more pop school," he said, "and a more structured school, and felt, at least at that point, like we'd better write some things that are listener friendly and that we can get on the radio."

Payne may have been thinking the same thing when he heard Fuller singing. "I thought Fuller fit into a certain area where we needed a more romantic voice," he recalled. "Paul handled the bluesier stuff fine, and he and Craig had a real nice blend, I thought. They traded off some stuff on 'Hate to Lose Your Lovin'' that was great. It was a really good mix of stuff."

Payne and company got to work, writing new songs. He, Barrere, Tackett, and Fuller met at Payne's place for brainstorming sessions, occasionally pulling in Martin Kibbee, who wound up cowriting two songs, including the title tune, "Let It Roll." The stakes, they all understood, were high. As Payne put it: "When we re-formed, I shared it with the band and said, 'Look, we're in competition with ourselves. If we don't come up with the right record, I don't care what Warners wants to do, or anybody we've brought in, if we don't feel this thing is happening, it ain't going out.' What I want is to have somebody coming to me and saying, 'Man, I heard this between the Beatles and the Stones, and boy, it sounded great.'"

As their collection of songs grew, they began looking for a manager. Thanks to their multiple musical connections, they were able to gain the attention of Peter Asher, who'd enjoyed long and prosperous runs with Linda Ronstadt and James Taylor. He'd known of the band and, in particular, Lowell George since Ronstadt began talking him up and proposing that she record "Willin'." Richie Hayward had played behind Ronstadt in her earlier years and, more recently, Asher had gotten to know Payne, who had played on several Ronstadt recordings.

"He played for me quite a bit and was a great friend," Asher said. "I love his playing. Because Lowell was so important, people forget that Billy was important as well." He noted Payne compositions like "Oh Atlanta": "I think there's a tendency to overlook him as a big part of the band. You hear people go, 'Oh, well, once Lowell died, forget it.' And actually a lot of the feel of the band came from the rhythm section."

Various Feats had come to know Asher and his staff. "I think it seemed logical, when they were looking for management, to go somewhere where they knew the people, knew that it wasn't a crooked operation," he said. "I think they came to me and said, 'We're going to get the band back together—do you want to manage?'"

Asher admitted to some skepticism. A long time had passed since George's death, since Little Feat's prime. But he heard their demo, with Fuller on lead vocals, and took it to Lenny Waronker, now the president of Warner Bros. Records. "We're getting the band back together," he recalled telling Waronker. "Are you interested?"

The longtime producer turned executive looked wary, Asher recalled, "until he heard the music, and he said, 'Absolutely, yes' on the spot. It was a good meeting."

As the news spread in 1987 about Little Feat's return, the response was predictably mixed. Many—even devoted fans of the band—echoed Bill Payne's remark from 1979: "Little Feat just does not exist without Lowell." But others flocked to the band's side. Lynn Hearne, who, as Shag, was so devoted to George, the Factory, and Little Feat through its various changes, was there. "My fervor for Feat music did not die with Lowell," she declared. "Instead, it has gained momentum and maturity."

But the music and media landscapes had changed dramatically since the midseventies. The Doobies and Led Zep had given way to U2 and Springsteen. Progressive rock radio, almost alone among formats in its support of Little Feat, was gone. In many markets in its place was "classic rock," playing the hits of the sixties and seventies. Because Little Feat had no hits, they were not in any playlist or rotation.

Still, there were diehards like Gary Bennett, a DJ on KSHE in St. Louis. He dated back to the days and nights of underground, free-form radio, when announcers, many of them fleeing the restrictions of Top 40 radio, lit up and said and played whatever they wanted—as long as there were listeners and advertisers. Bennett fell in love with Little Feat over *Sailin' Shoes* and *Dixie Chicken*, and when the band disappeared, he kept them on the local air as much as he could. In fact, he began a daily feature, "Feats at Five," in 1985, two or three years before their reunion.

When KSHE had become tightly programmed, Bennett followed the new format five evenings a week. When asked to work Saturday afternoons as well, however, he took action: "I didn't really want to work on Saturdays, but since I did, I wanted to throw a Little Feat song in at five—just slide it in, just one song." When, after a few weeks, the program director noticed what he was doing, Bennett talked him into letting him make it a regular segment. "It became a twenty-minute feature, where people would call in, write in requests, and we had T-shirts made, with the tomato lady on the front." The feature would continue to grow, and other radio rebels around the country would come to join the trend.

While fans (and critics) waited, the band gathered at the Complex, the studios George Massenburg had built. There they had another reunion with the engineer-turned-producer. Payne, who had asked Lowell George for a shot a coproducing, finally got his wish. He and Massenburg would coproduce the album.

They worked on *Let It Roll* for five weeks, six days a week. As Barrere recalled rather pointedly, "By planning things well, there weren't so many surprises in the studio as on past projects. There was no bullshit in the studio that would've gone on before. There weren't any petty arguments. It was more like, 'Okay, what do we need to get this thing done so it's the best it can possibly be?'"

When their work was finished, they had a gathering with Warner Bros. executives and staffers at the studio to listen to the final mixes. Barrere found the listening session "cathartic. . . . It felt like we were healed from that dark period—the passing of Lowell, the problems we all had as individuals and together. It felt great."

As they prepared to resume touring, the band received a gift from Jimmy Buffett. When Clayton informed his boss that a Feats reunion was in the works, Buffett not only understood that he'd be losing one of his percussionists but that the band might be able to use a boost. "Buffett said, 'I'll take you on tour with me,'" Clayton said. "And that was great. He would come out like before his show, with the opening band, to make sure his crowd was there. He'd sing the first two songs with us, make sure they were seated and in place and attentive. Then he would leave and let us play. It was excellent."

But the band's first concert was in New Orleans as part of the 1988 Jazz and Heritage Festival. "Fred Tackett . . . told us about New Orleans," Payne recalled. "He said, 'We ought to do our first gig there. We can sneak in there on one of the stages. Nobody will really notice.'" That was fine by them. But when they got to the Crescent City, they learned that Van Morrison had dropped out of a concert on a riverboat, the *Steamboat President*, and Little Feat had been drafted to fill his slot. "Now the spotlight was on us—and we're in there with Jimmy Buffett, Bonnie Raitt [who joined the band on stage], Ed Bradley, Steve Winwood, and all these kids, and we're goin', 'How the hell do they know all our lyrics?' They were all in front of the stage singing."

One of the audience members, according to Tackett, was weeping during the performance of "Willin'": "Right in the front row . . . tears coming down his face." And not just any rock fan. "He was a Hell's Angels kind of a biker dude." All around and behind him people were holding up lit matches and lighters and waving their arms to the song.

Welcome to the eighties.

On their first time out on the road Fuller had no problems filling in, in effect, for Lowell George. "I was accepted with open arms, because I think it was pretty obvious that I wasn't trying to sound like Lowell." At the same time, he was in George's vocal range and could emulate a vocal, if he wanted, to reflect a George performance on a record.

Only once, he said, did he get any kind of "You ain't Lowell" guff. At a concert on Long Island he found himself yelling back at an audience member. "I'm usually a very nice guy," he said, "but the guy pissed me off. He was kind of drunk, so I just said, 'Hey, man, ain't gonna be another Lowell.'" The passage of years between the previous and the revived Little Feat dimmed some memories. And, as Barrere noted, many of the younger people they performed for didn't even know about Lowell.

The album was a mellow affair compared with the original Feats albums. With Fuller up front, there was more country, less jazz; more romance, less edge. And it was a hit. But critics couldn't help bringing up the Lowell George angle. Some, however, like J. D. Considine, reviewing the album for *Rolling Stone*, moved on quickly, finding the band "sounding almost as fresh as it did the first time around." He said he could imagine "Hate to Lose Your Lovin'" on *Dixie Chicken*. He found the Payne-Kibbee song "Cajun Girl" pedestrian but thought "One Clear Moment," by Payne, Barrere, and Fuller, reminiscent of the "romantic unease" of some of George's songs. Overall, he said, *Let It Roll* more than lived up "to what the band name promises."

Their efforts were rewarded at record shops. *Let It Roll* went gold, reaching the album chart of *Billboard* again, peaking at number thirty-six.

The next year, the band released another album, *Representing the Mambo*, again produced by Payne and Massenburg, this time recorded at George Lucas's Skywalker Ranch north of San Francisco. (This, Payne believes, was because Lucas had dated Ronstadt, who continued to work closely with Massenburg.)

It was "Day at the Dog Races" all over again—at least on two or three tracks, including "Silver Screen" and "Daily Grind." To Warner Bros.'s ears, Payne let his love of jazz-fusion take over too much of the album, and the Big Bunny's music division was not happy. "I thought it was a good album," Payne said, but he was called into Lenny Waronker's office. "He says, 'Man, don't you guys have anything that's more . . . rock 'n' roll?'"

Payne tried to convince the label chief that several of the nonjazz cuts, like "Texas Twister" and "That's Her She's Mine," could make it onto the radio. Although he was right about the countryish rocker, "Texas Twister," which featured Barrere on lead vocals and got onto album-rock (known as AOR) radio for several weeks, that format, a blend of new and "classic" rock, was losing out to other, more contemporary pop formats. It couldn't be counted on to help expose and sell records.

It was odd that Little Feat would take such a left turn musically, defying a record company that had demonstrated a willingness to invest in the band. "It was my decision, and I kicked myself in the ass about it later," said Payne. "It wasn't exactly a disaster, but not the best move in terms of keeping our career going."

As the title of one of the songs declared, "Those Feat'll Steer You Wrong Sometimes."

Warners punished the band, Payne says, by limiting its support for the album. Little Feat then invoked what Payne vaguely called a "technicality" of their deal, and the band left the label. "I felt the worst about that in terms of Lenny Waronker, who was a true champion of the band," said Payne. "I felt we stabbed him in the back by leaving the way we did. He asked us to stay. But there were people there who were not on our side, and I just felt like we were like a canary in a cage."

Little Feat soon resurfaced on Morgan Creek Records, part of an independent film company. After the band produced an album, *Shake Me Up*, and did a few more tours, Craig Fuller stunned his bandmates in the fall of 1993 by announcing that he was leaving. He said he wanted to spend less time on the road and more at home with his family, especially as his wife, Vicki, was expecting another baby.

He said that he felt the band was on a "no-chance label" that had the members "working harder, with longer drives between shows, for less money." He soon would be the father of four children, "and I just felt that the best thing I could do to accumulate merit, as they say in Buddhism, is stay home with my kids."

Most of the band understood, although, he said, "Billy took it the hardest, I think, 'cause he thought I jumped ship. I guess he didn't feel the band was making less money, even though it was." He enjoyed the fun of traveling with the guys, but, he added, "I think everybody in that band likes to play live more than I do." Although he enjoys it too, he said, "especially when you're making a lot of money."

On September 1, 1993, Little Feat suffered another major loss. Neon Park died, at age fifty-three, of ALS, a degenerative disease also known as Lou Gehrig's disease. When Park was given the news of his diagnosis, he responded, "But I don't even play baseball!"

Members of Little Feat paid tribute to him in the fan magazine *FeatPrints*. Barrere signed off his piece: "I'll forever miss your wit, but your soul and spirit always remain with us. You were what's hip . . . a duck . . . with lips!!!" Years later, in a printed program for an exhibit of Park's work, Barrere promised, "As long as there's a Little Feat, we shall use one of your images to make us look good."

They would. In 1996 they paid further tribute to this master of cartoon consciousness by naming a live album after him. It sounded perfect: *Live at Neon Park*.

Chapter 15

THE LIGHTNING-ROD WOMAN

WHEN LITTLE FEAT FOUND ITSELF IN NEED OF A NEW VOCALIST, THE band's leadership—indisputably Bill Payne and Paul Barrere—turned to someone who was in the loop, who'd in fact sung with the band since their return. Shaun Murphy had joined in on background vocals on *Let It Roll, Representing the Mambo*, and *Shake Me Up*.

But as things turned out, in becoming Little Feat's lead vocalist, Murphy became, to borrow and twist a phrase from the Factory days, a Lightning-Rod Woman.

There's no question that Murphy, a blues shouter coming out of Omaha, Nebraska, was qualified for the job. She was a powerful vocalist who'd fronted her own band and served as vocal support behind the likes of Bob Seger and Eric Clapton as well as alongside Meat Loaf. That was in 1969, after she and Meat Loaf were cast mates in *Hair*, performing on Broadway as well as in Washington and Detroit. It was on opening night in Motor City when some people from Motown Records and its subsidiary, Rare Earth, decided that Shaun, who was going by the name "Stoney" at the time, might click with Loaf in an act called "Stoney & Meat Loaf," even though the two never had a scene together. They were signed and put into a studio with a Motown band, from which they produced an album, issued in 1971. A single, "What You See Is What You Get," reached the R&B charts.

But Murphy's ambitions lay more in musical theater than pop music. When she was young, she said, "I thought I was going to be an actress. I had no idea I would be in the singing field." But in tenth grade at Osborne High School in Detroit, where her parents had moved, her theater class staged a musical and asked if she could sing. She could, and so she wound up getting several lead roles, both in school and summer stock.

That work led to *Hair*, and after making the record with Meat Loaf, she mixed theater with rock vocals, beginning with sessions with Seger, a local star. Through Seger she got to meet Glenn Frey and Joe Walsh. "You know how the synchronicity goes," she says. "Everything sort of happens. It was just a wonderful time."

And once she was in the loop, synchronicity took over. When she moved to Los Angeles in 1985 the connections continued to work for her. By now she had worked with Bruce Hornsby, the Moody Blues, and Eric Clapton (in 1984 on his *Behind the Sun* album, which included percussion work by Ted Templeman). In Hollywood she made her first connections to Little Feat. "I ran into Catfish Hodge," she recalls. "I had known Catfish from Michigan, and I read in the paper that Catfish was playing at this club, and that's when I met Paul. He was hanging with Catfish."

Later, while performing at Josephina's, a club in the Valley, she met Richie Hayward, who'd dropped in to see the band. "We had some jam sessions," she recalls, even though at the time he was recovering from his second motorcycle accident. Then, on Seger's 1986 tour, Seger invited Barrere and Fred Tackett along, and that's how she met Tackett, who soon would be part of the reunited Little Feat.

When the band reformed, Shaun got a call to help out on backing vocals. But when Fuller told the band that he was leaving, she had no idea what was going on. "I don't want to say it was cryptic, but it was certainly subtle to the extreme," she recalled. "Paul called me up and said, 'Look, we're doing some demos at my house. Do you want to come over and sing some background?' That kind of thing. I came over. The next day I came back, and they said, 'Since you're here, we're doing this song, and we were wondering how you would sound on it. Can you take it home and come back tomorrow and sing it?' So I came back and sang the song, 'Romance without Finance,' and the next question was, 'How would you feel if you found yourself in the middle of the United States on a bus with six guys?'"

Shaun wasn't sure what they were saying. Was it a joke? But a few days later Payne and Barrere made it official. They wanted her in the band, and as a full partner. "I thought it was one of the greatest things I'd ever heard," she said. "I thought it was unbelievable of them."

"Billy and I thought she'd be a good addition," said Barrere. "In retrospect, maybe we should have hired her as a sideman as opposed to making her a full member . . . maybe we should have asked the rest of the band what they thought about it and so forth . . . but it was kind of like one of those executive decisions."

Barrere himself liked the idea of a female presence, "especially a strong one, who can hold her own, sound good on Little Feat material, has a good bluesy voice—it's an interesting new shade. And young men might enjoy looking at a female form on the stage."

As for hiring Murphy as a full-time band member, Payne and Barrere could have given her a part-time salary, because, even with Fuller, Little Feat had evolved into a multiple lead-vocals setup, with Barrere and Payne getting almost equal time up front. But, said Payne, "I'm not from the era of bringing in people piecemeal fashion. . . . If I'm going to say this person is in the band, they're in the band. It was years later that I realized that some band members were not enamored of her being there. I thought, *why'd they have to wait fifteen years to say anything?* The craziest thing about bands is, it's a comedy of human error and perception."

Although Murphy had known most of the Feat for years, she knew there might be some questions—both from the band members and their audience.

The boys in the band had thrived behind Craig Fuller. How would they do with a woman in the mix?

It's one thing to be buds with the boys in the band, another to take the spotlight—and a full share of the profits. "Everybody seemed happy," she said about the band after they got the word from Barrere and Payne. She believes that Feat fans never got any official announcement of Fuller's departure and her ascension. "There was a level of shock at first," she recalled. "There were some people who thought, 'How dare they put a woman in the band . . . ,' but most of those people, as soon as they saw that I was a fit, that I wasn't taking over everybody, that I just had my little niche in the band and brought a lot of energy—I turned a lot of minds around. But it was a process, definitely."

Actually, it was a process with some of the band too. Early on, said Barrere, he thought most of the guys were on board with Murphy, saying, "Talking to Sam, he loved having her around . . . "

"Well," said Sam, "I didn't have no say-so about it. It was like, 'Do you care?' 'Nah, I don't care.' It might help us to have some female personnel onstage, they might look at us different." But, he went on, "It's just that our band is more of a boys' band. Nothin' against Shaun—she sings great." In fact, Clayton said, "she's by far the superior vocalist. I'm not sayin' she's better than Lowell, but she's by far the superior vocalist."

Kenny Gradney thought back to the de facto announcement of Shaun's hiring and to his response: "A chick in the band. What can I say? As a person, I liked her. She's a very good singer. Without a doubt. As an artist, she was fine." And yet?

"A woman in the band. I wasn't into it all that much."

Hayward approved of Murphy's addition. "It definitely gave the band a tune-up," he told Robyn Flans of *Modern Drummer*. "It's a whole new direction and approach. I think Shaun's really exciting. She's more R&B, blues, and rock rooted than Craig was. Shaun has this knife edge to her performances that's really exciting."

Murphy wasted little time coming up with an agenda for the band, writing in *FeatPrints* that "I think I'm steering the band in a little different direction. Hopefully, it's back to where they originally started, maybe with a little more bluesy flair. They can do so many things, but some of their fans felt the later albums were sounding almost too perfect; everything was placed just right, and the tones were just right.

"When they play live, it's not like that at all," she continued. "There are a lot of raw edges, and that's what I wanted to get back to."

Lowell George's voice had raw edges that he could turn on and off at will, depending on the song. Murphy knew she would be expected to tackle a couple of his songs. Frankly, she wasn't sure how she'd handle them. "He was so incredible," she said. "His voice was amazing and his range was phenomenal. . . . He was just *wild* with his voice. He had no fear whatsoever; he just went everywhere, and it was great. I don't know if I can exactly capture what he did—I don't think anybody can replace him—but I just hope I complement his songs. . . . I hope he's up there smiling."

But there actually was less pressure on her than they might have thought. From the beginning, she said, she shared lead vocals with the others: "Paul was sort of Lowell George, he took over on all of Lowell's songs, and of course, Bill has a great voice, and he was doing a number of songs. Sam was in there, and occasionally even Richie was singing a song. It wasn't like I was just barreling in there singing all these songs . . . it was a nice ensemble, and a nice lineup."

And she wasn't expected to sing many Little Feat classics. "She had certain niches of things she could do," Barrere said, "and then others that she couldn't or wouldn't do, like 'Rocket in my Pocket.' I'd go, 'If this is not right for you, cool.'"

Murphy was also unlikely to tackle "Fat Man in the Bathtub," but she was willing to do whatever she was asked. "Paul realized that he just didn't want to sing every single song," she said. "If for no other reason, I was there to give Paul a break. And just give him a stab of energy here and there. It worked out really well."

Although Murphy had done numerous rock tours, she'd always been a backup. Between tours she fronted a blues and R&B band that played clubs in the San Fernando Valley. Frankly, she said, she preferred arenas. "I am much more comfortable in a ten-thousand-seat venue than I am in a little club," she said. "I have always been that way, since the first time I stepped on a stage. I get terrified giving a speech in a speech class and there's bright lights, and there's fifteen people there—it drives me to distraction. But set me in a huge crowd, and I just thrive on it."

She got those crowds her first times out, at the New Orleans Jazz and Heritage Festival in April 1994 followed by the Philadelphia Blues Festival. Linda Gibbon, editor of *FeatPrints*, gave her the fanzine's seal of approval, writing that "her powerful momentum belting out the blues just knocks you down."

Longtime Feats follower Lynn Hearne said, "The first time I heard Shaun sing 'On Your Way Down,' I had goose bumps on my goose bumps. Tears welled—I was completely taken by Feat's new vocalist."

With Murphy on board, Little Feat got busy recording and touring. Their deal with Morgan Creek had gone sour, so in 1994 they signed with Zoo Entertainment, a new record label founded by Lou Maglia, former president of Island Records. Zoo product was distributed by the conglomerate Bertelsmann Music Group (BMG), the parent company of RCA and other major labels.

On Feat's first album with Murphy on board, *Ain't Had Enough Fun*, issued in 1995, the newest member had five songwriting credits. Granted, they were cowriting credits, but she would earn eight more in the 1998 album, *Under the Radar*, and four more on 2000's *Chinese Work Songs*. (A live version of "Rock & Roll Everynight," of which she was one of five writers and which appeared on *Ain't Had Enough Fun*, was on the 1996 release, *Live from Neon Park*.)

None of the albums were big sellers, so the band found itself constantly on the road. The Featbase listing of concerts showed 63 dates in 1994 and an astounding 154 in 1995, with the Feats going around the country several times and then jumping over to England, Ireland, Scotland, the Netherlands, Belgium, Denmark, Switzerland, Austria and Germany, Norway, Sweden and Finland, and then returning to play the Fillmore Auditorium in San Francisco and, back home in Los Angeles, the House of Blues.

Murphy recalled playing seventeen shows in twenty-one days and having a puzzling time in Dublin in an indoor amphitheater. "Of course, there was a pub attached," she said. "And we're playing, and after the song there's polite little claps, and we thought, 'Oh, that was weird,' like they were already in their cups. And these are *my* people—I know them, they get rowdy. We play another song, and again, a little bit more, but there's still polite applause.

"And all of a sudden it just changed to this wild thing, and every-body was standing and screaming and yelling and hootin' and holler-in'. And after the show we were really puzzled by this reaction, and we went over to the pub, and it turned out that they thought that we were a Little Feat tribute band."

When did it dawn on them that they were hearing the real thing? "It must have been something Paul was singing, that just hit the note, 'cause he has such a distinctive voice. That must have been it . . . then, all of a sudden, they just lost it."

Little Feat would have more noteworthy dates, including the clos-ing ceremonies of the 1996 summer Olympics in Atlanta. They played in Centennial Olympic Park—the scene, just a week earlier, of the explosion of a pipe bomb that killed a woman, injured 111 others, and was blamed for causing the death of a fleeing man, who had a heart attack.

"This was one of the most amazing experiences I've ever had," said Clayton on the *Little Feat Radio Hour*, "and I thought we wouldn't have a chance to play it, because of that bomb thing that they had. . . . The Olympics was great. I'm really athletic myself, and I wish I coulda been there as an athlete, but it really fulfilled a dream of mine. I hold that high in my memories."

When Murphy arrived at the park, which served as the "town square" for the Olympics, she was surprised. "We had no idea that we would be playing for one of the largest crowds, outside of the Olympics themselves. I guess we had about eighty thousand, which was pretty darn good. And they were all rockin', having a great time."

A few months later the rockin' was happening in one of the band's favorite cities, Washington, DC. This time they weren't at the Lisner Auditorium but instead were part of Bill Clinton's second inaugura-tion in 1997. They'd also played for Clinton when he first won the White House in 1992.

Their connection was Tackett. Both he and the president played in the Arkansas state band when Clinton took first chair in the sax-ophone section. Barrere remembers being brought down to earth the evening before the 1993 inauguration where, at one event, they opened for Aretha Franklin: "We were at the Arkansas Blue Jean Ball, checking out the Cate Brothers. We were standing behind these little old ladies, and they were like, 'Is that Little Feat?'"

The second time around, said Barrere, "We were treated a little more high end. They had a dressing room for us. But Judy Collins sequestered herself in it and wouldn't let us in." Little Feat, dressed close to the nines, performed at three of the fifteen galas. The president and Hillary Clinton, along with Al and Tipper Gore, joined Little Feat on stage at the New England Ball, but only briefly; they had places to go. "We got to shake hands, all that stuff," said Barrere. "It was very cool."

Back home they had more band business to attend to. Peter Asher, their manager since their reunion, had been appointed senior vice president at Sony Music Entertainment and thus parted ways with Little Feat. They then signed with Gold Mountain, an agency in Los Angeles, whose clients included Bonnie Raitt and Lyle Lovett.

While the band worked on their next album, an independent project was under way, seeking to pay tribute to Lowell George. *Rock and Roll Doctor* was the brainchild of a Feat fan, Jamie Cohen, who in the early nineties was an A&R executive—read "talent scout"—for a record label, Private Music. He shopped his idea of an all-star tribute to George throughout the industry and around the country, talking to record companies and potential financial backers. Cohen, who continued his pursuit after leaving Private Music, made more than forty pitches and got no takers.

All-star musicians sounded great, but who was Lowell George? "I just assumed that he'd go to Warner Bros., and Warners would say, 'Oh, great,'" said Ira Ingber. "Well, by that time Warners was already gutted." In the aftermath of Time Inc.'s purchase of Warner Communications in 1989 as well as a series of shakeups in the executive suites, Mo Ostin, Lenny Waronker, and other key figures left. "The artist-first" era of Warner Bros. Records was long over. "Looking back on that time," said Ingber, "they probably didn't even know who Lowell was."

Ingber is the younger brother of Elliott Ingber, and both had met George in the midsixties. Elliot connected with George through the Mothers of Invention and Fraternity of Man. Ira, who, like Elliott, was a guitarist, was also in a band that George tried to connect with Atlantic Records. Ingber says George produced a few demos, but the band went unsigned.

Ingber then met Jamie Cohen, who died in 2008, through Martin Kibbee and, when Cohen finally found a taker—a Japanese label called Kaigan Entertainment—he jumped on board as a producer. While Elizabeth George, who administered her husband's publishing interests, and Valerie Carter, who'd become a friend of hers, began contacting potential artists, Ingber corralled J. D. Souther, whom he'd backed on a tour, into a studio and worked up "Roll Um Easy." Kibbee along with Neon Park's widow, Chick Strand, joined in on the project, and the result was a thirteen track CD, all recorded at different sites, with a lineup including Bonnie Raitt, Jackson Browne, Taj Mahal (Payne guested on his 1993 album, *Dancing the Blues*), Randy Newman (with Carter), Eddie Money, Chris Hillman (with Jennifer Warnes), and Allen Toussaint. R&B artist Phil Perry joined with Merry Clayton, the sister of Sam, on "Spanish Moon," which he cocomposed with Lowell George. Little Feat backed Raitt on "Cold Cold, Cold" and, with Shaun Murphy up front, accounted for "Honest Man," which George wrote with Tackett and recorded for his solo album.

Inara George, who by this time had become a singer, first with a prog-rock band called Lode and then on her own, sang "Trouble," backed by Van Dyke Parks (who also arranged and produced) and Ry Cooder. Elizabeth used to sing the calming ballad to Inara and would later sing it to her grandchildren.

> 'Cause your eyes are tired and your feet are too
> And you wish the world was as tired as you . . .

Because a performance of "Willin'" failed to meet the producers' standards, George's best-known song is not on *Rock and Roll Doctor*. And, Ingber said, because of distribution problems, "hardly anybody ever heard of" the collection. "It's kind of the curse of Lowell," he said.

But there would be another all-star tribute to come. Meanwhile, Little Feat continued to work. After issuing *Chinese Work Songs*, including covers of the Band ("Rag Mama Rag") and Dylan ("It Takes a Lot to Laugh, It Takes a Train to Cry") on CMC International, another label under the BMG umbrella, the band decided in 2003 to form its own label, Hot Tomato Records. Shaun Murphy would be on all the initial releases, including the anthologies *Raw Tomatos* and *Ripe Tomatos*.

But trouble was brewing.

Martin Kibbee, whose role with Little Feat diminished as the band members began writing with others, was still keeping an eye— and both ears—on them. He was a strong supporter of Murphy and, in an interview in *FeatPrints*, called her "probably the best singer the group has had in terms of pure vocal ability." He said he was "very disappointed to see what some of the reaction to her seems to be."

He was talking more about the band than the audience. As Craig Fuller put it: "I thought the fans were generous to Shaun. I think there were some people who really didn't think it worked at all, but people had an open mind."

Further, two of the band's staunchest supporters, Linda and Dick Bangham, who published their fanzine, *FeatPrints*, liked her. But, she added, "I think a lot of people just never really loved her with them. People that liked them for a really long time just never really liked Shaun with them that much. . . . You'd talk to people and they'd be, 'Yeah . . . I just don't know.'"

The perceived problems were threefold: financial, musical, and— there was no getting around it—aesthetic: Shawn Murphy's appearance.

This was unfair. Critics didn't judge Lowell George's weight, white painter's overalls, or the size of his feet when they wrote about Little Feat's music. Murphy was an excellent singer, capable of a blues mama's sensuality and a balladeer's sensitivity. She was at ease up front or harmonizing with Barrere, Payne, and others. But it was those shirts and slacks, and the first snipes came from within the band.

Clayton, talking about the band's audience, told me: "I don't think they dug the way she presented herself onstage. I think they wanted her to be a little more sexy and stuff." Clayton liked her, he emphasized, but, he added, "A lot of girls will have these risqué outfits and stuff, like women do." Murphy? "She'd make a shirt. She's a great seamstress. She made shirts for people in the band. She's excellent. But that's one of the reasons why I think that didn't work. They wanted someone who was a little more flashy. I really think that, 'cause it sure wasn't about her talent."

Murphy was totally and immediately aware of the attention. "I mean, that's the first thing anybody is thinking about when they are going to have a female lead singer, that she is going to be scantily clad or just be that will-of-the-wisp. . . . But I've never been like that." Singing behind Seger, she said, she and other women wore "scanty items." But up front? "That's just not me." In fact, she went the other way, stating, "I think the first year I just wore black pants and Harley-Davidson T-shirts."

Her bandmates, who all dressed more for comfort than for show, never spoke to her about her wardrobe. "They knew I was kind of shy in that regard, and I wouldn't want to put that kind of element on that stage," she said. "It would have really changed the dynamic if I was to come out there in a Madonna outfit."

But Murphy said the main reason for her departure was financial. "They were having some problems getting booked and getting enough money to live on, and that was what was told to me."

Barrere agreed with Murphy. "It was first and foremost a financial decision," he said. The band had signed with new managers. The first time they attended a concert, Barrere said, "they saw the band without Shaun because she was off doing a Seger thing. Then they saw it with Shaun, and they said, 'Why do you have her in the band?' And financially it made more sense. We wouldn't have been able to afford the tour with seven people. We're talking about the expenses of a tour and everybody in the band making a wage that's decent enough to warrant going on the road."

The reason the new managers questioned Murphy's value was that her role had diminished dramatically over her fifteen years with the band. "I was kinda weeded out, every show, a little less, a little less," she said. "I don't want to say anything bad about anybody. I was always fighting to do more stuff and was kinda shot down." A typical Little Feat concert comprised about fifteen songs. Murphy was happy when she would sing five leads and do harmonies and backgrounds on other songs.

On the first album, *Ain't Had Enough Fun*, she was dominant with her bluesy-rock vocals—too dominant, perhaps: "I went to Bill and said, 'I got too many songs on this record. I don't want to cause any problems here.' 'No, No,' he said. 'This is the way we wanted to go.'"

But from five lead vocals, she was, near the end in 2008, down to about two. Now she was complaining about too few songs, but "nothing ever really got done about it. . . . I was pretty disappointed by it. I was a full member, but I wasn't running the band."

To the band's leaders it wasn't only the paucity of Murphy's participation onstage; it was the songs she chose. To critics, concerts became disparate segments: Little Feat's and Murphy's. She might do a Feat song like "Cold, Cold, Cold" or "Mercenary Territory," but she often did the blues or her showcase number, her cover of Dylan's "It Takes a Lot to Laugh, It Takes a Train to Cry."

Barrere remembers Murphy leaning on Dylan and on more recent songs she and Payne had written for her to sing. To him, she wasn't sufficiently interested in Little Feat music. "She didn't dive in to find old Feat songs," he said. "We would have to suggest certain ones to her. She would do them, but we would always have to bring it up. She never really went for it."

The band had a meeting without Murphy, took a vote, then gave her the news. Said Payne: "It was a painful thing on all levels to have to do. She wasn't overreacting or anything. I was more emotional about it than she was."

Murphy chose not to recount to me how she was let go. "I just want to thank them so much for allowing me to be in the band for fifteen years," she said. "I learned so much from them."

In retrospect, she said, it was fine that she was let go. "I am so happy where I am at right now. They did me a big favor 'cause it forced me to get out there and do my own thing." She has released four albums since leaving Little Feat. "I'm doing blues and loving it."

Chapter 16

'NET GAINS

SHAUN MURPHY WAS GONE, AND SOME OF THE COMMENTS SUR-
rounding her dismissal echoed the financial realities of rock 'n' roll,
of keeping a band together without the benefit of substantial record
sales and media attention. And Little Feat had been dealing with
those realities for years yet had managed to stay together, thanks to
devoted fans, developing technology, and one Hunter S. Thompson.

Not that the gonzo journalist, famed for his "Fear and Loathing"
pieces in *Rolling Stone*, personally came to their rescue. But he was
an inspiration for what became known as the Grassroots Movement.

"The model I landed on was the Hunter Thompson model," Payne
said, referring to Thompson's chronicle of the 1972 presidential campaign in *Fear and Loathing on the Campaign Trail*. Volunteers for the
Democratic candidate George McGovern fanned out across the country, spreading the word on a grassroots level. Thompson "described
very accurately how to do that," Payne said. "And that was where I
took my impetus, to begin that process of calling people."

Of course, there was another model: the Grateful Dead. In the
early seventies the San Francisco band gave birth to the Dead Heads
movement by slipping a message into their live album, released in

1972. "Dead Freaks Unite," they encouraged, asking for names and addresses. They began issuing a *Dead Heads Newsletter*, including drawings and writings from Jerry Garcia and Robert Hunter.

But Payne had something else in mind. He wanted Feats fans to do most of the work. In an open letter published in 1997 in *Feat-Prints*, he candidly explained the band's quandary. Little Feat, he said, had been living on word of mouth: "It has been an odd marriage of isolation and reaching out. What do I mean? Little Feat falls into a special and frustrating area because of our isolation to the 'musical scene.' We don't fit into the music industry's idea of what a nice presentable package should be: we play too many styles of music, we have too many lead vocalists, we don't present a flashy show . . . it goes on and on."

The band, he said, had relied on record companies to market and sell its records and promote the band. But, he wrote, "all good intentions aside, we have been hurt and hurt badly by our counter-part not doing their job." (At that time Zoo Records had folded, and the Feats were about to slide over to CMC International.)

"It got to the point that in some cities, people were asking if it [was] the 'real' Little Feat playing some venues," Payne wrote. Ah, memories of Dublin.

Payne went on to name two Feat fans the band had come to know, Cat Bauer in upstate New York and Dr. Jay Herbst, in Florida, who would oversee "volunteer regional reps throughout the country and around the world to pass out information on Little Feat."

In the late nineties the Internet was still new to the general public. Fortunately, Little Feat fans were among the net's earliest adopters. Bauer, a paralegal in upstate New York, created a Feats-centric website, The Blue Highway, including a chat room on AOL. An electronic mailing list, known as a listserv, was gathering hundreds of fans from around the world; they could send messages to fellow "Feat Heads," as they inevitably became known, and get digests of all members' e-mails.

The new mixed with the old. *FeatPrints* had begun publishing in 1990, and regional reps carried clipboards at concerts, gathering addresses for both snail- and e-mail lists. Before Little Feat came to a town, locals handed out fliers and put up posters, alerted local media and called radio stations, and helped promote new albums as well as upcoming shows.

Payne also pushed to have Little Feat albums—CDs, by now—available for sale at their shows. Management, he said, scoffed at the idea of selling CDs at shows. "What?" said Payne. "It's only reserved for country artists?" When the band began selling at their concerts, they moved as many as fifty copies a night—far more than any stores were even carrying.

With his call for help and his stated goal to "make Little Feat more interactive," Payne was a kick-starter for the Grassroots Movement. Within a year a few dozens of fans had become an organization of some eight thousand members. The *New York Times* took note with an article in late 1998, when reporter Bill Kent quoted Michael Tearson, a DJ at WMMR in Philadelphia, crediting the band with creating "a global fan community on the Internet called the Grassroots Movement that is unlike anything any rock band has ever done. If Grassroots is successful—and the signs so far have been very encouraging—it has the potential to change the way some of the music will be made and heard in the next century."

By 2000 the movement had an international online reach of some 15,000 Feat fans. Now, according to Chris Cafiero, archivist and keeper of the band's website, about 1,400 people visit Littlefeat.net every day, the band's e-mail list is at 24,000, and its Facebook page has gathered over 130,000 of those coveted "likes." And that's just the main page. Feat Heads can also visit FeatPhotos, FeatCampers, Feat Friends, and Feats at Five.

According to Tearson, the Philly DJ, Grassroots members did everything from promoting to booking the band, stating, "The fans are blazing a trail around the mainstream music industry that will soon be followed by other bands that aren't getting the attention that they and their fans feel they deserve."

The *New York Times* credited Dr. Herbst for creating the organization in mid-1997, but Herbst pointed to Fred and Amy Miller, who were in California by way of New England, as the originators. Fred, a musician and a Feats fan since 1974, moved to Los Angeles in 1977, and one of the first people he met was Fred Tackett. Later he also met Lowell George, who expressed interest in producing a blues-rock band Miller had joined, called Tombstone. But that was just before George died.

Miller, a keyboard player who jammed on occasion with members of Little Feat, discovered the Internet in the early nineties. "I saw listservs for the Grateful Dead and Jimmy Buffett, but nothing for Little Feat. So I called up Fred Tackett and said, 'Wanna start a listserv?' He said, 'We have this little group going on AOL.'" (That would be Bauer's chat room.)

Fred and Amy Miller, whom he'd met in 1980 (Amy had been a Feats fan since her teens in Connecticut), created a listserv that would become the Hoy Hoy Digest early in 1995. They did the clipboard thing at concerts, gathering addresses. Soon the list of e-mailing correspondents grew to a thousand Feat fans worldwide, and it would peak at about fifteen hundred active users before other social media networks like Facebook took over. But under the umbrella of the Little Feat website, the listserv continues on, with some seven hundred members. "It has the feel of a community of people who know one another," said Amy.

Dr. Jay Herbst, a surgeon in Florida specializing in skin cancer, was twelve when an older brother turned him onto *Sailin' Shoes*. Then, starting in the late eighties, he and his wife, Donna, a nurse he met in med school, attended numerous Feat concerts, enough that they began to meet a couple of the band members. By the time he began tinkering with the Internet and ran into Fred Tackett in the AOL chat room, they knew each other.

"We started talking," Herbst said, "but there was no organized online presence." He soon heard from Fred Miller (who used "Red" as his onstage name): "Red e-mailed me one day and said, 'I want to start this mailing list, and do you know anybody who might be interested in testing this out?' And I believe we got eleven people together to start that mailing list—or listserv." Dr. Herbst began conducting a weekly Little Feat chat, sometimes involving thousands of fans, on what had become the Hoy Hoy Digest.

Tapped by Bill Payne to coordinate volunteers, he and Donna helped build a network of Points of Contact (POCs), fans on the street level who would collect contact information and hand out promotional materials, sell CDs, and even send out holiday cards—at their own expense. Even when the mailing list headed toward six thousand, the Herbsts created and sent out the cards. "It got to be very expensive," he agreed, "but we loved the band, and they were very good to us, and we didn't mind spending the money to do this once a year."

Dr. Herbst also became one of the band's volunteer concert promoters. It happened when Payne called one day in September 2000 to say the band was coming to Florida and had a gap in its schedule. Might he find them a gig in the Fort Meyers area? Given two weeks' notice, Dr. Herbst found a theater, called the Ricochet Night Club, and negotiated a deal for the venue. The club owner would get all the money from food and beverages, and the band would get all the door. He advertised the show and sold about a thousand tickets. Herbst would go on to produce two more dates over the next three years. "We never made a profit," he said, but "it worked out okay." And Little Feat had no "weird" requests, he said. "I didn't have to pull out the red M&M's."

Dr. Herbst noted one more benefit Little Feat reaped from its outreach to fans. One day he and Payne were talking about a new live album the band had completed but had not yet named. After tossing around a couple of ideas, one of them suggested opening the naming to Feat fans. An online contest was announced, and the winner turned out to be Tony Stott, who was the band's regional volunteer coordinator in Australia.

His suggestion: *Live from Neon Park.*

One of Little Feat's most vital Grassrooters, Chris Cafiero, thrived on recordings of the band's concerts. In fact, he used to tape them illegally. But he had an excuse: he was raised on the Grateful Dead, who always allowed fans to tape their shows and exchange tapes with each other. "I was a Deadhead," said Cafiero, who was born in 1959, meaning he was about six when the Warlocks became the Grateful Dead. He caught up quickly, though, catching some 250 concerts. But in high school some friends hipped him to Little Feat, and he taped his first show in Upper Darby, Pennsylvania, in May 1977. "I had to hide the tape deck to get through security," he recalled.

"The band wasn't taper-friendly for a long time," said Jay Herbst. As in, say, twenty-five or so years. "It stemmed from years ago," said Barrere. "Lowell hated the fact that we had so many bootlegs out there, and people were selling our music and we weren't making a dime off of it." The biggest Feat bootleg was *Electrif Lycanthrope*, taken from two radio appearances the band made on WLIR in Long Island in 1973 and 1974. In 1981 the band would include three songs from those broadcasts in their own legit album, *Hoy-Hoy!* "We thought, we might as well make some money out of it," said Barrere.

But it would be about sixteen more years before they came around to the advantages of allowing fans to record their concerts. "We got some good information from the Grateful Dead," said Barrere. "They said, 'You don't understand. They trade the tapes, but they buy everything of yours they can get their hands on.'"

Jay and Donna Herbst were among the Grassrooters who spoke with Bill Payne about allowing taping, saying, "We finally convinced them that it might be useful to stimulate the fan base to allow them to tape and trade shows."

Finally, in mid-1997, twenty years after Cafiero had surreptitiously taped his first Feat concert, the band relented, and Feat Heads were allowed to record directly from the sound board, beginning with a concert in Tallahassee, Florida.

And it wasn't just taping that Little Feat were slow to approve. Several Grassroots pioneers say that band members, as Cafiero put it, "didn't understand the value of Grassroots. They were always a friendly bunch of guys, but there was a period when they did not extend themselves out into the public."

Payne appreciated the efforts of the fans, but he says it was management that needed to sign off on the various initiatives that the Grassrooters were taking on. "They said, 'We'll get back to you,' and never did." After reading the Hunter Thompson book, however, he said he decided to join forces with the fans. "Some of the band took a while to get what was going on," Payne recalled. "This was unknown territory to everybody." Still, in connecting with the fans on an organized level, "we were well ahead of the curve on many levels." And

Cafiero welcomed the band's approval of his activities. He had begun as a fan and a taper, but he would go on to do a lot more on Feat's behalf.

By day a commercial real estate developer in the suburbs of Philadelphia, Cafiero joined the Grassroots Movement and, in 2000, became the band's official archivist, the keeper of Little Feat's concert recordings and set lists (begun by Fred Miller). Since 2008 he has been the webmaster for the band's home page, Littlefeat.net.

Over the years the various Feat sites on the Internet have changed in name, scope, purpose, and personnel. They were not always easy to sort out and locate. But now they all are accessible by links from Littlefeat.net, which carries news; the band's history; reviews; blogs; photo and video archives; song lyrics; CDs and other merchandise, links to a YouTube channel, to Lowell George tributes, radio shows; and, of course, set lists and recordings of past concerts, which fans can download for free. Cafiero, whose entire collection is on the site, says he just likes to share. But he also enjoys tracing the band's shifting styles. "They've evolved over time," he said. "There is not one set way to play 'Fat Man in the Bathtub.' They've played it at least six different ways throughout their career, so having access to listen to multiple eras of the band is wonderful."

Still, there's nothing like seeing a favorite band live and close up, and one of Little Feat's least technological but most effective ways of connecting with fans is its annual fan fest in Jamaica. Since 2003 Feat Heads—at least those who can afford the trip—have been able to spend a long weekend with the band and special musical guests.

Between concerts, either at the hotel or on the beach, the Feats open rehearsals to their fans, host a "blues brunch," do Q&A sessions, and pose for photographs. One year Shaun Murphy did a cooking demonstration; other years Payne, Gradney, and Hayward did casual clinics on keyboards, bass, and drums, respectively.

Cafiero has attended the first ten gatherings. "It's the closest thing to being dropped off on a private island with your favorite band," he says. The gathering is limited to one hotel, which has two hundred or so rooms. It's in Negril, a fairly remote beach resort, on the island's west coast. "No one has anywhere to go," said Cafiero, "but to stay and get along with each other and eat and drink and be friends and listen to good music."

For a seriously devoted fan—like, say, a former Deadhead—who is used to traveling to follow favorite bands from town to town, it's paradise. "You just walk to your hotel room and the next show's gonna be right there. . . . It is the closest thing to a Little Feat fan convention. There's fans from Ireland, from Norway, from Germany, fans from all over the United States."

To Diane Pelis, who hops down from Schereville, Indiana (that's near Chicago), with her husband, Jerry, it's a working vacation, but with minimal work. She's a Point of Contact and, in Negril, helps sell merchandise, just as she does when she attends Feat concerts closer to home. And she's seen plenty of them. In 2004 she took the summer off and caught thirty-two concerts in sixteen different states. "There's something about the groove of the music that just captures you and draws you in," she said.

Like other POCs, she's happy to do a little work before the shows. "In Jamaica for the last nine years," she said, "we've done a little raffle for various charities. I'm the one that sells the raffle tickets and gets all the money together." Then, with the raffle over, she and Jerry enjoy what amounts to an annual reunion. "The first year," she recalled, "my husband made a comment: 'All these people are here, and there's not an asshole in the bunch!' A lot of the same people go back all these years, and the only place you get to see them is in Jamaica."

Diane and Jerry, who married in 2001, decided to renew their vows in Jamaica in 2012. When the band heard about their plans, they joined the ceremonies. "Billy was kind enough to walk me down the aisle, and the other band members and spouses came, and they are wonderful people."

IT WAS BAD LUCK, bad timing, or both, that one of Little Feat's most impressive points of contact with its fans, the newsletter-turned-magazine *FeatPrints*, ceased publication in 2002, just before the first Jamaican fan fest.

In its time, beginning in 1990, the publication did a superb job of reflecting the band. After a couple of issues that were composed of the usual fan newsletter fodder, including clippings of reviews and news articles from newspapers and magazines, *FeatPrints* began carrying interviews with band members. Early on, Payne popped up, explaining why, after *Representing the Mambo*, the band was leaving Warner Bros. Records. And when a Feat fell sick, it was covered. In 1999, when Barrere required neck surgery to remove a bone spur, he spoke with *FeatPrints*, saying, "I've got to tell myself that I'm not 25 anymore. No more crowd surfing!"

FeatPrints' graphics and sense of design helped make it stand out among fanzines. Its editor, Linda Gibbon, was a graphic designer who became a fan of Little Feat in the seventies while working as a secretary and receptionist at WHFS in Bethesda, Maryland. After starting up *FeatPrints*, she got help from a fellow artist, Dick Bangham, who met the band while he was in his own band, Root Boy Slim and the Sex Change Band, and worked with George Massenburg at his Track Recorders Studio in Maryland. Bangham worked in Washington, DC, where he specialized in designing album covers.

Whereas Bangham had a chance to see Little Feat live in the mid-seventies, Gibbon never did. So when the band reformed, she said, she had extra impetus to see them, stating, "I loved them so much, and I thought that they never really got the recognition they should have. I thought, any little thing I could do to get them some them more attention."

She started the newsletter, calling it "the unofficial & unapproved news exchange for Little Feat Fans." But she soon drew support, both from fans and volunteers like Bangham, who provided cover art that was cleverly focused on shoes that had eyes and tongues as well as other variations on themes Neon Park had created.

Soon after Gibbon approached Park for an interview, he began contributing poetry as well as items from his massive collection of illustrations. When he fell ill and could no longer draw but still had use of his index fingers, he began writing a story, "Tattooed Tears," that ran as a serial in *FeatPrints*.

FeatPrints, which published two or three times a year with no set schedule (at least not one they successfully met), would grow its circulation to some fifteen hundred, plus free copies given out at concerts and record shops. Linda and Dick, who worked days and nights together on the magazine, would eventually marry, and when Neon Park passed away in 1993, they picked up his brush, with the band's blessings and, they believe, Park's.

Near the end, they visited Park. "He'd give us these pointers on painting," said Linda, now known as Linda Bangham. "We went through a lot of his artwork and started scanning it so we could use it for future Little Feat covers and incorporate something of Neon's in the covers."

When Little Feat were preparing the live set that would be called *Live at Neon Park*, Payne invited the Banghams out for dinner. "He started talking about picking up where Neon had left off. And bringing something of our own to it," Linda said.

The Banghams do, although sexy tomatoes and tongue-tied sailin' shoes are never far below the surface. (A gallery of *FeatPrints* covers is at www.ripbang.com/FeatPrints, where back issues are available for sale.)

Another vital part of the Grassroots Movement was the *Little Feat Radio Hour*. In St. Louis Gary Bennett managed to get "Feats at Five" on the air, and Buffett's site still carries "Feats at Five" on weekends. But it was David Moss, a Feat fan in Humboldt County in Northern California, who created, produced, and hosted the most fanatical radio show on behalf of the band. From KHUM in the small town of Humboldt in 1998, "the Mossman," as he called himself, produced a weekly program for almost eight years. On this program he interviewed band members as well as fellow musicians like Jackson Browne, Robert Palmer, Bob Weir, David Lindley, Dave Matthews, Leftover Salmon, Inara George, and Leo Nocentelli (of the Meters, who teamed with Allen Toussaint on "Two Trains" on the *Rock and Roll Doctor* tribute album).

As with all the Grassroots fans, Moss worked for the fun of it, giving away his show to KHUM and other stations, some of them found through the band's Points of Contact. He hooked up with a Public Radio Network satellite and got the show on about fifty stations around the country. He presented rare concert recordings, played Little Feat appearances on other radio broadcasts, Bill Payne's show-and-tell piano sessions at a university, and spread Little Feat news and tour information.

One gem aired on the program was a rebroadcast from a 1973 visit the Feats made to the Ultra Sonic Studio in Hempstead, New York. It was taped for airing on Long Island's WLIR and was a snapshot of the band in more harmonious times. George was at his self-effacing and mischievous best, downgrading Feat as "just another band from L.A." Introducing the band, he got to Barrere and couldn't resist adding, "formerly of Led Enema." Seconds later he looked around the studio and at a small audience that had gathered for the broadcast, and asked, "What is that aroma, oh my god."

The announcer interjected, "Hey, speaking of aromas, how come you put 'Willin'' on two albums?"

George, curious: "'Speaking of *aromas*'?"

Chapter 17

FEATS WALK ON

Live from Neon Park served to introduce Feat fans to Inara George, who joined the band onstage at the House of Blues in Los Angeles late in 1995. She sang behind Barrere on "Dixie Chicken" and with Shaun Murphy on "Sailin' Shoes," taking a solo for a verse.

At that point Inara had just begun to sing in public. After high school she went to Boston to study classical theater and acting. As a kid, she had done Shakespeare at the outdoor Theatricum Botanicum in Topanga Canyon. Home from her freshman year at college, she began playing in a band with some high school friends, "kind of like as a joke, 'cause I'd written a couple of songs on the guitar" even though, she swore, she'd never played one before. The band was called Lode and could be called "hippie or prog—more in the vein of my father's music than anything I do now, but obviously not as good, by a long shot." They continued through the summer, and when she went back to school she learned that there was interest in her band from two major record companies, Capitol and Geffen Records.

"It was exciting," said Inara. "The problem was I didn't really like the music that much"—nor the rock lifestyle. "The band was smoking pot all the time. There was something about it that turned me off.

So I signed the deal, but I really didn't want to do it." After producing an EP called *Legs & Arms* in 1996, Lode broke up, and Inara broke off a relationship with a band member and moved to New York, again pursuing acting. "Funny," she said. "I got to New York, and I ended up playing more music. And when I got home I realized I liked that music thing much more than I did the acting thing."

Inara turned out to be a prolific composer of jazzy, indie-sounding pop songs with twists. She was half of a duo called Merrick, which produced two albums. She made a solo album, *All Rise*, and met Greg Kurstin, with whom she formed the duo The Bird and the Bee. Their debut in 2006 showcased both her charming voice, which could sound both innocent and bent, and her writing skills. A song called "F*cking Boyfriend" hit *Billboard*'s Club Play chart.

Inara was also part of an indie pop trio, the Living Sisters, and in 2008 she made an album, *An Invitation*, with Van Dyke Parks, wedding her songs with his orchestral, near-classical arrangements. Parks also played piano and accordion, and the players included Don Heffington on percussion—the same Heffington who toured with Inara's father and babysat her while others dealt with his death in Arlington.

Inara has three stepbrothers: Jed, Forrest, and Luke. All are smart and creative, but Inara stands out as the bearer of her father's legacy. As Elizabeth George told me: "she . . . carries her dad in her heart and has explored her own avenues without being the daughter of Lowell George."

"I'd like to think I got the best parts of both my parents," Inara says. "I know there are certain weird things I do like . . . I don't like to wear my glasses, and I squint at the TV, and I guess my dad was like that as well. But in terms of my personality, I don't think I'm like him. I'm probably much quieter. I'm musical, that's what I do, and I'm sure I got some of that from my dad, but my mom is musical as well. Fortunately I don't think I got the excess. I had some moments in my twenties, but I never could get into it as far, as deep . . . " (Inara is married to Jake Kasdan, a filmmaker who produced the hilarious *Walk Hard: The Dewey Cox Story* and has been a producer of the sitcoms *The New Girl* and *Freaks and Geeks*.)

Thinking back to when she was with Lode and when two record companies came calling, I asked whether she felt that part of their interest was because she is the daughter of Lowell?

"I think that was definitely a big part of the interest," she agreed. "And then as I did other music, it was so different, and we had such a different audience, it became less of an issue and less comparison. It was more just like, 'Oh, your dad was in the band Little Feat,' and I'd say 'Yes,' and that would be that. And younger journalists have no idea who that is. They don't really care."

Inara has maintained a good relationship with Little Feat, which has performed with her on several occasions, beginning with a benefit for the Theatricum Botanicum. It was 1992, as David Moss of the *Little Feat Radio Hour* recalls, and she had just begun to sing with her rock band. "Little Feat introduced her for the first time, and I was blown away," Moss said. "She could sing those blues, and her tone—it reminded me of Lowell." One of her featured songs from the beginning was the one her mother had sung to her: "Trouble." And she would perform it on Little Feat's 2008 album, *Join the Band*. That one was the result of Jimmy Buffett's unwavering support for the band.

By that point Little Feat, with its own Hot Tomato label, had issued one studio album, *Kickin' It at the Barn*, recorded in Tackett's home studio in Topanga Canyon, and a solo effort from Payne, *Cielo Norte*. But during that time, early in its DIY days, the band knew it could use some help, so Payne had reached out to Buffett, who'd employed Sam Clayton for years, had Little Feat as his opening act, and was interested in Payne's help on a country album he was cutting in late 2003, *License to Chill*. (The album, Buffett's twenty-sixth, was the first and still only one to top the *Billboard* charts.) By then Buffett and Payne had been talking about a Little Feat project that would involve selected guest artists and would be recorded at Buffett's Shrimpboat Sound Studios in Key West, Florida.

Although it would come to include, among others, Dave Matthews, Bob Seger, Brooks & Dunn, Béla Fleck, Emmylou Harris, Chris Robinson, Brad Paisley, and Vince Gill, it was not a tribute album. It wasn't limited to Feat songs, and the band would sing on some but not all the tracks. Buffett offered his studios and sang on a couple of tracks, but his most important role was as executive producer. In other words, he was bankrolling it by giving the band studio time and paying for transportation to Shrimpboat. (Additional recording and mixing took place at other studios.)

Buffett had been a Feat fan from way back. He remembers going out with Glenn Frey of the Eagles to see the band at the Roxy. This would have been during the run in April 1976, when they appeared to mark their Hollywood star outside that lingerie emporium Frederick's. "I was swept away by the whole thing and became an immediate fan." Buffett, who's from Alabama and Mississippi and once performed on New Orleans streets, could hear his past in Feat's playing. "I could certainly hear that in the music—influences coming from Professor Longhair, from Allen Toussaint, people like that." Of the early Feat songs his favorite was one he performs with Payne on *Join the Band*: "Time Loves a Hero." "It really spoke to me. I just loved the lyrics, the setting in Puerto Rico, and it just had this great little groove to it."

On *Join the Band* Buffett pairs with Barrere on "Champion of the World" by Emmylou Harris's guitarist, Will Kimbrough. "I just loved the lyrics," he said. "It sounded just like a Lowell George song to me."

For the rest of the album, some of the guest bookings were serendipitous. One night an employee of Buffett's caught a Black Crowes concert. The encore number was "Willin'." When Payne heard that, he called Chris Robinson to invite him on board, and they wound up sharing vocals on one of Payne's proudest songwriting moments, "Oh Atlanta." ("Willin'" was already accounted for, by Brooks & Dunn.)

Inara George performed her vocal on "Trouble," accompanied only by Payne on piano, in Los Angeles. Recording this song was yet another Little Feat full circle: the studio, Ocean Way Recording, was in the same complex of studios where Little Feat made its first album at United-Western Recorders.

But this full circle coincided with an end of a line. On August 12, 2010, Richie Hayward died. He had been diagnosed with liver cancer more than a year before, and he died from complications of a lung disease while waiting for a liver transplant. He was sixty-four.

Although Van Dyke Parks referred to Lowell George as the king of rock 'n' roll and John Sebastian likened him to Elvis, to many, Hayward was the real deal. Carl Scott, who helped book and manage Little Feat in the early days, called Hayward "the bad boy. If there was shit to get into, he got in it. He represented rock 'n' roll." The rest of the band, he said, "had a serious attitude about the music, about the future. Richie wanted to play the fuckin' drums and get loaded and hang out, drink, and have a good time. And he was a nice man."

Hayward fessed up to his chosen lifestyle on the *Little Feat Radio Hour*: "We were pharmacological test pilots for about ten years," he said.

Fred Tackett wasn't on those flights. He toured with Hayward, and they were neighbors in Topanga, but they didn't hang out much. "He kind of avoided me," Tackett said, "'cause I was always a health nut, and he was the total opposite." Hayward smoked and favored cheeseburgers. "'Come on,'" Tackett told Hayward, "'you're eating like a fuckin' teenager.' And he'd swear to god he'd had a physical, everything was just great."

"And then he got sick," said his percussion partner, Sam Clayton. Hayward was diagnosed with liver cancer in mid-2009. On the road he told Payne that he would not be able to perform beyond an early August date in Billings, Montana. "Richie was deathly ill," said Payne. "His liver was basically shot. His breathing problems were mounting." But he made it through the concert in Billings. Clayton recalled, "I'm making him stay with me. I know that it's bearing on his strength, and I got to keep it there the way it's supposed to be. I could tell he was getting tired, and he didn't want us to have mercy. He wanted to play it, just play the song. And it's up to him to keep up. And I couldn't just feel sorry. I'm gonna play, and you're gonna be right there with me."

He was. "That night had to count as a last statement," said Payne. "He was brilliant."

The band's last time in public together with Hayward was a year later, in July 2010, at the Vancouver Island Music Fest in Courtenay, British Columbia. Hayward was too ill to perform a set, but the band wanted him there anyway, if only to see him one more time.

Gabe Ford, who had been with Little Feat for two years as Hayward's drum technician, had been filling in for Hayward in concert. And before his diagnosis Hayward had married again. He wife, Shauna, had created a website to keep friends and fans up to date on Richie. She reported on that evening in Canada: "Then the gig. The weather had turned a bit cold, and the wind picked up. . . . We kept Richie warm . . . then Paul invited him up to sing the Jamaican national anthem! It was amazing. . . . Richie was beaming. He played three songs: 'Spanish Moon,' 'Skin It Back,' and 'Fat Man.' I cannot touch with words all that happened. Just know that it was the magic of love, everywhere."

Payne recalled that for "Willin'," Barrere called Hayward out to sing a line that the band had come to interject into the song, taken from "Don't Bogart That Joint." Hayward did, accompanied by the audience. He then took over the drums from Ford, played his three songs, and retreated to the side of the stage, where, during the encore, he added a bit of percussion to "Oh Atlanta."

Hayward, said Payne, had a habit of asking, after concerts, how he'd done. This time he didn't. "Richie had a smile on his face as large as the Big Sky above us," Payne wrote in a tribute to the drummer. "He knew he had played as well as he ever had in his life."

Hayward was singular, said Barrere: "That's the thing that was so cool about Little Feat: all the different players are very unique in their styles, and somehow they managed to mesh and create this thing that's bigger than the sum of the parts. It was funny, because we used to rag on him because he'd go and do sessions with people and play straight and just be right in the pocket, and we'd go, 'Why can't you do that with us?' And he'd go, ''Cause this is Little Feat. I get to do what I want.'"

Lowell George didn't always appreciate that, but many others did. In a tribute essay music critic Don Snowden called Hayward "the prime motor that made your body move." Even when Kenny Gradney and Sam Clayton joined—ostensibly to keep Hayward's timing in check, "Hayward was the foundation," said Snowden, "the fulcrum it all revolved around, negotiating the tricky time signatures and intricate song structures, yet always keeping the flow loose and organic, and doing all that while singing high vocal harmonies!"

Hayward, said Robyn Flans in *Modern Drummer*, "was among the most musically stylish and quietly influential drummers of the classic rock era, equal parts monster technician and old-soul groove master . . . the drum world will never see another Richie Hayward."

A FEW MONTHS AFTER the loss of Richie Hayward Little Feat received a morale boost, an honor, a laurel that had nothing to do with re-cord sales or chart positions, Grammys, or the Rock and Roll Hall of Fame. It was about their live album, *Waiting for Columbus*, which had come out more than thirty years before.

It had been performed, song for song, note by note, in concert, by Phish.

The jam band from Vermont, which was the nineties version of the Grateful Dead, liked surprising its concert audiences, wheth-er with goofy props or replications of classic albums, usually on Halloween.

For All Hallows' Eve in 2010 the band chose to perform, as the second of its three sets at the Boardwalk Hall in Atlantic City, all of *Columbus*, minus only the drug hangover–induced near violence of "Black Wednesday."

They played every song from the original vinyl album, from "Join the Band" and "Fat Man in the Bathtub" through "Feets Don't Fail Me Now." To represent the Tower of Power horns, Phish brought on a five-piece horn section, and then they also added Giovanni Hidalgo on percussion. What's more, they included an a cappella rendition of "Don't Bogart That Joint" at the end of "Willin'." And in *Phish-bill*, the program booklet patterned after *Playbill*, drummer Jonathan Fishman wrote an appreciation of Hayward. "There has probably been no greater direct influence on my drumming than Richie Hay-ward," he wrote.

In a similar vein, Trey Anastasio told *Rolling Stone* editor David Fricke, who wrote the essay for the program: "We may have learned more from Little Feat than any other band."

To replicate *Waiting for Columbus* the band had to learn and master fifteen songs. But they had previously performed "Time Loves a Hero," "Dixie Chicken," "Rocket in My Pocket," and "Spanish Moon."

Bassist Mike Gordon, who played on "This Land Is Your Land" on the Feat album *Join the Band*, was the first to add Feat songs to the Phish playlist. "I liked that Trey's originals were getting strange," he said, "but I said I wanted to balance it with some gutsy, bluesy music." He meant Little Feat.

Page McConnell, Phish's keyboard player since 1985, had become a fan years beforehand by way of a bootleg tape from a 1975 concert in Boston (ironically, on Halloween that year). "I just wore that thing out, I loved it so much, and I couldn't believe that a band sounded that good playing together." Payne, he said, emerged as a hero for him. "He's such a great player. I know there are all sorts of different styles of rock keyboard . . . but in terms of the players I've tried to learn from, Bill Payne is right up there, so I was really happy when we chose the album and could get into it even more."

Little Feat, McConnell told me, posed a greater challenge than previous bands Phish has covered. "With *Exile on Main Street*, it's all pretty much blues-rock, and there's not a lot of compositional elements to it," he said. "Whereas there are a few parts in these [Feat] songs that have some cool time changes. That's the thing about these guys and the musicianship in this band—they're so extraordinary, the songwriting is so great. . . . They are one of the great bands."

McConnell has a tour de force on "Dixie Chicken," but, as part of Phish's shenanigans, the band switched instruments on "Willin'," and McConnell wound up playing bass while Mike Gordon handled keyboards. Jon Fishman ended up doing lead vocal, though it was slightly pitchy—and he knew it. Late in the song he sang "And I'm still . . . " and then said, "in a whole lot of trouble!"

As with all their Halloween tricks, Phish didn't announce its treat until its audiences arrived and received their *Phishbill*. Little Feat were also out of the loop. "We didn't know," said Payne. "We found out the next day when our manager told me. I thought it was a tremendous tip of the hat."

"Now," said Barrere, "we get a lot of the younger generation coming out to see us, the young hippie-types. They say they'll be back, and they'll tell their friends."

It's a different kind of grass roots, but welcome, nonetheless.

Barrere does admit that when he looks out into the audience, it's not all youngsters. The Little Feat demographic now ranges, he says, with not a little amazement in his voice, from "eighteen to eighty." At a show in Las Vegas, he recounted, "there was a lady in the front row who had a walker. And she was standin' up in her walker . . . boogiein'."

Although the Grassroots Movement continues apace, the band, like its audience, has spread out and slowed down in recent years. It can hardly be helped: five of the six Feats are in their sixties, and only the presence of their drummer, Gabe Ford, who's forty, brings down their median age.

Ford seems older than he is, but in a good way. He brought into the band a family pedigree steeped in blues music. His father and two uncles, all from northern California, were in a blues band. One uncle, Robben Ford, broke out as a virtuoso guitarist (credits include Bob Dylan, George Harrison, Bonnie Raitt, and Joni Mitchell). The other uncle is Mark Ford, a harmonica player, and his father, Patrick, played drums with Mark and Robben in the Charles Ford Band, named after their father.

Gabe took up drums, but he learned quickly that gigging with local bands didn't pay the bills. He wound up working as a stagehand at the Fillmore Auditorium and did drum technician work for the band Living Colour. While at the Fillmore he had met Cameron Sears, then working with the Dead, when he was doing odd jobs at the band's warehouse. After Sears and partner John Scher took over management of Little Feat, Sears told Ford about an opening as Richie Hayward's drum tech, and Ford joined the Feat family in 2006.

Within a few years Hayward was ailing, so Ford found himself having to learn some sixty songs in two weeks before hitting the road with the band. Given Feat's music and Hayward's singular style, it wasn't easy even though Ford knew the songbook. "If I had to replicate every single thing he did, there's no way I could have done it," he said. "There are such intricate drum parts, so I would just from memory throw in stuff that I remember him doing." He smiled. He was thinking of Hayward. "When I pulled off one of his licks, I'd go, 'Right on, man, that's for you.'"

Although the band did consider other drummers after Hayward had to take a leave, they soon settled on the kid who'd been around for years. Sam Clayton, for one, approved. "It's easier to play with Gabe," he said, "because Gabe is thinking along my lines. A lotta drummers came to see Richie, they called him Mr. Fantastic, and Lowell would get on his butt all the time about staying on the thing [the beat]." Ford, he said, "plays more funk, more straight ahead."

Set up in an isolated drum room at a homey studio in Los Angeles—partly because it was a converted garage in back of the home of musician and engineer Johnny Lee Schell—Ford appeared totally at ease as he worked on Little Feat's latest album, *Rooster Rag*. His father had a blues label, so Ford began doing sessions at age nineteen. In that room, he said, "I had to get my mind ready and be open for anything. And it worked out all right. It ended up sounding like a Little Feat album. I didn't know if that was possible. But it sounds like a Little Feat album, so I was very happy with that."

Rooster Rag, released in 2012, was the band's first studio album, not counting the Jimmy Buffett all-star project, since 2003's *Kickin' It at the Barn*. Buffett's was crowded, the *Barn* was laid back and cozy, and *Rooster* was comfortably in between, aided and abetted not by any big-name guest artists but instead with a new (and big-named) songwriter.

Robert Hunter's credits included "Dark Star," "Casey Jones," "Uncle John's Band," "Box of Rain," "Touch of Grey," and "Ripple." And, once again thanks to their comanager Sears's strong ties to the Dead, Little Feat was able to connect with Hunter.

Sears let Payne and Barrere know that Hunter was interested in writing some songs with them. But when they saw some lyrics the composer sent, they reacted in radically different ways. "I didn't like 'em," said Barrere. "I said, 'Can I change 'em?' And he said 'No.'"

Payne liked a song called "Waiting for the Rain" and began writing music for it. Before long they had come up with four songs for the new album (although "Waiting" will have to wait) and have another seven worked up. "We're on a pretty good roll."

Why was Hunter interested in working with Feat? "When he presented the lyrics," said Payne, "he said, 'I've been listening to this Little Feat song, and it took me off in this direction.'" Although some musicians might find that to be insulting, Payne checked out the lyrics Feat had inspired and composed music for them. "I don't try and analyze his songs," he said. "What I do is look at certain key phrases, like in 'Rooster Rag'—'Tubal-Cain was the god of fire' and 'leave this old world a better place'—and I'll say, '"Tubal-Cain" sounds almost religious to me,' and I thought it'd be a good time to insert some ragtime chords into the process. . . . So that's what I did there." Later Hunter turned the tables and asked Payne to send him some music he could write lyrics to. One result was "Way Down Under," with Hunteresque lines like "Have you ever gone down under / way down beneath the liquid thunder / under the blue-black rolling sea / with a broken heart in revery."

Payne welcomed the partnership with Hunter; he hadn't written music since *Kickin' It at the Barn*, and, he would admit, the band was lacking in new material.

Hunter's songs pumped some poetic new life into the Feat repertoire, but Tackett, a proven composer, also stepped up, contributing four songs, all of them taken from recent solo albums of his (*Silver Strings* and *In a Town Like This*) and fleshed out, Feat style. Barrere teamed with the late Texas singer-songwriter Stephen Bruton (who'd cowritten "Corazones y Sombras" for a previous Feats album) for "Just a Fever," which, Barrere said, was autobiographical—about both men. "We shared a common ailment," said Barrere, who was diagnosed with Hepatitis C in 1994. "One day we were sitting around joking about our 'problem,'" and came up with perhaps the only use ever of the phrase "delirium tremens" in a song—a love song, at that:

Having visions / seeing demons / shakin' apostles /
delirium tremens

Little Feat had originally conceived *Rooster Rag* as a blues album, and the band members' and associates' ten songs are sandwiched by sizzling performances of Mississippi John Hurt's "Candy Man Blues" and Willie Dixon's "Mellow Down Easy," with Sam Clayton handling lead vocals. Clayton also swaps phrases with Tackett on the bluesy Tackett song "One Breath at a Time." After a relatively sedate *Kickin' It at the Barn*, the gumbo was back.

The band took only a couple of months to rehearse and record the album at Ultratone Studio, the glossy name for the garage facility owned and operated by Johnny Lee Schell in Studio City. Schell, a highly regarded songwriter and guitarist, engineered the sessions, and Payne and Barrere coproduced.

They worked in a cramped space, dominated by Schell's control board and related gear and machinery. The décor, such as it is, is western and blues, with a Beale Street sign, posters, and memorabilia celebrating Roy Rogers and the Lone Ranger sharing the walls with framed certificates signifying Schell's Grammy Award nominations for his work with Taj Mahal and Bonnie Raitt.

Viewing the scene, it took a while to spot Barrere, who, set up next to Schell, was barely visible behind a bank of equipment. Payne, standing behind a KORG keyboard, pointed to a neighboring Steinway baby grand. "That was Richard Manuel's piano," he said. Suddenly we were in a rock museum. Schell, Payne would explain, knew the piano from 1979, when he was playing on a session for Ian McLagan, one of the Rolling Stones' favorite keyboard players, at Shangri La Studios in Malibu. How the piano, which Manuel and Garth Hudson found at a piano store in Poughkeepsie, New York, in the late sixties, found its way to Malibu is a mystery. From there, Payne discovered through research, it was sold when Shangri La itself was sold, traveled to Connecticut, then was put in storage in Tarzana, California, before Schell acquired it.

Schell made some repairs and had the piano restrung, but it's still the piano that Manuel, who died in 1986, played as he pounded out "The Weight," "I Shall Be Released," and "The Night They Drove Old Dixie Down"—in short, rock of ages. And now, forty-something years after the Band members had found the piano, Bill Payne was playing it. His first reaction: "The damn piano near plays itself." And then: "It is a very soulful piano." Schell himself observed that this compact Steinway seemed suitable for a wide range of music, including rock, jazz, and ballads—in other words, suitable for Payne and Little Feat.

While awaiting the arrival of Clayton, who is called "One-Take Sam," from San Diego, the rest of Feat work on "Rooster Rag" (Rooster is the name of Schell and his wife's dog). Between takes the talk, like the music on the album, is all over the place, easy flowing, and good humored. The chatter ranges from Tackett talking about being confronted, as a teenaged musician in Little Rock, by National Guard officers as he headed home from a gig—"I guess it was against the law for whites to play with blacks," he said—to Schell noting that his wife's uncle was the legendary Broadway composer Jules Styne.

In the forced intimacy of the studio, the Feats seem happy to cram themselves onto a sofa and talk about the World Series or Gradney's parents' run-ins with the KKK. They sound like guys hanging out in a sports bar—minus the alcohol.

For a rock band who has had a generous share of thrills and spills, highs and lows, breakups and makeups, Little Feat is a collection of models of good health and domestic stability. Fred and Patricia Tackett have been married since 1968, Paul and Pamela celebrated their twenty-fifth anniversary in mid-2013, Sam and Joni Clayton had notched thirty years by then, Kenny and Johanna ("Josje") Gradney were at thirty-five, and the new kid, drummer Gabe Ford, married Alicia in 2004, and they have a son, Joaquin. Bill and Polly Gray Payne were wed in 2011. (Payne married Fran Tate, the recording engineer and singer, in 1977; she passed away in 1997.)

Rooster Rag was released in the summer of 2012 (with Rounder Records serving as distributors) and quickly leapt onto charts maintained by blues and Americana music sites, tallying airplay on college, public, and alternative radio stations. Given the fragmentation of pop music, the dominance of downloads over CDs, and Feat's resolute place outside the pop music world, these rankings had to suffice as barometers of success—those, and reactions from critics and Feat fans.

Payne was knocked out by the response. "I felt we'd hit a real home run," he said. "I haven't heard that kind of thing since *Let It Roll*." He was especially gratified that the raves came from people who had come to think of Feat as primarily a live act.

But soon that crucial element of Little Feat was in jeopardy.

In late 2012 Paul Barrere announced on the band's website that he would be taking time off to begin treatments for Hepatitis C. "For the past twenty years I have managed to control the effects of the disease with lifestyle changes and the love and support of my family and friends," he wrote. "During this time I've had regular checkups with a team of specialists at UCLA. These doctors have now advised that I should begin a treatment designed to eradicate the virus from my body. The treatment requires that I stay off the road for the next year, in order to give it the best possible chance for a successful result."

He went on: "Music is my life and I still have plenty left in me that I plan on sharing. I have a solo project that I have been working on for seven years that I plan on releasing. . . . I also hope to be able to do the occasional gig if the planets line up."

If they did, it'd most likely be an acoustic show with Tackett. The two have been working together, between Feat tours, since 1999, when they opened for John Lee Hooker at a music convention in Los Angeles. As a duo, they have issued two albums.

Barrere sounded fine when we spoke after the announcement. "There is hope there with some new drugs just on the horizon," he said. "I'm trying to get into a clinical trial study of one; I have friends on the east and west coasts who have taken it and are virus free in less than a month with no side effects. They both say that their energy level has risen a lot. . . . I was just glad they found that the interferon could cause liver damage while killing the virus and therefore they didn't put me on it. It would suck to beat the virus only to die from liver damage." Hep C, he ventured, "is a lot like HIV in its early stages—rampantly spreading in a generation that was, how should I say, a bit loose in their cleanliness . . . so they are trying a slew of drugs trying to get a handle on it."

Barrere quickly issued the solo project he had mentioned, called *Riding the Nova Train*. But Little Feat, he said, is officially "on hiatus," with band members free to do session work and other projects until they're called to rejoin the band.

Gradney, for one, will stand by. "If you're in a position to play whatever you want," he reasoned, "would you give it up?"

Ford also looks forward to Barrere's—and Feat's—return. He knows he won't find a similar band any time soon. Other acts, he said, "play the same set. Every single thing is the same every night, and with Little Feat, it's a different thing every night, and the jams we go into every night are always different too. I think people enjoy that live aspect of this band, and a lot of bands aren't doing that . . . unless you're talking the jazz world. And these guys have always done their own thing. They play all kinds of styles, and it can go anywhere."

There had been some talk about Little Feat simply disbanding, calling it a career, hanging up their sailin' shoes. Payne sees no point in such a move. Other bands can take long breaks between recordings and tours, so why not Little Feat?

Why not keep the name out there, in the music public's consciousness, and keep the music playing, keep the discourse going about Little Feat and why they never got bigger?

"They should have had a huge hit," says Jimmy Buffett. "Little Feat had great songs, and it's a bit of a mystery why they couldn't get to that plateau." His guess is bad management and wrong decisions by record companies in the past. "But the band just kept playing and writing."

"Possibly, they were too musically sophisticated," conjectured Bonnie Raitt. "I mean, they thought 'Spanish Moon' was gonna be a hit." Early on, she thinks, the band didn't care about hit singles. "They just wanted to do what they did, like the Grateful Dead, to just be a band that was respected as musicians and not have to be put into some promo-hype thing." Still, she said, "I think that if Lowell had lived and the band could have made up, if things got clean and all that, the same turnaround that I've had in my life . . . I think they could have been huge."

Cerphe Colwell, the radio announcer at WHFS in Bethesda, Maryland, says he interviewed George the night before he died. It was a return visit, after his drop-in with Linda Ronstadt and friends.

Colwell recalled little of their last conversation except to note that George went on a "rant" about "Louie Louie." That is, George loved the song and even played a bit of it on the guitar he'd brought in. "This is revisionist history," Colwell said, "but if Lowell were alive, he'd be right up there with all the current Americana, he was so much into that. And his style of playing, his writing was so inventive, the musician community really responded to that, and there's no way to imagine the effect that he would have if he were still alive."

Martin Kibbee, George's old buddy and cowriter, added, "If he's considered a minor figure, it's just because Little Feat was never a Fleetwood Mac. But the stuff holds up critically, and the chances are that in fifty years people will go, 'Hey, this guy was really on the money.'"

That's the stuff of a hall of famer. So far, to the puzzlement and chagrin of its supporters, the Rock and Roll Hall of Fame has yet to come calling.

"You know," says Barrere, "our fans have written letters, sent e-mails—they don't understand why we're not in." The museum in Cleveland now has a pair of George's overalls in hand along with some handwritten Little Feat lyrics. But the band, which qualified to be nominated twenty-five years after its first recording—that is, in 1996—has not even been nominated. "We haven't even been on the ballot." Barrere shrugged. "You know, that's for other people to consider. It's not for me to say we should or we shouldn't or whatever." But, of course, he knows otherwise.

Diane Pelis and several fellow Feat fans have purchased bricks from the Legacy Brick Program at the Rock and Roll Hall of Fame and Museum. They acquired eight bricks. One each will carry the names of Lowell George, Bill Payne, Richie Hayward, Paul Barrere, Sam Clayton, Kenny Gradney, and Fred Tackett. The eighth brick will be shared by Craig Fuller, Shaun Murphy, Gabe Ford, and Roy Estrada. "One way or another, we're going to make sure our favorite band is in the Hall of Fame," she said.

IN THE END IT'S ABOUT FAMILY, in the various definitions of that word. It began with a family led by a headstrong Mother of Invention. It became a houseful of rock hopefuls, living and playing together. It became a gathering of Prices and other priceless dreamers on Fountain Avenue. It became Little Feat, led by a force so creative and productive that his voice cannot be dimmed.

"Lowell is a part of our family whether he's here or not," says Payne. "We play his music out of respect to Lowell. The family thing is what started this band. It was a sense of community if you will, and it's only grown. The evidence is with Inara and Miles [Tackett, the multi-instrumentalist son of Fred] when they join us onstage.

"There are kids much younger than them who love the music this band plays, sort of like new families we have. Lowell is irreplaceable, and the best way to honor somebody like that is get up there and play his music in the spirit in which it was meant to be, which is free, loose—and it's what we do."

Family is the Grassroots Movement, tens of thousands of people united in support of a band of musicians who do a simple thing: make people feel good.

And family is one person.

"Lowell is my soul mate," says Elizabeth George. "We were soul mates, and I think about him every single day."

Like Inara, Luke George won't say he inherited his father's musical talents. If anything, he says, he got "his ability to have ultimate focus almost all the time." As we spoke, Luke was focused on producing a tribute album for a father he lost when he was nine years old. Like his stepmother, Liz, he thinks of him often. "And the one bright spot out of all of this that a lot of people don't get is I can always hear my Dad's voice."

As his father, with his stepbrother, Jed, wrote,

I've got twenty million things to do, twenty million things
All I can do, is think about you
With twenty million
Twenty million things to do

BIBLIOGRAPHY

Books

Brackett, Nathan, and Christian Hoard. *(The New) Rolling Stone Album Guide*. New York: Fireside, 2004.

Brend, Mark. *Rock and Roll Doctor: Lowell George, Guitarist, Songwriter, and Founder of Little Feat*. London: Backbeat Books, 2002.

Burgess, Chuck, and Bill Nowlin. *Love That Dirty Water!: The Standells and the Improbable Red Sox Victory Anthem*. Cambridge, MA: Rounder Books, 2007.

Burks, John, and Jerry Hopkins. *Rolling Stone Special Report: Groupies and Other Girls*. New York: Bantam Books, 1970.

Cornyn, Stan, and Paul Scanlon. *EXPLODING: The Highs, Hits, Hype, Heroes, and Hustlers of the Warner Music Group*. New York: Harper Entertainment and Rolling Stone Press Book, 2002.

Flanagan, Bill. *In My Soul: Rock's Great Songwriters Talk About Creating Their Music*. Chicago: Contemporary Books, 1986.

Frame, Peter. *Rock Family Trees, Volume 2: Charting the History and Development of Rock Bands from The Merseybeats to Motorhead, Manfred Mann to Adam Ant*. London: Omnibus Press, 1983.

Hoskyns, Barney. *Hotel California: The True-Life Adventures of Crosby, Stills, Nash, Young, Mitchell, Taylor, Browne, Ronstadt, Geffen, the Eagles, and Their Many Friends*. Hoboken, NJ: John Wiley & Sons, 2006.

McNally, Dennis. *A Long Strange Trip: The Inside History of the Grateful Dead*. New York: Broadway Books, 2002.

Palmer, Robert. *Rock & Roll: An Unruly History*. New York: Harmony Books, 1995.

Pareles, John, and Patricia Romanowski. *The Rolling Stone Encyclopedia of Rock & Roll.* New York: Summit Books, 1983.

Rolling Stone. *The Rolling Stone Record Review.* New York: Pocket Books, 1971.

Rolling Stone. *The Rolling Stone Record Review, Volume II: The Authoritative Guide to Contemporary Records.* New York: Pocket Books, 1974.

Slaven, Neil. *Electric Don Quixote: The Definitive Story of Frank Zappa.* New York: Omnibus Press, 1996.

Trager, Oliver. *The American Book of the Dead: The Definitive Grateful Dead Encyclopedia.* New York: Fireside Books, 1997.

Walley, David. *No Commercial Potential: The Saga of Frank Zappa.* New York: Da Capo Press, 1996.

Whitburn, Joel, ed. *The Billboard Book of Top 40 Albums.* New York: Billboard Books, 1995.

Zappa, Frank, and Peter Occhiogrosso. *The Real Frank Zappa Book.* New York: Poseidon Press, 1989.

Magazine, Newspaper, and Online Articles

Bell, Max. "Little Feat: Time Loves a Hero." *New Musical Express,* May 21, 1977.

Charone, Barbara. "Presenting the Open Crotch, Maximum Uplift." *Sounds,* May 29, 1976.

Childs, Andy. "Huge Stars, Big Hearts and Little Feat." *ZigZag,* March 1975.

Considine, J. D. "Let It Roll." *Rolling Stone,* November 17, 1988.

Costa, Jean-Charles. "The Last Record Album." *Rolling Stone,* January 29, 1976.

Cregar, Michael. "Beyond Little Feat: The Music of Lowell George." *Topanga Messenger,* May 1979.

Crescenti, Peter. "In Time, Everyone Will Love Little Feat." *Circus,* June 1977.

Erskine, Pete. "The Last Lowell George Interview." *New Musical Express,* August 4, 1979.

Flanagan, Bill. "The Legend of Lowell George and Little Feat." *Musician,* March 1982.

Flans, Robyn. "Richie Hayward." *Modern Drummer,* October 2010.

Flans, Robyn, and William F. Miller. "Little Feat's Richie Hayward: No Stopping Now." *Modern Drummer*, October 1995.

Gans, David. "Ted Templeman: Super Producer." *BAM*, 1982.

Gelinas, J. P. "Perfect Imperfection." *Perfect Sound Forever*, August 2008.

Gerson, Ben. "Feats Don't Fail Me Now." *Rolling Stone*, October 24, 1974.

Gilmore, Mikal. "Is Lowell George Willin' to Succeed?" *Rolling Stone*, April 3, 1979.

Gleason, Holly. "Time Heels All Wounds." *BAM*, September 9, 1988.

Greenwald, Matthew. "Little Feat: Talkin' About Past, Present and Future." *Discoveries*, December 2000.

Gunnin, John. "Neon Park." *Juxtapoz*, Summer 1995.

Herbst, Peter. "Time Loves a Hero." *Rolling Stone*, June 30, 1977.

Hoskyns, Barney. "Album by Album: Little Feat." *Uncut*, August 2008.

Hoskyns, Barney. "Little Feat: The One That Got Away." *MOJO*, July 1994.

Houghton, Mick. "Little Feat Albums." *Let It Rock*, March 1975.

Kendall, Paul. "My Name's Lowell George, and I'm Here to Talk About Little Feat." *ZigZag*, August 1976.

Kendall, Paul. "The Pitter Patter of Lowell George and His Barefooted Little Feat." *ZigZag*, August 1976.

Kent, Bill. "Fans Who Do Much More Than Applaud." *New York Times*, November 15, 1998.

Leviton, Mark. "Little Feat's Life After Lowell." *BAM*, December 1, 1979.

Leviton, Mark. "Lowell George: A Feat of His Own." *Blank Space*, December 1978.

Leviton, Mark. "Lowell George Walks Alone." *BAM*, September 1, 1978.

"Little Feat's Last Record Album." *Rolling Stone*, November 1, 1979.

Mattox, T. E. "Time Loves a Hero—Remembering Lowell George." Travelingboy.com, July 1978.

McLane, Daisann. "Home and Deranged." *Crawdaddy!*, April 1979.

McLane, Daisann. "Lowell George, 1945–1979." *Rolling Stone*, August 9, 1979.

McLane, Daisann. "Tribute to Lowell George Draws 20,000." *Rolling Stone*, September 20, 1979.

Moore, Steve. "Little Feat: Still Out There Among the Great Unknown Bands." *Rolling Stone*, n.d.

Murray, Charles Shaar. "Little Feat." *New Musical Express*, December 1975.

Palmer, Robert. "Lowell George and New Band." *New York Times*, June 25, 1979.

Palmer, Robert. "The Pop Life." *New York Times*, November 30, 1979.

Pareles, Jon. "Hoy-Hoy!" *Rolling Stone*, October 29, 1981.

Platt, Alan. "Thanks I'll Eat It Here." *Rolling Stone*, June 28, 1979.

Ramball, Paul. "Lowell George: Thanks I'll Eat It Here." *New Musical Express*, April 7, 1979.

Ray, Randy. "Adventures in Tower of Power." Jambands.com, September 30, 2009.

Reilly, Sue. "Lowell George's Little Feat Have Always Done Their Stuff, But Only Now Are They a Shoo-in." *People*, April 10, 1978.

Rensin, David. "Little Feat: Giant Steps Across the Sea." *Rolling Stone*, April 10, 1975.

Rensin, David. "Little Feat Keeps on Truckin'." *Crawdaddy!*, June 1973.

Rockwell, John, "Coast Tribute to Lowell George." *New York Times*, August 6, 1979.

Rockwell, John. "Lowell George, 34, Folk-Rock Musician, Suffers Heart Attack." *New York Times*, June 30, 1979.

Rockwell, John. "Lowell George Since Leaving Little Feat." *New York Times*, June 22, 1979.

"Rolling Stone Readers Poll on the 10 Best Live Albums of All Time," RollingStone.com, November 21, 2012, http://www.rollingstone.com/music/pictures/readers-poll-the-10-best-live-albums-of-all-time-20121121/10-bob-seger-and-the-silver-bullet-band-live-bullet-0114011.

Snowden, Don. "Feats Don't Fail: Richie Hayward R.I.P." *Rock's Backpages*, August 2010.

Snowden, Don. "Little Feat: The Rock and Roll Doctors." *Rock Around the World*, July 1977.

Snowden, Don. "Lowell George: Artists Salute." *Los Angeles Times*, July 8, 1979.

Sutherland, Sam. "Lowell George & Little Feat." *Phonograph Record*, December 1975.

Swaney, Dave. "Bizarre Isn't the Word. . . ." *Teenset*, March 1969.

Sweeting, Adam. "Time Loves a Hero." *The Guardian*, August 29, 2000.

Swenson, John. "Lowell's Retreat from Little Feat." *Rolling Stone*, July 14, 1977.

Tober, John. "Van Dyke Parks." *Hot Wacks*, November 9, 1973.

White, Timothy, "New Little Feat LP: Lowell Says It Oughta Be 'Rich'." *Crawdaddy!*, 1977.

Williams, Richard. "Lowell George: The Rock 'n' Roll Doctor." *Melody Maker*, July 7, 1979.

INTERVIEWS

Little Feat

Paul Barrere
Sam Clayton
Roy Estrada

Gabe Ford
Craig Fuller
Kenny Gradney

Shaun Murphy
Bill Payne
Fred Tackett

Musicians

Greg Adams
Denny Bruce
Jimmy Buffett
John Fleckenstein
Elliot Ingber
Ira Ingber
Tom Johnston

Rickie Lee Jones
Martin Kibbee
Warren Klein
Page McConnell
June Millington
Van Dyke Parks
Bonnie Raitt

Linda Ronstadt
John Sebastian
Larry Tamblyn
Allen Toussaint
Ivan Ulz
Bob Weir

Family of Lowell George

Elizabeth George
Hampton George

Inara George
Luke George

Patte George Stahlbaum

Producers

George Massenburg   Ted Templeman   Russ Titelman

Staffers, Managers, and Record Execs

Peter Asher   Carl Scott   Lenny Waronker
Georgia (Jo) Bergman   Joe Smith
Howard Burke   Gene Vano

Grass Roots Movement

Linda Bangham   Lynn Hearne   Fred Miller
Dick Bangham   Jay Herbst   David Moss
Chris Cafiero   Amy Miller   Diane Pelis

Media

Gary Bennett   Daisann McLane   JoAnne Ostrow
Don "Cerphe" Colwell   Ed O'Connell

INDEX